Let's Study!

The Grammar School 1

JMTR

지금까지 이런 맛은 없었다!

Iam books

Contents

Features

새로운 중학교 교과 과정 반영
자기주도 학습을 통한 내신 완벽 대비
내신 기출문제 분석
명확한 핵심 문법 해설
Workbook – 다양하고 풍부한 문법문제 수록

Unit 문법 설명

· 새로운 교과 과정이 반영된 교과서를 분석하여 꼭 알아야 할 문법 사항을 예문과 함께 정리하였습니다.

· 쉬운 설명으로 문법의 기초를 다질 수 있습니다.

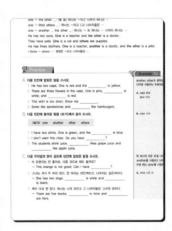

Practice

· 다양한 주관식 문법 문제를 통해 배운 문법 사항을 문제로 풀어보며 익히도록 하였습니다.

· 핵심 문법 설명을 토대로 배운 문법 사항을 Practice를 통해 확실하게 점검할 수 있습니다.

Review Test

· 해당 Chapter에서 배운 문법 사항을 통합하여 다양한 주관식 문제를 통해 복습하며 점검하도록 하였습니다.

· 학습 내용을 바탕으로 문제를 해결하며 응용력을 키울 수 있도록 하였습니다.

Chapter Test

· 해당 Chapter에서 배운 내용들을 학교 시험 유형으로 구성하였으며 출제 비율이 높은 문제를 선별하여 종합문제로 제시하였습니다.

· 학교 시험에 나올만한 내신 대비 문제와 주관식 문제를 수록하여 내신을 완벽하게 대비하도록 하였습니다.

· 종합문제를 통해 자신의 실력을 점검하도록 하였습니다.

Workbook

· 해당 Chapter에서 배운 문법 사항과 관련된 추가 문법 문제로 구성하였습니다.

· 주관식 문제를 대폭 수록하여 많은 문제를 풀어보며 실력을 쌓을 수 있도록 하였습니다.

문장의 구성 요소

1. 8품사

* 품사 : 성질이나 문법적 역할이 같은 단어끼리 모아 놓은 것을 품사라고 한다.

(1) 명사 : 사람, 동물, 사물, 장소나 개념 등을 나타내는 말로, 문장에서 주어, 목적어, 보어로 쓰인다.

　① 셀 수 있는 명사

　　－ 보통명사 : 하나씩 구분할 수 있는 명사(cat, chair, house 등)

　　－ 집합명사 : 사람이나 사물이 여럿 모여 집합체를 이루는 명사(family, team 등)

　② 셀 수 없는 명사

　　－ 고유명사 : 이름이나 지명 등 세상에 하나밖에 없는 명사(Korea, Sunday 등)

　　－ 물질명사 : 모양이나 크기가 없는 물질이나 재료로 이루어진 명사(water, air 등)

　　－ 추상명사 : 모양이 없이 추상적인 개념을 나타내는 명사(love, happiness 등)

(2) 대명사 : 사람이나 사물의 이름을 대신하는 말로, 문장에서 주어, 목적어, 보어로 쓰인다.

　① 인칭대명사 : 사람이나 동물, 사물을 대신하여 나타내는 말(I, me, my, mine 등)

　② 지시대명사 : '이것' 또는 '저것'이라고 대상을 가리키는 말(this, that 등)

(3) 동사 : 사람, 동물, 사물의 동작이나 상태를 나타내는 말이다.

　① be동사 : '~이다, ~에 있다'라는 뜻을 나타내는 동사(am, are, is 등)

　② 일반동사 : 동작이나 상태를 나타내는 대부분의 동사(go, see, eat 등)

　③ 조동사 : be동사나 일반동사 앞에서 동사의 뜻을 더해 주는 동사(can, will 등)

(4) 형용사 : 사람이나 사물의 성질, 성격, 상태 등을 나타내는 말이다.(good, pretty, red, tall 등)

(5) 부사 : 방법, 정도 등을 나타내며 동사, 형용사, 부사 또는 문장 전체를 꾸며 주는 말이다.(very, really, late, early 등)

(6) 전치사 : 명사나 대명사 앞에 쓰이며 장소, 시간, 목적, 수단 등을 나타내는 말이다.(in, on, under, by, at, to, from 등)

(7) 접속사 : 단어와 단어, 구와 구, 절과 절을 이어주는 말이다.(and, but, so 등)

(8) 감탄사 : 기쁨, 슬픔, 놀람 등의 감정을 나타내는 말이다.(oh, wow, ouch 등)

2. 문장의 구조

(1) 주부와 술부

① 주부 : '~은/는, ~이/가'에 해당하는 주어를 포함한 부분을 주부라고 한다. 주부는 주어만으로 이루어
질 때도 있고 수식어구를 포함할 때도 있다.

The woman is a doctor. 그 여자는 의사이다.

The woman on the chair is a doctor. 그 의자에 앉아 있는 여자는 의사이다.

② 술부 : '~이다, ~하다'에 해당하는 동사를 포함한 부분을 술부라고 한다. 술부는 동사만으로 이루어질
때도 있고 목적어, 보어, 수식어구를 포함할 때도 있다.

I eat. 나는 먹는다.

I eat an apple. 나는 사과를 먹는다.

I eat an apple in the park. 나는 공원에서 사과를 먹는다.

＊주어 : 동사의 주체가 되는 말

＊동사 : 주어의 상태나 동작을 나타내는 말

＊목적어 : 동작의 대상이 되는 말

＊보어 : 주어나 목적어의 성질이나 상태를 나타내는 말

(2) 구와 절

① 구 : 「주어+동사」를 포함하지 않은 둘 이상의 단어가 모여 명사, 형용사, 부사의 역할을 하는 것을 말
한다.

－ 명사구(명사 역할) : I enjoy eating pizza. (목적어)

－ 형용사구(형용사 역할) : The cat on the sofa is cute. (명사 수식)

－ 부사구(부사 역할) : I put the car in the garage. (동사 수식)

② 절 : 「주어+동사」를 포함한 둘 이상의 단어가 문장의 일부를 이루는 것을 말한다.

He is tall, but his brother is short. 그는 키가 크지만 그의 형은 키가 작다.

＊절도 구처럼 명사, 형용사, 부사의 역할을 한다.

－ 명사절 : I know that he is honest. (목적어)

－ 형용사절 : The man who is sitting on the chair is Tom. (명사 수식)

－ 부사절 : Let's meet tomorrow if you are busy now. (문장 전체 수식)

be동사란 무엇인가?
be동사는 '~이다, ~하다, ~(에) 있다'라는 뜻으로 주어의 상태나 성격, 위치 등을 나타낼 때 사용한다.
You **are** a best teacher.
My sister **is** on the bench.

인칭대명사란 무엇인가?
인칭대명사는 사람이나 동물, 사물의 이름을 대신해서 나타내는 말로 인칭과 수에 따라 나눈다. 또한 문장에서 역할에 따라서 주격, 목적격, 소유격으로 쓰인다.
Mark is **my** brother. **He** likes **her**.

Chapter 1. be동사와 인칭대명사

01 be동사의 의미와 형태

- be동사는 '~이다, (상태가) ~하다, ~(에) 있다'의 뜻으로 주어의 인칭과 수에 따라 am, are, is를 쓴다.

I **am** a doctor.　　　You **are** a cook.

He **is** happy.　　　She **is** beautiful.

They **are** in the park.

	단수(축약형)	복수(축약형)
1인칭	I am(I'm)	We are(We're)
2인칭	You are(You're)	You are(You're)
3인칭	He is(He's) She is(She's) It is(It's)	They are(They're)

*Tom, my brother, Korea 등 1인칭과 2인칭이 아닌 것은 모두 3인칭이다.

*셀 수 있는 것이 하나이면 단수, 둘 이상이면 복수라고 한다.

 Practice

A. 다음 괄호 안에서 알맞은 것을 고르시오.

1. I (am / are / is) sick now.

2. They (am / are / is) clean.

3. (He / They / I) is a singer.

4. We (am / are / is) good friends.

B. 다음 밑줄 친 부분을 줄여 쓰시오.

1. <u>It is</u> a good book.　　2. <u>They are</u> very sleepy.

3. <u>I am</u> in the theater.　　4. <u>She is</u> a kind girl.

C. 다음 문장의 주어를 괄호 안의 말로 바꿔 다시 쓰시오.

1. She is tired today. (I)
→ _____

2. It is very long. (They)
→ _____

3. They are under the tree. (He)
→ _____

4. You are in the park. (We)
→ _____

Grammar Tip

be동사 뒤에 명사가 오면 '~이다'라는 뜻이고, 장소를 나타내는 전치사가 오면 '~에 있다'라는 뜻이다. 또한 be동사 뒤에 형용사가 오면 '~하다'라는 뜻이다.

A. sick 아픈
　singer 가수

B. sleepy 졸린
　theater 극장

C. tired 지친

02 be동사의 부정문

· be동사의 부정문은 「주어+be동사+not ~.」의 형태로 '~이 아니다, ~이 없다'의 뜻이다.

I'm **not** a farmer.

He **isn't** happy. (isn't=is not)

They **aren't** in the room. (aren't=are not)

		주어+be동사+not	축약형	
단수	1인칭	I am not	I'm not	
	2인칭	You are not	You're not	You aren't
	3인칭	He/She/It is not	He's/She's/It's not	He/She/It isn't
복수		We/You/They are not	We're/You're/They're not	We/You/They aren't

Practice

A. 다음 괄호 안의 단어를 바르게 배열하여 문장을 다시 쓰시오.

1. (not, I, am) a math teacher.

   → _____

2. She (is, beautiful, not).

   → _____

3. They (are, not, easy) problems.

   → _____

4. (We, not, are) at school.

   → _____

B. 다음 밑줄 친 부분을 줄여 쓰시오.

1. I am not a farmer.　　　2. They are not at the station.

3. He is not from Japan.　　4. You are not an artist.

C. 다음 문장을 부정문으로 바꿔 쓰시오.

1. She is in the garden. → _____

2. It is a popular movie. → _____

3. They are very sad. → _____

Grammar Tip

is not은 isn't로, are not은 aren't로 줄여 쓴다. am not은 amn't로 줄여 쓰지 않는다. (I'm not)

A. problem 문제

B. farmer 농부
station 역
artist 화가, 예술가

C. garden 정원
movie 영화

03 | be동사의 의문문

- be동사의 의문문은 「Be동사+주어 ~?」의 형태로 '~이니?, ~이 있니?'의 뜻이다.

  She is tired now. 주어와 be동사의 위치를 바꾸고 문장 뒤에 물음표를 넣는다.

  Is she tired now?

- 의문문에 대한 대답은 긍정이면 「Yes, 주어+be동사.」, 부정이면 「No, 주어+be동사+not.」으로 한다.

  Are you hungry? – Yes, I am. / No, I'm not.

  * 부정의 대답은 축약형을 사용한다.

  Is she a nurse? – Yes, she is. / No, she isn't.

 ## Practice

A. 다음 괄호 안의 단어를 배열하여 의문문을 만드시오.

1. (he, is, an actor)?

2. (are, busy, you, today)?

3. (they, in the library, are)?

B. 다음 대화의 빈칸에 알맞은 말을 쓰시오.

1. *A*: Are they new gloves?   *B*: Yes, they _____.

2. *A*: Is he kind to you?   *B*: No, _____.

3. *A*: _____ in the office? *B*: Yes, I am.

4. *A*: Is it an expensive bike?   *B*: No, _____.

C. 다음 문장을 의문문으로 바꿔 쓰시오.

1. The shoes are on the table.

   → _____

2. She is a good chef.

   → _____

3. They are baseball players.

   → _____

4. Mike is in the bookstore.

   → _____

Grammar Tip

be동사 의문문의 대답이 부정이면 「No, 주어+be동사+not.」으로 쓰는데, 「be동사+not」은 축약형으로 쓴다.

A. actor 배우

B. expensive 비싼

C. chef 요리사
　　bookstore 서점

Unit 04 인칭대명사

- 사람이나 동물, 사물의 이름을 대신하여 가리키는 말로 인칭, 수, 격에 따라 형태가 달라진다.

  *주격 : 문장에서 주어로 쓰이며 '～은, 는, 이, 가'의 뜻이다.

  *목적격 : 문장에서 목적어로 쓰이며 '～을, ～에게'의 뜻이다.

  *소유격 : '～의'라는 뜻으로 소유를 나타낸다.

	단수			복수		
	주격 (～은, 는, 이, 가)	목적격 (～을, ～에게)	소유격 (～의)	주격 (～은, 는, 이, 가)	목적격 (～을, ～에게)	소유격 (～의)
1인칭	I	me	my	we	us	our
2인칭	you	you	your	you	you	your
3인칭	he	him	his	they	them	their
	she	her	her			
	it	it	its			

 Practice

A. 다음 밑줄 친 부분을 인칭대명사로 바꿔 쓰시오.

1. <u>Cathy and you</u> are from Canada.

2. <u>The rabbit's</u> tail is short.

3. Jack is very kind. They like <u>Jack</u>.

4. <u>The woman</u> is a good actress.

B. 다음 괄호 안의 단어를 알맞은 형태로 바꿔 빈칸에 쓰시오.

1. Soccer is _____ favorite sport. (I)

2. I know _____. Her name is Jenny. (she)

3. Look at that. That is _____ farm. (we)

4. My mother teaches _____. (they)

C. 다음 밑줄 친 ①~④ 중 어법상 어색한 것을 고르시오.

1. They <u>are</u> <u>my</u> <u>sneakers</u>. I like <u>their</u>.
   　　①　　②　　③　　　　　④

2. <u>We</u> know <u>him</u> phone number. <u>He</u> is <u>kind</u>.
   　①　　　　②　　　　　　　③　　④

3. <u>Your</u> doll <u>is</u> on the sofa. <u>Its</u> <u>not</u> under the table.
   　①　　　②　　　　　　③　④

4. I like <u>him</u> very much. <u>He</u> is <u>me</u> best friend.
   　①　②　　　　　　　③　　④

Grammar Tip

사람 이름 and I는 인칭대명사 we로, 사람 이름 and you는 you로, 사람 이름 and 사람 이름은 they로 바꾸어 쓸 수 있다.

A. tail 꼬리
　actress 여배우

B. farm 농장
　teach 가르치다

C. sneakers 운동화
　phone number 전화번호

05 소유대명사, 명사의 소유격

· 소유대명사는 '~의 것'이라는 뜻으로 「소유격＋명사」의 역할을 한다.

This bike is not **mine**. It's **yours**.

	단수			복수		
	주격	소유격	소유대명사	주격	소유격	소유대명사
1인칭	I	my	mine	we	our	ours
2인칭	you	your	yours	you	your	yours
3인칭	he	his	his	they	their	theirs
	she	her	hers			
	it	its	–			

· 명사의 소유격은 「명사＋'s」 또는 「of＋명사」로 나타낸다.
  (1) 사람이나 동물의 소유격 : 「명사＋'s」 This is **Jenny's** jacket.
  (2) 사물이나 장소의 소유격 : 「of＋명사」 The roof **of the house** is blue.
    ＊명사의 소유대명사는 명사의 소유격과 같다. This is **Jenny's** hat. = This hat is **Jenny's**.

 Practice

A. 다음 괄호 안에서 알맞은 것을 고르시오.
  1. The socks are (your / yours).
  2. This book is mine. That book is (her / hers).
  3. (My neighbor / My neighbor's) name is Ann.
  4. Our car is blue and (their / theirs) is white.
  5. The colors (of / for) the rainbow are beautiful.
  6. The nice watch is (Tony / Tony's).

B. 다음 우리말과 같도록 빈칸에 알맞은 말을 쓰시오.
  1. 내 가방은 오래되었지만, 너의 것은 새 것이다.
    → My bag is old, but _____ is new.
  2. 저 예쁜 장갑은 Sarah의 것이다.
    → Those pretty gloves are _____.
  3. 이것은 나의 사전이다. 저것은 그녀의 것이다.
    → This is _____ dictionary. That is _____.
  4. Peter의 집은 크고 깨끗하다.
    → _____ house is big and clean.
  5. 그 책의 제목은 '어린 왕자'이다.
    → The title _____ the book is *The Little Prince*.

Grammar Tip

소유격은 「소유격+명사」의 형태로 명사와 함께 쓰이지만 소유대명사는 단독으로 쓰인다.

A. neighbor 이웃
rainbow 무지개
watch 손목시계

B. dictionary 사전
title 제목

 **Review Test**

 01~ 05

 Grammar Tip

A. 다음 빈칸에 알맞은 말을 <보기>에서 골라 쓰시오.

<보기> are They're It's is isn't

1. We _____ very busy today.

2. She _____ a pilot. She is a pianist.

3. Look at this picture. _____ very good.

A. pilot 조종사
pianist 피아니스트

B. 다음 괄호 안의 지시대로 문장을 바꿔 쓰시오.

1. They are his grandparents. (부정문)

→ _____

2. Tony and Steve are late for school. (의문문)

→ _____

3. I'm a famous cook. (부정문)

→ _____

4. He is a soccer player. (의문문)

→ _____

B. late 늦은
famous 유명한

C. 다음 밑줄 친 부분을 바르게 고치시오.

1. Is him your best friend?

2. We know Tim address.

3. Are the cats yours? – Yes, it is.

4. This yellow doll is my. That white doll is her.

소유대명사는 「소유격+명사」의 역할을 하며 문장에서 단독으로 쓰일 수 있으며, 소유격은 뒤에 명사와 함께 쓴다.

C. address 주소
doll 인형

D. 다음 우리말과 같도록 괄호 안의 말을 알맞게 배열하시오.

1. 그녀는 게으르지 않다. (not, lazy, is, she)

→ _____

2. 그들의 아들들은 용감하다. (brave, their, are, sons)

→ _____

3. 그녀는 나의 미술 선생님이시다. (she, my, art teacher, is)

→ _____

4. 그 의자는 내 아버지의 것이다. (is, my father's, the chair)

→ _____

D. lazy 게으른
brave 용감한

15

1. 다음 중 두 단어의 관계가 나머지와 다른 것은?

① I – my　　② they – their

③ she – her　　④ he – him

⑤ we – our

2. 다음 중 밑줄 친 부분을 줄여 쓸 수 없는 것은?

① You are very sleepy.

② I am not a student.

③ It is my toy car.

④ She is a math teacher.

⑤ They are not in the park.

3. 다음 밑줄 친 부분의 의미가 나머지와 다른 것은?

① She is my aunt.

② It is not her bag.

③ We are good friends.

④ My sisters are in the room.

⑤ He is a great singer.

4. 다음 빈칸에 isn't가 들어갈 수 있는 것은?

① He and she _____ busy.

② We _____ from Canada.

③ They _____ her sneakers.

④ You _____ in the library.

⑤ The bike _____ expensive.

5. 다음 문장의 빈칸에 올 수 없는 것은?

_____ are very tired.

① She　　② Amy and you

③ They　　④ Peter and I

⑤ He and she

6. 다음 중 밑줄 친 her[Her]의 쓰임이 <보기>와 다른 것은?

<보기>　They know her name.

① They meet her.

② It is her computer.

③ Her hair is black.

④ Are you her sons?

⑤ Is her car white?

7. 다음 빈칸에 공통으로 알맞은 말을 쓰시오.

My uncle has a daughter. _____ is a student. _____ is very tall.

8. 다음 중 어법상 어색한 것은?

① He's from New York.

② Tom and I are brothers.

③ They are on the table.

④ It is my glasses.

⑤ She is a great painter.

[9-10] 다음 대화의 빈칸에 알맞은 대답을 고르시오.

9.
> A: Are you from Korea?
> B: _____ I'm from China.

① Yes, I am.　　② Yes, we are.
③ Yes, you are.　　④ No, you aren't.
⑤ No, I'm not.

10.
> A: Is it your house?
> B: _____ It is Tony's.

① Yes, it is.　　② Yes, they is.
③ No, it isn't.　　④ No, they isn't.
⑤ No, they aren't.

11. 다음 중 대화가 어색한 것은?
① A: Is John his brother?
　B: Yes, he is.
② A: Are they your cousins?
　B: Yes, they aren't.
③ A: Am I pretty?
　B: Yes, you are.
④ A: Is your father a chef?
　B: No, he is a doctor.
⑤ A: Is Sally smart and kind?
　B: Yes, she is.

12. 다음 중 부정을 나타내는 not이 들어갈 곳은?

> ① She ② is ③ very ④ hungry ⑤.

13. 다음 빈칸에 공통으로 알맞은 것은?

> · The store _____ closed. It is open.
> · Jenny _____ stupid. She is smart.

① is　　② are
③ isn't　　④ wasn't
⑤ am not

14. 다음 중 밑줄 친 부분의 쓰임이 <보기>와 다른 것은?

> <보기>　Amy's sweater is pink.

① They are Kevin's books.
② Lisa's brother is a lawyer.
③ Today's her birthday.
④ Harry's school is near here.
⑤ The man is Steve's uncle.

[15-16] 다음 문장에서 틀린 부분을 찾아 바르게 고치시오.

15.
> Emily is from the U.S. She is fourteen years old. Hers mother is a nurse.

_____ → _____

16.
> This is my puppy. It name is Spot. I love Spot very much.

_____ → _____

17. 다음 빈칸에 알맞은 것은?

> I like _____ very much.

① his   ② she
③ them   ④ your
⑤ its

18. 다음 대화의 빈칸에 알맞은 것은?

> A: Is this your umbrella?
> B: Yes, it's _____.

① my   ② his
③ mine   ④ yours
⑤ her

19. 다음 빈칸에 들어갈 말이 나머지와 다른 것은?
① My mother _____ sick.
② I _____ in the bookstore.
③ He _____ at the restaurant.
④ Jake's brother _____ tired now.
⑤ The tall man _____ a scientist.

20. 다음 우리말을 영어로 바르게 옮긴 것은?

> 그 그림들은 우리의 것이 아니다.

① The pictures are ours.
② The pictures aren't ours.
③ The pictures isn't ours.
④ The pictures aren't yours.
⑤ The pictures isn't theirs.

〈서술형 문제〉

[21-22] 다음 문장을 우리말과 같도록 바꿔 쓰시오.

21. My dolls are in the box.
→ _____
(나의 인형들은 그 상자 안에 있지 않다.)

22. He is a famous actor.
→ _____
(그는 유명한 배우인가요?)

[23-24] 다음 표를 보고, 빈칸에 알맞은 말을 쓰시오.

	Julie	Brian
Age	13	17
Hometown	Paris	London

23. Julie _____ 13 years old. _____
_____ 17 years old.

24. Julie _____ from Paris.
Brian _____ from _____.

25. 다음은 수진이의 남동생 민호의 자기소개 글이다. 이를 바탕으로 수진이가 남동생 민호를 소개하는 글을 완성하시오.

> Let me introduce myself. My name is Minho. I'm 14 years old. I'm from Busan, Korea. I'm not tall, but my favorite sport is basketball. I'm good at basketball.

→ Let me introduce (1) _____
_____. (2) _____ _____
is Minho. He is 14 years old. He is from Busan, Korea. He is not tall, but
(3) _____ _____ _____
is basketball. (4) _____ good at basketball.

일반동사란 무엇인가?

동사는 크게 be동사와 일반동사, 조동사로 나눌 수 있다. be동사는 주어의 성질이나 성격, 상태를 나타내는 동사이고 일반동사는 be동사와 조동사를 제외한 대부분의 동사로 동작이나 상태를 나타낸다. 일반동사는 인칭과 수에 따라 형태가 변한다.

I **play** the piano.

She **plays** the piano.

Chapter 2. 일반동사

06 일반동사의 의미

- 일반동사는 주어의 동작이나 상태를 나타내는 말이다.

  * 일반동사의 현재형은 주어의 반복되는 동작이나 습관을 나타낸다.

  I **am** a student. I **go** to school by bike.

  * 일반동사는 주어의 인칭과 수(단수, 복수)에 따라 형태가 달라진다.

  (1) 주어가 1, 2인칭(단수, 복수)인 경우에는 동사원형을 쓴다.

     I **like** apples. We **live** in Seoul.

  (2) 주어가 3인칭 복수인 경우에는 동사원형을 쓴다.

     They **know** my name.

Practice

A. 다음 중 일반동사가 쓰인 문장이면 ○표, 그렇지 않으면 ×표 하시오.

1. She is his science teacher.   (   )
2. I have three dogs.   (   )
3. You read the English books.   (   )
4. He and she go to school.   (   )
5. The doll is under the chair.   (   )

B. 다음 문장에서 일반동사를 찾아 밑줄을 그으시오.

1. Eagles fly in the sky.
2. I wash my hair every day.
3. They study in the classroom.
4. My brother and I clean the room.
5. The students dance on the stage.

C. 다음 빈칸에 알맞은 말을 〈보기〉에서 골라 쓰시오.

〈보기〉 go   play   live   eat   swim

1. They _____ soccer after school.
2. My parents _____ Italian food.
3. They _____ in New York.
4. Tim and I _____ to the library.
5. You _____ in the swimming pool.

07 일반동사의 3인칭 단수형

- 일반동사의 현재형은 동사원형을 그대로 쓰지만, 주어가 3인칭 단수인 경우에는 보통 동사원형에 -s나 -es를 붙인다.

  I **want** a blue skirt.

  She **wants** cookies.

- 일반동사의 3인칭 단수 현재형 만드는 방법

대부분의 동사	동사원형+-s	want → wants, work → works, see → sees, like → likes, sing → sings, come → comes
-o, -x, -(s)s, -sh, -ch로 끝나는 동사	동사원형+-es	go → goes, mix → mixes, pass → passes, wash → washes, teach → teaches
「자음+y」로 끝나는 동사	y를 i로 고치고+-es	study → studies, carry → carries, fly → flies
불규칙 변화	(예외적인 경우)	have → has

Practice

A. 다음 동사의 3인칭 단수형을 쓰시오.

1. swim   → _____
2. stay   → _____
3. relax   → _____
4. do   → _____
5. sleep   → _____
6. cry   → _____
7. make   → _____
8. have   → _____

B. 다음 괄호 안에서 알맞은 것을 고르시오.

1. My sister (have / has) short hair.
2. Ashley (go / goes) to the zoo by bus.
3. They (watch / watches) a movie on Sundays.
4. Mr. and Ms. Brown (need / needs) their help.
5. She (send / sends) an email to her son.

C. 다음 밑줄 친 부분을 현재형으로 바르게 고치시오.

1. My uncle <u>fix</u> the old bike.
2. Julie <u>drink</u> some milk every morning.
3. The student <u>sing</u> a long song.
4. The old woman <u>miss</u> her hometown.
5. Jonathan <u>listen</u> to music with his friend.

Grammar Tip

「모음+y」로 끝나는 동사의 3인칭 단수형은 동사원형에 -s를 붙인다.
buy → buys, play → plays

B. help 도움
send 보내다

C. fix 고치다
hometown 고향

08 일반동사의 부정문

- 일반동사의 부정문은 주어의 인칭에 따라 동사원형 앞에 do not[don't]이나 does not[doesn't]을 써서 나타낸다.

 * doesn't를 써서 부정문으로 나타낼 때 뒤에 동사는 동사원형으로 쓴다.

	형태	예문
부정문	〈주어가 1, 2인칭 또는 복수일 때〉 주어+do not[don't]+동사원형 ~.	I like cats. → I **do not[don't]** like cats.
	〈주어가 3인칭 단수일 때〉 주어+does not[doesn't]+동사원형 ~.	He likes cats. → He **does not[doesn't]** like cats.

A. 다음 괄호 안에서 알맞은 것을 고르시오.

1. Lisa (don't / doesn't) eat pizza.

2. They (don't / doesn't) like scary movies.

3. We (don't / doesn't) play soccer now.

4. Tony (don't / doesn't) solve the problem.

5. My brother doesn't (wash / washes) his face.

B. 다음 밑줄 친 ①~④ 중 어법상 어색한 것을 고르시오.

1. I <u>know</u> the man, but my sister <u>don't</u> <u>know</u> <u>him</u>.
   　　①　　　　　　　　　②　　③　　④

2. I <u>have</u> a camera. <u>Sam</u> <u>doesn't</u> <u>has</u> a camera.
   　①　　　　　　　②　　③　　④

3. She and he <u>are</u> heathy. <u>They</u> <u>doesn't</u> <u>drink</u> coffee.
   　　　　　　①　　　　②　　③　　④

C. 다음 문장을 부정문으로 바꿔 쓰시오.

1. Kevin rides a bike very well.

   →

2. You want a new computer.

   →

3. The coat has many pockets.

   →

Grammar Tip

do는 '~을 하다'라는 뜻의 일반동사로도 쓸 수 있고, 일반동사의 부정문이나 의문문을 나타낼 때 일반동사를 돕는 조동사로도 쓸 수 있다.

A. scary 무서운
   solve 풀다
   problem 문제

B. know 알다
   healthy 건강한

C. ride 타다
   pocket 주머니

09 일반동사의 의문문

· 일반동사의 의문문은 주어의 인칭에 따라 문장의 맨 앞에 Do나 Does를 써서 나타낸다.

＊Does를 써서 의문문으로 나타낼 때 뒤에 동사는 동사원형으로 쓴다.

	형태	예문
의문문	〈주어가 1, 2인칭 또는 복수일 때〉 Do+주어+동사원형 ～? - Yes, 주어+do. 〈긍정〉 　No, 주어+don't. 〈부정〉	You play the violin. → **Do** you play the violin? 　- Yes, I do. / No, I don't.
	〈주어가 3인칭 단수일 때〉 Does+주어+동사원형 ～? - Yes, 주어+does. 〈긍정〉 　No, 주어+doesn't. 〈부정〉	She plays the violin. → **Does** she play the violin? 　- Yes, she does. / No, she doesn't.

 Practice

A. 다음 괄호 안에서 알맞은 것을 고르시오.

1. Do you (finish / finishes) your homework?

2. Does she (know / knows) his address?

3. (Do / Does) your mother cook well?

B. 다음 밑줄 친 부분을 바르게 고치시오.

1. A: <u>Do</u> she jog every morning?
   B: Yes, she <u>do</u>.

2. A: <u>Does</u> you speak English well?
   B: Yes, I <u>doesn't</u>.

3. A: <u>Do</u> the boy study hard?
   B: No, he <u>don't</u>.

4. A: <u>Does</u> your uncles remember my name?
   B: No, they <u>do</u>.

C. 다음 괄호 안의 지시대로 문장을 바꿔 쓰시오.

1. You buy many flowers. (의문문으로)

   → _____

2. He finds a wallet on the street. (의문문으로)

   → _____

3. Do you want a backpack? (주어를 your sister로)

   → _____

Grammar Tip

3인칭 단수 주어가 있는 문장을 의문문으로 만들 때는 Does를 사용하는데, 뒤에 오는 동사는 반드시 동사원형을 써야 한다.

A. address 주소

B. remember 기억하다

C. wallet 지갑
backpack 배낭

A. 다음 밑줄 친 부분을 바르게 고치시오.

1. Ann and Jamie <u>has</u> many dogs.

2. The old man <u>fix</u> the piano.

3. Ms. White <u>don't</u> run to the market.

4. <u>Do</u> your mother like cloudy days?

B. 다음 질문과 대답을 바르게 연결하시오.

1. Do you walk to school? •   • (a) Yes, she does.

2. Does she study hard? •   • (b) No, he doesn't.

3. Does Nick eat breakfast? •   • (c) No, we don't.

4. Do they clean the room? •   • (d) Yes, they do.

C. 다음 우리말과 같도록 빈칸에 알맞은 말을 쓰시오.

1. Sally는 여름 스포츠를 즐긴다. (enjoy)
  → Sally ＿＿＿＿＿＿ summer sports.

2. Sam과 그의 아들은 벤치에 앉는다. (sit)
  → Sam and his son ＿＿＿＿＿＿ on the bench.

3. 그는 그 트럭을 운전하지 않는다. (drive)
  → He ＿＿＿＿＿ ＿＿＿＿＿ the truck.

4. 그녀는 패스트푸드를 좋아하니? (like)
  → ＿＿＿＿＿ she ＿＿＿＿＿ fast food?

D. 다음 문장을 부정문과 의문문으로 바꿔 쓰시오.

Jack sells books at the bookstore.

1. (부정문) → ＿＿＿＿＿＿＿＿＿＿＿＿＿＿

2. (의문문) → ＿＿＿＿＿＿＿＿＿＿＿＿＿＿

Grammar Tip

A. market 시장
  cloudy 흐린

B. breakfast 아침 식사
  clean 청소하다

일반동사의 현재형은 동사원형을 그대도 쓰고, 주어가 3인칭 단수인 경우에만 동사원형에 -s나 -es를 붙인다.

C. summer 여름
  drive 운전하다
  fast food 패스트푸드

D. sell 팔다
  bookstore 서점

1. 다음 중 동사의 3인칭 단수형이 잘못 짝지어진 것은?
   ① stay – stays   ② have – has
   ③ mix – mixs   ④ go – goes
   ⑤ carry – carries

2. 다음 중 어법상 옳은 것은?
   ① Do your sister study hard?
   ② You don't like rainy days.
   ③ Does she has dinner with them?
   ④ They drinks milk in the morning.
   ⑤ He don't know her phone number.

3. 다음 빈칸에 알맞은 것은?

   _____ likes vegetables.

   ① The students   ② He and she
   ③ They   ④ Joan
   ⑤ Mark and I

4. 다음 밑줄 친 부분의 형태가 바르지 않은 것은?
   ① Joseph enjoys tennis.
   ② Tom goes to school on foot.
   ③ She teaches history at school.
   ④ Jack speaks English very well.
   ⑤ The girl have many dolls.

5. 다음 중 빈칸에 Do가 올 수 없는 것은?
   ① _____ they have a nice camera?
   ② _____ the kids read these books?
   ③ _____ you come home early?
   ④ _____ Ann and you cook spaghetti?
   ⑤ _____ your sister a popular singer?

[6-7] 다음 빈칸에 알맞지 않은 것을 고르시오.

6.
   Alice _____ in the park.

   ① wait for James
   ② helps the man
   ③ plays badminton
   ④ meets Emily
   ⑤ rides her bike

7.
   Does _____ sell apples in the market?

   ① Cathy   ② his father
   ③ Mr. Jason   ④ Tim and you
   ⑤ your uncle

8. 다음 빈칸에 have를 쓸 수 없는 것은?
   ① I _____ a robot.
   ② Kevin _____ a good pen.
   ③ They _____ a big garden.
   ④ You _____ many flowers.
   ⑤ His brothers _____ a nice room.

[9-10] 다음 대화의 빈칸에 알맞은 것을 고르시오.

9.
A: Mike, _____ Susie know him?
B: Yes, she does.

① is   ② are
③ do   ④ does
⑤ doesn't

10.
A: Do you like summer?
B: _____ I like cold weather.

① Yes, I do.   ② Yes, I does.
③ No, I don't.   ④ No, I do.
⑤ No, I doesn't.

11. 다음 중 어법상 어색한 것은?
① I don't go to the movie theater.
② Many people don't like the actor.
③ They doesn't play computer games.
④ My father doesn't drink coffee.
⑤ Mr. Brown doesn't work at a hospital.

12. 다음 빈칸에 들어갈 do의 형태가 나머지와 다른 것은?
① _____ you play baseball?
② _____ Harry jog every morning?
③ _____ she walk to school?
④ _____ the child like my brother?
⑤ _____ Kate watch TV in the room?

13. 다음 문장을 부정문으로 바르게 나타낸 것은?

She listens to music.

① She isn't listen to music.
② She don't listens to music.
③ She don't listen to music.
④ She doesn't listens to music.
⑤ She doesn't listen to music.

[14-15] 다음 우리말과 같도록 괄호 안의 단어를 이용하여 쓰시오.

14.
나의 여동생은 침대에서 잠을 잔다.
My sister _____ on the bed. (sleep)

_____

15.
Billy는 집에서 인터넷을 사용하지 않는다.
Billy _____ the Internet at home. (use)

_____

16. 다음 문장을 <보기>와 같이 바꿔 쓰시오.

<보기> They make an apple pie.
    → Do they make an apple pie?

She cleans her house every day.

→ _____

17. 다음 밑줄 친 부분 중 어법상 옳은 것은?

① I don't fixes an umbrella.

② Does Sam buy the bag?

③ He don't answer the question.

④ My father don't go to bed early.

⑤ Does Jill meets the old woman?

[18-19] 다음 빈칸에 들어갈 말이 순서대로 짝지어진 것을 고르시오.

18.
> A: Does he _____ at the hotel?
> B: No, he doesn't. He _____ to the zoo.

① stay – go   ② stay – goes

③ stays – go   ④ stays – goes

⑤ staies – goes

19.
> A: Does she _____ bread every day?
> B: Yes, she does. She _____ bread every day.

① eat – eats   ② eat – eat

③ eats – eats   ④ eats – eat

⑤ eates – eates

20. 다음 대답에 대한 질문으로 알맞은 것은?

> No, I don't. I have a daughter.

① Do you live with her?

② Does she have a daughter?

③ Do you like your sons?

④ Do you have a daughter?

⑤ Do you have a son?

21. 다음 밑줄 친 부분 중 어법상 어색한 것은?

> Alex ① gets up late in the morning on Sundays. He ② don't ③ have breakfast. He ④ meets his friends in the afternoon. He ⑤ jogs in the evening.

〈서술형 문제〉

[22-23] 다음 밑줄 친 동사를 이용하여 빈칸에 알맞은 말을 쓰시오.

22.
> Henry wants a present for his sister's birthday. She _____ a new hat. But she _____ _____ sneakers.

23.
> The first airplane leaves at 6 a.m. But this morning, It _____ _____ at 6 a.m. It _____ at 6:30.

[24-25] 다음 표를 보고, 빈칸에 알맞은 말을 쓰시오.

	나	Dan
좋아하는 운동	soccer	baseball
싫어하는 운동	basketball	volleyball

24. I play soccer after school. I like soccer, but I _____ basketball.

25. Dan plays baseball after school. He likes baseball, but he _____ volleyball.

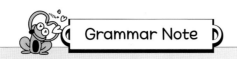

다음 빈칸에 알맞은 말을 쓰시오.

1. 일반동사의 3인칭 단수 현재형 만드는 방법

대부분의 동사	동사원형+-s	want → wants, work → _____, see → _____, like → _____, sing → sings, come → _____
-o, -x, -(s)s, -sh, -ch 로 끝나는 동사	동사원형+-es	go → _____, relax → _____, pass → _____, wash → _____ teach → _____, mix → _____
「자음+y」로 끝나는 동사	y를 i로 고치고+ -es	study → _____, carry → _____, fly → _____, cry → _____
불규칙 변화	(예외적인 경우)	have → _____

2. 일반동사의 부정문

주어의 인칭에 따라 동사원형 앞에 do not[don't]이나 does not[doesn't]을 써서 나타낸다.

	형태	예문
부정문	〈주어가 1, 2인칭 또는 복수일 때〉 주어+do not[_____]+동사원형 ~.	I like cats. → I do not[_____] like cats.
	〈주어가 3인칭 단수일 때〉 주어+does not[_____]+동사원형 ~.	He likes cats. → He does not[_____] like cats.

3. 일반동사의 의문문

주어의 인칭에 따라 문장의 맨 앞에 Do나 Does를 써서 나타낸다.

	형태	예문

의문문	〈주어가 1, 2인칭 또는 복수일 때〉
	_____ +주어+동사원형 ~?
	– Yes, 주어+do. 〈긍정〉
	  No, 주어+_____. 〈부정〉
		You play the violin.
		→ _____ you play the violin?
		  – Yes, I do. / No, I _____.

	〈주어가 3인칭 단수일 때〉
	_____ +주어+_____ ~?
	– Yes, 주어+does. 〈긍정〉
	  No, 주어+doesn't. 〈부정〉
		She plays the violin.
		→ _____ she _____ the violin?
		  – Yes, she does. / No, she doesn't.

명사란 무엇인가?

명사는 사람이나 동물, 사물 등의 이름을 나타내는 말로 셀 수 있는 명사와 셀 수 없는 명사가 있다. 또한 셀 수 있는 명사가 하나인 것을 단수라고 하고 둘 이상인 것을 복수라고 한다.

house, family, Korea, sugar, love 등

관사란 무엇인가?

관사는 명사 앞에서 명사의 성격을 정해주는 말로 부정관사 a, an과 정관사 the가 있다.

There is **a** boy. **The** boy is my brother.

Chapter 3. 명사와 관사

10 명사의 단수와 복수 I(규칙 변화)

· 명사는 사람이나 사물, 장소 등의 이름을 나타내는 말로 하나는 단수, 둘 이상은 복수라고 한다.

  I have a **pencil**.   He has three **pencils**.

· 명사의 복수형은 일반적으로 명사의 끝에 -(e)s를 붙여서 복수형을 만든다.

대부분의 명사	명사+-s	book → books, orange → oranges, girl → girls, lion → lions, ring → rings
-o, -x, -(s)s, -sh, -ch로 끝나는 명사	명사+-es	tomato → tomatoes, box → boxes, bus → buses, dish → dishes, bench → benches 예외) pianos, photos
「자음+y」로 끝나는 명사	y를 i로 고치고 +-es	baby → babies, lady → ladies, city → cities, candy → candies
「모음+y」로 끝나는 명사	명사+-s	monkey → monkeys, toy → toys, boy → boys
-f, -fe로 끝나는 명사	-f, -fe를 v로 고치고 +-es	knife → knives, leaf → leaves, wife → wives 예외) roofs

Practice

A. 다음 빈칸에 명사의 복수형을 쓰시오.

1. car → _____
2. bottle → _____
3. knife → _____
4. toy → _____
5. piano → _____
6. fox → _____
7. dress → _____
8. family → _____
9. baby → _____
10. key → _____

B. 다음 괄호 안에서 알맞은 것을 고르시오.

1. Put some onions and (potatos / potatoes).
2. We have six (class / classes) on Tuesday.
3. Look at these big (shoe / shoes).
4. He buys many (flowers / floweres) at the shop.

C. 다음 밑줄 친 부분을 바르게 고치시오.

1. My uncle has three <u>baby</u>.
2. We can see many yellow and red <u>leaf</u>.
3. There are ten <u>orange</u> on the table.
4. They travel to a lot of <u>countrys</u>.
5. She eats two <u>tomato</u> every day.
6. I need an eraser and two <u>pencil</u>.

Grammar Tip

셀 수 있는 명사는 단수와 복수를 구분할 수 있고, 복수형은 규칙적으로 또는 불규칙적으로 변한다.

A. bottle 병
    key 열쇠

B. onion 양파

C. country 나라, 시골
    eraser 지우개

11 명사의 단수와 복수 2(불규칙 변화)

· 셀 수 있는 명사 중에는 복수형을 만들 때 -(e)s를 붙이지 않고 불규칙적으로 변하는 명사도 있다.

단수와 복수의 형태가 다른 경우 (단수형 ≠ 복수형)	man → men, woman → women, tooth → teeth, foot → feet, child → children, mouse → mice, goose → geese, ox → oxen
단수와 복수의 형태가 같은 경우 (단수형 = 복수형)	sheep → sheep, fish → fish, deer → deer, Chinese → Chinese Japanese → Japanese

· 짝을 이루거나 중요 부분이 두 개인 것은 항상 복수형으로 나타낸다.

glasses, shoes, sneakers, pants, gloves, socks, scissors

The boy always wears glasses.

Practice

A. 다음 빈칸에 명사의 복수형을 쓰시오.

1. foot → _____
2. Chinese → _____
3. goose → _____
4. woman → _____
5. ox → _____
6. sheep → _____

B. 다음 괄호 안의 명사를 알맞은 형태로 바꿔 빈칸에 쓰시오.

1. Look at those little _____. (child)
2. My father raises four _____. (deer)
3. The eleven _____ are soccer players. (man)
4. The baby has only two _____. (tooth)
5. _____ don't like cats. (mouse)

C. 다음 우리말과 뜻이 같도록 빈칸에 알맞은 말을 쓰시오.

1. 우리는 겨울에 눈사람들을 만든다.
   → We make _____ in winter.
2. 그들은 그 연못에서 물고기들을 본다.
   → They look at _____ in the pond.
3. 요즘 많은 중국 사람들이 한국을 방문한다.
   → Nowaday many _____ visit Korea.
4. 남자들은 일반적으로 스포츠를 즐긴다.
   → _____ usually enjoy sports.
5. 그녀의 이는 정말 하얗다.
   → Her _____ are really white.

Grammar Tip

명사의 복수형 중 불규칙적으로 변하는 명사에는 단수형과 복수형이 같은 것이 있고 형태가 달라지는 것도 있다.

A. goose 거위

B. raise 기르다
deer 사슴
only 오직, 단지

C. snowman 눈사람
visit 방문하다

12 셀 수 없는 명사

- 셀 수 없는 명사에는 고유명사, 물질명사, 추상명사가 있다. 셀 수 없는 명사는 셀 수가 없기 때문에 복수형이 없고 단수 취급한다.

고유명사	사람의 이름, 지명, 요일, 월 등 고유한 것을 나타내는 명사로 첫 글자는 대문자로 쓴다. Kate, Jane, Seoul, London, Korea, Monday, July
물질명사	일정한 모양이 없는 물질을 나타내는 명사(기체, 액체, 고체, 가루 등) sugar, water, air, money, coffee, juice, milk, paper
추상명사	추상적인 의미를 나타내는 명사(추상적인 개념, 감정) love, beauty, peace, hope, health, luck, news

- 물질명사는 단위 명사를 써서 수량을 나타내며 복수형은 단위에 -(e)s를 붙여서 나타낸다.

a cup of	a cup of coffee → two cups of coffee	a glass of	a glass of water → three glasses of water
a bottle of	a bottle of juice → four bottles of juice	a piece of	a piece of cake[paper] → two pieces of cake[paper]

Practice

A. 다음 괄호 안에서 알맞은 것을 고르시오.

1. The children need (love / loves).
2. The news (is, are) on the television.
3. We have a lot of (rain / rains) in summer.
4. They need some potatoes and (salt / salts).
5. I want two (cup / cups) of coffee.

B. 다음을 복수형으로 바꿔 쓰시오.

1. a piece of paper → three _____
2. a glass of water → five _____
3. a bottle of juice → six _____
4. a cup of green tea → two _____

C. 다음 밑줄 친 부분을 바르게 고치시오.

1. Airs is very important on earth.
2. He likes a milk and sugar very much.
3. The man has a lot of moneys.
4. The capital city of korea is seoul.
5. Drink two glass of juices every day.
6. We order two piece of cakes.

 Grammar Tip

A. 다음 빈칸에 명사의 복수형을 쓰시오.

1. tooth → _____
2. man → _____
3. knife → _____
4. piano → _____
5. bench → _____
6. watch → _____
7. class → _____
8. deer → _____
9. city → _____
10. wolf → _____
11. lady → _____
12. Japanese → _____

A. watch 손목시계
　 wolf 늑대

B. 다음 괄호 안에서 알맞은 것을 고르시오.

1. Put some onions and (pepper / peppers).

2. Cats can catch (mice / mouse) well.

3. How about these (shoe / shoes)?

4. (A friendship / Friendship) is important to us.

5. There are many (goose / geese) on the farm.

B. pepper 후추
　 catch 잡다
　 friendship 우정

셀 수 없는 명사는 명사의 복수형으로 만들 수 없으며 문장에서 단수 취급한다. 물질명사는 단위에 복수형을 넣어 복수형으로 나타낼 수 있다.

C. 다음 밑줄 친 부분을 바르게 고치시오.

1. The cook needs some <u>sugars</u>.

2. I don't have much <u>papers</u>.

3. My grandfather knows many <u>storys</u>.

4. I ate two <u>piece of pizza</u>.

5. She wants a ruler, pencils and <u>scissor</u>.

C. cook 요리사
　 story 이야기

D. 다음 밑줄 친 부분 중 어법상 어색한 것을 고르시오.

> A lot of ①<u>animals</u> are useful to us. For example, ②<u>sheep</u> give wool and ③<u>cows</u> give ④<u>milks</u> to us.

D. useful 유용한
　 example 예, 보기
　 wool 양털, 모직

Unit 13 부정관사 a, an

- 부정관사 a, an은 '하나'라는 개념으로 정해지지 않은 것을 나타낼 때 사용하며 셀 수 있는 명사 앞에 쓴다. 첫 소리가 자음인 단어 앞에는 a, 첫 소리가 모음인 단어 앞에는 an을 쓴다.

하나의	I have **a** sister.	I eat **an** apple for lunch.
막연한 하나	He is **a** teacher.	She is **an** actress.
매 ~, ~마다	I go to church once **a** week.	

＊단어의 첫 글자가 아니라 첫 글자의 발음에 따라서 a나 an을 쓴다. a European, an hour

- 부정관사와 명사 사이에 형용사가 오면 형용사의 첫소리에 따라 a나 an을 쓴다.

It's **an interesting** story.

He is **a famous** actor.

Practice

A. 다음 괄호 안에서 알맞은 것을 고르시오.

1. He is (a / an) kind boy.

2. I have (a / an) umbrella.

3. We have (a / an) English test today.

4. She is (a / an) honest student.

5. Brian works in (a / an) large office.

B. 다음 빈칸에 a나 an을 쓰고, 필요 없으면 ×를 쓰시오.

1. They wear _____ school uniforms.

2. I write _____ letter to my parents.

3. She has _____ MP3 player.

4. We visit our uncle once _____ month.

5. Judy looks at _____ eagles in the sky.

C. 다음 우리말과 뜻이 같도록 빈칸에 알맞은 말을 쓰시오.

1. 그는 그들을 공원에서 한 시간 동안 기다린다.

   → He waits for them _____ hour in the park.

2. 나는 좋은 친구가 필요하다.

   → I need _____ good friend.

3. 우리는 하루에 세 끼를 먹는다.

   → We have three meals _____ day.

Grammar Tip

명사 앞에 형용사가 올 경우에는 명사가 아닌 형용사의 첫 글자의 발음에 따라서 a나 an을 쓴다.

A. honest 정직한
office 사무실

복수명사 앞에는 부정관사 a나 an을 붙일 수 없다.

B. once 한 번
eagle 독수리

C. wait 기다리다
meal 식사

Unit 14 정관사 the

· 정관사 the는 특정한 것이나 명확한 것을 나타낼 때 쓰며 명사의 종류나 단수, 복수에 관계없이 쓸 수 있다.

앞에 나온 명사를 다시 말할 때	I have a rabbit. **The** rabbit is very cute.
서로 알고 있는 것을 가리킬 때	Open **the** window, please.
수식어가 명사 뒤에서 꾸며줄 때	**The** bag on the table is red.
세상에 하나뿐인 것과 방위를 가리킬 때	**The** moon moves around **the** earth. ＊world, sea, sky, ground, country 앞에도 the를 쓴다.
악기 이름 앞에	I play **the** piano well.

· 정관사 the는 서수나 형용사의 최상급 앞에 쓴다.

The store is on **the second** floor.

Practice

A. 다음 빈칸에 a, an, the 중 알맞은 것을 쓰시오.

1. Pass me ＿＿＿＿＿＿ salt, please.

2. I have ＿＿＿＿＿＿ dog. ＿＿＿＿＿＿ dog is so small.

3. Julia plays ＿＿＿＿＿＿ violin.

4. His father is ＿＿＿＿＿＿ engineer.

5. The sun rises in ＿＿＿＿＿＿ east.

B. 다음 밑줄 친 부분을 바르게 고치시오.

1. A boy in our class is smart.

2. Nile is a very long river.

3. I have a pen. A pen is expensive.

4. My brother plays guitar very well.

5. An earth goes around the sun.

C. 다음 우리말과 뜻이 같도록 빈칸에 알맞은 말을 쓰시오.

1. 설탕 좀 건네줄래?
   → Can you pass me ＿＿＿＿＿＿ sugar?

2. 문 좀 열어 주세요.
   → Open ＿＿＿＿＿＿ door, please.

3. 너는 첼로를 잘 연주할 수 있니?
   → Can you play ＿＿＿＿＿＿ cello well?

Grammar Tip

악기 이름이나 세상에 하나뿐인 것, 방위 앞에는 정관사 the를 쓴다.

A. engineer 기술자
east 동쪽

바다, 강 등 특정한 고유명사 앞에 정관사 the를 쓴다.

B. expensive 비싼
guitar 기타

C. cello 첼로

Unit 15 관사를 쓰지 않는 경우

· 식사, 운동 경기, 과목, 교통수단을 나타낼 때는 명사 앞에 관사를 쓰지 않는다.

식사 앞에	I have **dinner** at seven p.m. → breakfast, lunch, dinner 등
운동 경기 앞에	She plays **tennis** with her friends. → tennis, soccer, basketball, golf 등
과목 앞에	They study **math** and **science**. → math, science, English, art, music 등
by+교통수단	We go to the museum by **bus**. → by+bus, subway, taxi, bike, car 등
건물이 본래의 목적으로 쓰일 때	Mike goes to **school** at eight. → go to church, after school, go to bed 등

 ## Practice

A. 다음 괄호 안에서 알맞은 것을 고르시오.

1. Jane plays (a / the / ×) badminton.
2. She goes to work by (a / the / ×) bus.
3. My favorite subject is (a / the / ×) math.
4. He meets her after (a / the / ×) school.
5. (A / The / ×) Seoul is my hometown.

B. 다음 빈칸에 알맞은 관사를 쓰고, 필요 없으면 ×를 쓰시오.

1. Kate is _____ great actress.
2. I go to _____ school by bike.
3. I don't have time for _____ lunch.
4. She walks her dog in _____ evening.
5. He plays _____ soccer with his friends.

C. 다음 우리말과 뜻이 같도록 빈칸에 알맞은 말을 쓰시오.

1. 나는 방과 후에 그들과 함께 농구를 한다.
   → I play _____ with them after _____.

2. Lisa는 일요일마다 교회에 간다.
   → Lisa _____ to _____ every Sunday.

3. 그녀와 그는 함께 점심을 먹는다.
   → She and he _____ _____ together.

4. 그는 지하철을 타고 그 동물원에 간다.
   → He goes to the zoo _____ _____.

Grammar Tip

지명이나 요일, 월 등의 고유명사 앞에는 관사를 붙이지 않는다.

A. badminton 배드민턴
subject 과목

B. actress 여배우
walk 걷다, 걷게 시키다

C. together 함께
zoo 동물원

A. 다음 괄호 안에서 알맞은 것을 고르시오.

1. We play (a / an / the / ×) tennis after dinner.

2. The moon moves around (a / an / the / ×) earth.

3. I study math for (a / an / the / ×) hour.

4. Ann visits her aunt once (a / an / the / ×) month.

5. Sue goes to school by (a / an / the / ×) subway.

B. 다음 문장에서 <u>틀린</u> 부분을 찾아 바르게 고치시오.

1. A jacket on the sofa is mine.

2. I have a computer. A computer is new.

3. James usually plays the soccer in the evening.

4. She is a honest girl. I like her.

5. Sarah plays a violin very well.

C. 다음 우리말과 같은 뜻이 되도록 빈칸에 알맞은 말을 쓰시오.

1. Sam과 나는 방과 후에 야구를 한다.
   → Sam and I play baseball _____ _____.

2. 그들은 일요일마다 함께 저녁 식사를 한다.
   → They _____ _____ together every Sunday.

3. 태양은 서쪽으로 진다.
   → The sun sets _____ _____ _____.

D. 다음 밑줄 친 부분 중 어법상 <u>어색한</u> 것을 고르시오.

> During vacation, I usually visit my grandparents ① <u>by</u> <u>bus</u>. There is ② <u>a big farm</u> and it has a lot of vegetables and fruit. I can see many cows there. My grandparents work on ③ <u>a farm</u> all day long and I help them. I'm very tired, so I ④ <u>go to bed</u> early.

Grammar Tip

A. moon 달
month 월, 달
subway 지하철

수식어가 명사를 뒤에서 꾸며줄 때는 정관사 the를 쓴다.

B. usually 보통
honest 정직한

식사, 운동 경기, 과목, 교통수단을 나타낼 때는 명사 앞에 관사를 쓰지 않는다.

D. vacation 방학
farm 농장
vegetable 야채

1. 다음 중 단수와 복수가 잘못 짝지어진 것은?

① bus – buses   ② piano – pianoes

③ woman – women   ④ sheep – sheep

⑤ foot – feet

2. 다음 중 밑줄 친 명사의 복수형이 잘못된 것은?

① Ms. White has three <u>sheep</u>.

② Ellen travels many <u>countries</u>.

③ I don't know those <u>men</u>.

④ I bought two <u>sandwiches</u>.

⑤ The <u>leafs</u> turn yellow in fall.

[3-4] 다음 빈칸에 알맞지 <u>않은</u> 것을 고르시오.

3.
> The child needs a _____.

① pencil   ② hat

③ guitar   ④ orange

⑤ friend

4.
> There are two _____ in the kitchen.

① tomatoes   ② eggs

③ children   ④ women

⑤ table

5. 다음 <보기>와 같은 관계가 되도록 빈칸을 채우시오.

> <보기>
> monkey : monkeys = foot : feet

puppy : _____ = mouse : _____

6. 다음 중 빈칸에 a 또는 an을 쓸 수 <u>없는</u> 것은?

① I have _____ apple.

② He is _____ famous artist.

③ Tony plays _____ violin every day.

④ We buy _____ new computer.

⑤ I like _____ honest man.

[7-8] 다음 중 어법상 어색한 것을 고르시오.

7. ① Alice is in the bedroom.

② Tony has an interesting book.

③ I wash the dishes once the week.

④ The shoes on the box are not mine.

⑤ The moon doesn't have air.

8. ① His feet are very clean.

② I drink a glass of water.

③ She has many deer on her farm.

④ We have a lot of snows in winter.

⑤ My mother wears glasses.

9. 다음 빈칸에 들어갈 말이 바르게 짝지어진 것은?

> · This is _____ old house.
> · Carol is _____ good actor.
> · Pass me _____ pepper, please.

① an – an – the ② a – an – the
③ the – a – the ④ an – a – the
⑤ a – a – the

10. 다음 빈칸에 공통으로 알맞은 말을 쓰시오.

> · This is an umbrella. _____ umbrella is yellow.
> · The earth moves around _____ sun.

11. 다음 중 빈칸에 the(The)를 쓸 수 없는 것은?
① We can see many stars in _____ sky.
② She plays _____ guitar every day.
③ I go to the museum by _____ bus.
④ _____ world is wide.
⑤ _____ tree in his garden is very tall.

12. 다음 빈칸에 공통으로 알맞은 것은?

> · I have _____ lunch with Emily.
> · She goes to _____ bed late.

① a ② an
③ the ④ some
⑤ 필요 없음

13. 다음 빈칸에 알맞은 말을 <보기>에서 골라 알맞은 형태로 쓰시오.

> <보기> cup   health   deer

(1) I drink two _____ of tea.
(2) They see some _____ in the field.
(3) We exercise for our _____.

14. 다음 중 빈칸에 a나 an을 쓸 수 있는 것은?
① _____ moon comes out at night.
② There is a coin on _____ ground.
③ He plays soccer after _____ school.
④ She sends _____ letter to him.
⑤ _____ bird on the roof is cute.

15. 다음 우리말과 같은 뜻이 되도록 빈칸에 알맞은 말을 쓰시오.

> 나는 양말 한 켤레가 필요하다.

→ I need _____ socks.

16. 다음 대화의 빈칸에 들어갈 말이 바르게 짝지어진 것은?

> A: Do they have _____ child?
> B: Yes, they do. They have two _____.

① a – children ② the – child
③ a – childs ④ an – children
⑤ 필요 없음 – children

17. 다음 대화의 밑줄 친 ①~⑤ 중 어법상 어색한 것은?

> A: Do you have a ①pet?
> B: ②Yes, I do. I have two ③puppies and one ④rabbits. I like ⑤them very much.

18. 다음 중 어법상 옳은 것은?

① He drinks a lot of milks.
② Two horse run very fast.
③ Ryan has five tomatos.
④ Are they your potatoes?
⑤ It's cold. Put on these glove.

19. 다음 중 빈칸에 들어갈 말이 나머지와 다른 것은?

① Many birds fly to _____ sky.
② The men go to _____ south.
③ _____ earth is round.
④ I visit my uncle once _____ month.
⑤ There is a girl. _____ girl is Sue.

20. 다음 중 빈칸에 관사가 필요 없는 것은?

① I meet _____ famous musician.
② Open _____ window, please.
③ I'm looking for _____ shirt.
④ Take medicine three times _____ day.
⑤ We go to _____ school at eight.

〈서술형 문제〉

[21-22] 다음 문장을 괄호 안의 지시대로 바꾸어 쓰시오.

21.
> I see a deer in the woods. (a를 four로)

→ _____

22.
> He eats a piece of cake. (a를 two로)

→ _____

23. 다음 문장을 〈보기〉와 같이 바꿔 쓰시오.

> 〈보기〉 She is a pretty woman.
> → They are pretty women.

It is a sweet candy.

→ _____

24. 다음 빈칸 중 필요한 곳에 the를 쓰시오.

> I am busy today. I play _____ piano for _____ two hours and have _____ lunch with my friend, Jack. After lunch, I study _____ science with him.

25. 다음 글의 빈칸에 a, an, the 중 알맞은 것을 쓰시오.

> He is _____ middle school student. He wears _____ uniform, but he doesn't like _____ uniform. He plays _____ guitar very well.

대명사란 무엇인가?

앞에 나온 명사를 대신할 때 대명사로 바꾸어 사용할 수 있는데
인칭대명사는 사람이나 동물, 사물을 대신해서 나타내며 지시대명
사는 사람이나 사물을 가리키는 대명사이다. 또한 부정대명사는
불특정한 대상을 가리킨다.

This is my friend, Jane.

I don't have a pencil. I need **one**.

Chapter 4. 대명사

Unit 16 지시대명사

- 지시대명사는 사물이나 사람을 가리키는 대명사로 this, that, these, those가 있다. this와 that은 be동사 is, these와 those는 be동사 are와 쓰인다.

가리키는 대상	단수	복수
가까이 있는 사물이나 사람	This(이것, 이 사람)+is	These(이것들, 이 사람들)+are
떨어져 있는 사물이나 사람	That(저것, 저 사람)+is	Those(저것들, 저 사람들)+are

- 의문문에서 this나 that으로 물으면 it으로, these나 those로 물으면 they로 대답한다.
  Is **this** your bag? – Yes, **it** is. / No, **it** isn't.
  Are **those** your hats? – Yes, **they** are. / No, **they** aren't.

- this, that, these, those는 뒤에 오는 명사를 수식하는 형용사로도 쓰이며, 이때는 '이 ~' 또는 '저 ~'의 뜻이다.
  This book is very interesting.

Practice

A. 다음 우리말과 같은 뜻이 되도록 빈칸에 알맞은 말을 쓰시오.

1. 이분은 나의 어머니입니다. → _____ is my mother.
2. 저 남자는 키가 매우 크다. → _____ man is very tall.
3. 저것들은 너의 장갑이니? → Are _____ your gloves?
4. 이 포도들은 달콤하다. → _____ grapes are sweet.

B. 다음 밑줄 친 부분에서 잘못된 것을 바르게 고치시오.

1. This pants are too long for me.   2. These are not my computer.
3. Those boys is Joe and Mike.   4. Are that her hamsters?

C. 다음 우리말과 뜻이 같도록 빈칸에 알맞은 말을 쓰시오.

1. 이 남자는 나의 삼촌이다.
   → _____ man _____ my uncle.
2. 저 운동화들은 매우 더럽다.
   → _____ sneakers _____ very dirty.
3. 이것은 재미있는 책이다.
   → _____ _____ an interesting book.
4. 저것들은 높은 빌딩들이다.
   → _____ _____ tall buildings.
5. 저 자전거는 나의 것이 아니다.
   → _____ bike _____ not mine.

Grammar Tip

this, that, these, those가 명사 앞에 와서 명사를 수식하는 지시형용사로 쓰일 수 있다.

A. grape 포도

B. pants 바지
   hamster 햄스터

C. sneakers 운동화
   dirty 더러운

Unit 17 비인칭 주어 it

- 대명사 it : 사물을 대신해서 나타내는 대명사로 '그것'이라는 뜻이다.

  I play basketball. I like **it**.

- 비인칭 주어 it : 시간, 날짜, 요일, 날씨, 계절, 거리, 명암 등을 나타낼 때는 문장의 주어로 비인칭 주어 it을 쓴다. 이때 it은 '그것'이라고 해석하지 않는다.

시간 : It's three o'clock.	날짜 : It's September 2nd.
요일 : It's Monday.	계절 : It's spring now.
날씨 : It's rainy.	거리 : It's four kilometers.
명암 : It's dark outside.	

Practice

A. 다음 문장의 It이 대명사인지 비인칭 주어인지 고르시오.

1. It's snowing outside. (대명사 / 비인칭 주어)

2. It's Sunday today. (대명사 / 비인칭 주어)

3. It's your camera. (대명사 / 비인칭 주어)

4. It's two kilometers from there. (대명사 / 비인칭 주어)

B. 다음 우리말과 뜻이 같도록 빈칸에 알맞은 말을 쓰시오.

1. 기차로 1시간 걸린다.

   → _____ takes an hour by train.

2. 오늘은 금요일이다.

   → _____ Friday today.

3. 그것은 무거운 상자이다.

   → _____ _____ a heavy box.

4. 밖은 밝고 따뜻하다.

   → _____ bright and warm outside.

5. 지금은 여름이다.

   → _____ _____ summer now.

C. 다음 문장을 바르게 해석하시오.

1. It is March third. → _____

2. It is cold in winter. → _____

3. It is my purse. → _____

4. It is twelve o'clock. → _____

18 부정대명사 one

· 부정대명사는 불특정한 사람이나 사물을 나타내는 대명사이다. 부정대명사 one은 앞에 나온 것을 가리킬 때 사용되거나 일반적인 사람을 나타낼 때 사용된다.

(1) 앞에 나온 셀 수 있는 명사와 같은 종류의 것을 가리킬 때 쓰며 복수형은 ones이다.

I don't have a watch. I need **one**. (one = a watch)

I have gloves. She has the the same **ones**, too. (ones = gloves)

(2) 일반적인 사람을 나타낼 때 쓰며 소유격은 one's이다.

One should keep **one's** promise.

= We should keep our promise.

· 서로 알고 있는 특정한 단수명사를 가리킬 때는 it을 사용한다. (복수명사일 경우에는 they 사용)

A: Do you have the smart phone?   *B*: Yes, I have **it**. (it = the smart phone)

 Practice

 Grammar Tip

A. 다음 괄호 안에서 알맞은 것을 고르시오.

1. Look at the car. (It / One) is very fast.

2. Do you have an umbrella? – No, I need (it / one).

3. The shoes are expensive. Do you have cheap (one / ones)?

4. Her bag is very old. She doesn't like (it / one).

5. She has a beautiful ring. I want the same (it / one).

B. 다음 밑줄 친 부분을 바르게 고치시오.

1. My car is old. I need a new <u>ones</u>.

2. I have a storybook. <u>One</u> is interesting.

3. One should do <u>ones</u> best.

4. I have three ball; a red one and two blue <u>one</u>.

C. 다음 우리말과 뜻이 같도록 빈칸에 알맞은 말을 쓰시오.

1. 나는 자가 필요해. 너는 하나 가지고 있니?

→ I need a ruler. Do you have _____?

2. 나는 로봇을 가지고 있다. 그것은 새것이다.

→ I have a robot. _____ is new.

3. 나는 그 피자를 원한다. 나는 그것을 좋아한다.

→ I want the pizza. I like _____ very much.

4. 나는 그 바지를 좋아하지 않는다. 나는 그 파란 것이 좋다

→ I don't like the pants. I like the blue _____.

Grammar Tip

앞에 나온 일반적인 것을 나타낼 때는 one을 사용하고 특정한 것을 나타낼 때는 it을 사용한다.

A. cheap 값이 싼
   same 같은

일반적인 사람을 나타낼 때는 one을 사용하며 복수형은 ones이고 소유격은 one's이다.

B. storybook 이야기책
   best 최선, 최고

C. ruler 자
   robot 로봇

Unit

19 another, other

- another는 'an+other'의 형태로 '다른 하나, 하나 더'라는 뜻으로 단수 취급한다.

  I don't like this one. Show me **another**.

- other는 '다른 것(사람)'의 뜻으로 사람이나 사물에 모두 사용한다.

  one ~ the other ...: (둘 중) 하나는 ~이고 나머지 하나는 …

  one ~ (the) others ...: 하나는 ~이고 (그) 나머지들은 …

  one ~ another ... the other ...: 하나는 ~ 또 하나는 … 나머지 하나는 …

  He has two sons. **One** is a teacher and **the other** is a doctor.

  They have pets. **One** is a cat and **others** are puppies.

  He has three brothers. **One** is a teacher, **another** is a doctor, and **the other** is a pilot.

  * Some ~ others …: 몇몇은 ~이고 나머지들은 …

Practice

A. 다음 빈칸에 알맞은 말을 쓰시오.

1. He has two caps. One is red and the _____ is yellow.

2. There are three flowers in the vase. One is pink, _____ is white, and _____ is red.

3. This skirt is too short. Show me _____.

4. Some like sandwiches and _____ like hamburgers.

B. 다음 빈칸에 들어갈 말을 〈보기〉에서 골라 쓰시오.

〈보기〉 one   another   other   others

1. I have two shirts. One is green, and the _____ is blue.

2. I don't want this chair. Do you have _____?

3. The students drink juice. _____ likes grape juice and _____ like apple juice.

C. 다음 우리말과 뜻이 같도록 빈칸에 알맞은 말을 쓰시오.

1. 이 오렌지는 안 좋아요. 다른 것으로 해도 될까요?

   → This orange is not good. Can I have _____?

2. 그녀는 개가 두 마리 있다. 한 마리는 하얀색이고, 나머지는 검은색이다.

   → She has two dogs. _____ is white and _____ is black.

3. 책이 다섯 권 있다. 하나는 나의 것이고 그 나머지들은 그녀의 것이다.

   → There are five books. _____ is mine and _____ are hers.

Grammar Tip

another, other도 불특정한 것을 나타낼 사용하는 부정대명사이다.

A. vase 꽃병
skirt 치마

B. chair 의자

'또 하나의 다른 것'을 나타낼 때는 another를 사용하고 나머지를 나타낼 때는 other를 사용한다.

C. mine 나의 것

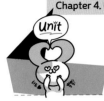

20 재귀대명사

- 재귀대명사는 '~ 자신', '~ 자체'의 뜻으로 주어의 동작이 주어 자신에게 미치거나 주어의 행동을 강조할 때 쓴다.
- 인칭대명사의 소유격(1, 2인칭)이나 목적격(3인칭) 뒤에 단수형에는 -self, 복수형에는 -selves를 붙인다.

	단수	복수
1인칭	myself	ourselves
2인칭	yourself	yourselves
3인칭	himself / herself / itself	themselves

Practice

A. 다음 우리말과 같도록 괄호 안에서 알맞은 것을 고르시오.

1. She cut (herself, her) with a knife.
   그녀는 칼에 베였다.

2. Heaven helps those who help (themself, themselves).
   하늘은 스스로 돕는 자를 돕는다.

3. Brian always thinks of (himself, his).
   Brian은 항상 자신만을 생각한다.

4. The door opened of (itself, itselves).
   문이 저절로 열렸다.

5. Jane draws (himself, him) in a soccer uniform.
   Jane은 축구 유니폼을 입은 그를 그린다.

6. Eric draws (himself, him) in a soccer uniform.
   Eric은 축구 유니폼을 입은 자신을 그린다.

7. I make the model airplane (myselves, myself).
   나는 스스로 그 모형 비행기를 만든다.

B. 다음 빈칸에 알맞은 재귀대명사를 넣어 문장을 완성하시오.

1. I make spaghetti _____. (I)

2. She talks about _____. (she)

3. He says to _____ "I am happy." (he)

4. A: May I have some more cookies?
   B: Sure, help _____. (you)

5. A: Let's me introduce _____. I'm Mark. (I)
   B: Nice to meet you.

6. We enjoy _____ at the concert. (we)

A. 다음 우리말과 같도록 주어진 단어를 이용하여 완성하시오.

1. 이분은 나의 수학 선생님이시다. (this, math, teacher)

→ _____

2. 저 소녀들은 Ashley의 여동생들이다. (those, Ashley's, sisters)

→ _____

3. 이것들은 너의 고양이들이니? (these, cats)

→ _____

4. 여름에는 덥다. (it, hot, summer)

→ _____

B. 다음 빈칸에 one(s)이나 it 중 알맞은 것을 쓰시오.

1. This cap is nice. John gives _____ to me.

2. I don't have an eraser. Can I borrow _____?

3. I make a card and give _____ to Joe on his birthday.

4. Give me two red pencils and I don't need three blue _____.

5. She doesn't have this ring, so she needs _____.

6. I raise three cats – a black one and two white _____.

C. 다음 빈칸에 알맞은 대명사를 쓰시오.

1. He needs the book, so he orders _____.

2. Do you have a dictionary? – No, I don't have _____?

3. This example is not good. Show me _____.

4. One student likes math, but _____ don't.

5. They have two flowers. _____ is a rose and the _____ is a tulip.

D. 다음 밑줄 친 부분을 바르게 고치시오.

1. Is this your bike? – Yes, <u>this</u> is.

2. <u>That</u> is January 12th. It is cold.

3. These <u>tower</u> are very old and tall.

4. He sometimes cuts his hair <u>him</u>.

Grammar Tip

대명사 it이 비인칭 주어로 쓰일 때는 '그것'이라고 해석하지 않는다.

A. summer 여름

B. eraser 지우개
raise 기르다

C. order 주문하다
dictionary 사전
example 견본

의문문에서 this나 that으로 물으면 it으로, these나 those로 물으면 they로 대답한다.

D. January 1월
tower 탑

1. 다음 대화의 빈칸에 들어갈 말이 순서대로 짝지어진 것을 고르시오.

   A: _____ are very old.
   B: Yes, but _____ house is not old.

   ① Those – these
   ② This – that
   ③ These – that
   ④ That – those
   ⑤ That – these

2. 다음 밑줄 친 it의 쓰임이 나머지와 다른 것은?

   ① It's not far from here.
   ② It's snowing now.
   ③ It's bright outside.
   ④ It's a very funny story.
   ⑤ It's Monday today.

3. 다음 대화의 밑줄 친 부분 중 어색한 것은?

   A: Is ①this your umbrella?
   B: Yes, ②this is.
   A: I don't have ③an umbrella.
      ④How's the weather?
   B: ⑤It's raining outside.

4. 다음 문장에서 틀린 부분을 찾아 바르게 고치시오.

   It is June 22nd in Seoul. That is June 21st in Los Angeles.

   _____ → _____

5. 다음 대화의 빈칸에 알맞은 것은?

   A: Is that your bag?
   B: _____ It is Dan's.

   ① Yes, it is.
   ② No, it isn't.
   ③ Yes, that is.
   ④ No, that isn't.
   ⑤ No, they aren't.

6. 다음 질문에 대한 대답으로 알맞은 것은?

   How's the weather today?

   ① It's sunny and warm.
   ② It's April 25th.
   ③ It's my birthday.
   ④ It's two kilometers from here.
   ⑤ It's the weather.

[7-8] 다음 밑줄 친 부분의 쓰임이 나머지 넷과 다른 것을 고르시오.

7. ① Do you know this girl?
   ② This watch is my uncle's.
   ③ This is my friend, Julia.
   ④ This ring is expensive.
   ⑤ This man plays the piano well.

8. ① It is seven kilometers.
   ② It is dark in the cave.
   ③ It is summer now.
   ④ It is ten o'clock p.m.
   ⑤ It is a nice jacket.

[9-10] 다음 빈칸에 알맞은 것을 고르시오.

9.

> We had a fun party.
> We enjoyed _____.

① myself   ② yourself
③ herself   ④ ourselves
⑤ yourselves

10.

> The young man _____ cooks every meals.

① myself   ② yourself
③ himself   ④ herself
⑤ themselves

11. 다음 빈칸에 들어갈 말이 나머지 넷과 <u>다른</u> 것은?
  ① Her idea is a good _____.
  ② The bike is old. I want a new _____.
  ③ You have a hat. She has same _____.
  ④ I lost my purse. I need _____.
  ⑤ You know many stories. Tell me _____.

12. 다음 밑줄 친 부분이 가리키는 것을 찾아 쓰시오.

> A: May I help you?
> B: Yes, please. I'm looking for a shirt.
> A: How about this <u>one</u>?
> B: Oh, I like it.

_____

[13-14] 다음 빈칸에 들어갈 말이 바르게 짝지어진 것을 고르시오.

13.

> A: Do you have a camera?
> B: Yes, I have _____. But I will give _____ to my brother.

① it – another   ② it – it
③ one – another   ④ one – it
⑤ one – one

14.

> There are many necklaces. _____ is cheap, but _____ are expensive.

① One – the others   ② One – the other
③ One – another   ④ One – other
⑤ One – it

[15-16] 다음 두 문장이 같은 뜻이 되도록 빈칸에 알맞은 말을 쓰시오.

15.

> This is a very useful dictionary.
> = _____ _____ is very useful.

16.

> The distance between my house and the library is two kilometers.
> = _____ _____ two kilometers from my house to the library.

49

[17-18] 다음 빈칸에 알맞은 것을 고르시오.

17.

He has two classes today. One is history and _____ is science.

① two ② ones
③ other ④ another
⑤ the other

18.

We have four apples. One is red and _____ are green.

① ones ② other
③ another ④ the others
⑤ they

19. 다음 밑줄 친 부분을 one(s)로 바꾸어 쓸 수 없는 것은?

① Do you have a pet? I want a pet.
② This is a nice boat. I like the boat.
③ Look at the cars. I like the red car.
④ Where are pencils? I need a pencil.
⑤ My socks are dirty. Do you have socks?

20. 다음 우리말을 영어로 바르게 옮긴 것은?

그녀는 캔버스에 그녀 자신을 그린다.

① She draw her on the canvas.
② She draws her on the canvas.
③ She draws herself on the canvas.
④ She draws on the canvas herself.
⑤ She herself draws on the canvas.

〈서술형 문제〉

[21-22] 다음 우리말과 같도록 알맞게 배열하시오. (지시대명사나 지시형용사를 포함하시오.)

21.

이 신발들은 매우 편하다.
(very, shoes, comfortable, are)

→ _____

22.

저것들은 매우 높은 건물들이다.
(are, buildings, very, tall)

→ _____

23. 다음 우리말과 같도록 문장을 완성하시오.

오후 7시이다. 그러나 아직 밖은 밝다.

_____ _____ seven o'clock p.m.
But _____ _____ still bright outside.

24. 다음 문장을 읽고, 문장을 완성하시오.

I have three friends from other countries.

(1) _____ from Canada.
(2) _____ from China.
(3) _____ from Japan.

25. 다음 글을 읽고, 밑줄 친 부분 중 어색한 부분을 찾아 각각 고치시오.

Today is my birthday. I make the birthday cake. ⓐ And I bake the cookies my. My friends come to my house. We have a fun party. ⓑ We enjoy us at the party.

ⓐ _____ → _____
ⓑ _____ → _____

50

시제란 무엇인가?

과거, 현재, 미래처럼 시간을 나타내는 것을 시제라고 한다. 영어에서는 동사의 형태를 바꾸거나 조동사를 이용하여 다양한 시제를 나타내는데 단순시제(과거, 현재, 미래), 진행시제, 완료시제가 있다.

They **played** soccer yesterday.

They **play** baseball.

진행시제란 무엇인가?

단순시제는 동작이나 상태가 이루어진 시점을 나타내며 진행시제는 동작이나 상태가 계속되고 있는 것을 나타낼 때 쓴다.

We **eat** dinner at seven.

We **are eating** dinner now.

Chapter 5. 동사의 시제

Unit 21. be동사의 과거형

Unit 22. be동사 과거형의 부정문

Unit 23. be동사 과거형의 의문문

Unit 24. 일반동사의 과거형 1(규칙 변화)

Unit 25. 일반동사의 과거형 2(불규칙 변화)

Unit 26. 일반동사 과거형의 부정문

Unit 27. 일반동사 과거형의 의문문

Unit 28. 진행형의 의미와 형태

Unit 29. 현재진행형과 과거진행형

Unit 30. 진행형의 부정문과 의문문

21 be동사의 과거형

- be동사의 과거형은 주어에 따라 was나 were를 쓰며 '~이었다, ~했다, (~에) 있었다'라는 뜻이다.

과거형	단수		복수	
	주어	be동사	주어	be동사
1인칭	I	was	We	were
2인칭	You	were	You	were
3인칭	He / She / It	was	They	were

I **was** at home yesterday.　　He **was** thirteen years old last year.

They **were** late for school two days ago.

- 과거시제는 주로 과거를 나타내는 부사(구)와 쓰인다.

→ yesterday, last night[week, month, year], two days[weeks, months, years] ago, then

Practice

A. 다음 괄호 안에서 알맞은 것을 고르시오.

1. I (am, was) so short when I (was, were) six.
2. The flowers (was, were) beautiful in the garden.
3. He and she (was, were) at home then.
4. They (are, were) in New York last month.

B. 다음 빈칸에 알맞은 be동사의 과거형을 쓰시오.

1. I _____ very tired yesterday.
2. My friend and I _____ in China last year.
3. The window _____ open then.
4. She _____ very sick last night.
5. They _____ busy last week.

C. 다음 우리말과 뜻이 같도록 빈칸에 알맞은 말을 쓰시오.

1. 그는 3년 전에 학생이었다.
   → _____ _____ a student three years ago.

2. 우리는 어제 매우 화가 나 있었다.
   → _____ _____ very angry yesterday.

3. 그들은 작년에 나의 반 친구들이었다.
   → _____ _____ my classmates last year.

4. 그녀의 생일은 지난 토요일이었다.
   → Her birthday _____ _____ Saturday.

Grammar Tip

과거시제는 과거에 있었던 일을 나타낼 때 쓰이며 last, ago, then 등의 부사나 부사구와 자주 쓰인다.

A. garden 정원

B. sick 아픈
　　busy 바쁜

C. classmate 반 친구
　　birthday 생일

22 be동사 과거형의 부정문

· be동사 과거형의 부정문은 「주어+be동사의 과거형+not ~.」의 형태로 '~이 아니었다, ~이 없었다'의 뜻이다.

주어	be동사 과거형+not	축약형
1, 3인칭 단수	was not	wasn't
복수 / 2인칭 단수	were not	weren't

I **was not**(wasn't) a teacher then.
He **was not**(wasn't) in his room.
We **were not**(weren't) hungry.

Practice

A. 다음 중 not이 들어갈 알맞은 위치를 고르시오.

1. He (①) was (②) a (③) good (④) doctor.
2. They (①) were (②) in (③) the gallery (④).
3. You (①) were (②) my (③) friend (④).

B. 다음 밑줄 친 부분을 바르게 고치시오.

1. He <u>not was</u> a soccer player last year.
2. They <u>was</u> not at the station last night.
3. The coffee <u>were</u> not very hot.
4. The women <u>not were</u> popular in Korea.
5. I <u>am</u> sick last year, but I'm very healthy.

C. 다음 문장을 과거형 부정문으로 바꿔 쓰시오.

1. Your trip is exciting.
   → _____

2. They are kind to everyone.
   → _____

3. I am interested in sports.
   → _____

4. The man is a great painter.
   → _____

5. My brother is good at history.
   → _____

Grammar Tip

A. gallery 미술관

B. popular 인기 있는
healthy 건강한

be동사 과거형 뒤에 not을 써서 부정문을 만들며 was not은 wasn't로, were not은 weren't로 줄여서 쓸 수 있다.

C. trip 여행
interested 관심 있는
history 역사

23 | be동사 과거형의 의문문

- be동사 과거형의 의문문은 주어와 be동사의 위치를 바꾸어 「Be동사의 과거형+주어 ~?」의 형태로 '~이었니?, ~이 있었니?'의 뜻이다.

  She was busy yesterday. → **Was** she busy yesterday?

  (주어와 be동사의 위치를 바꾸고 문장 뒤에 물음표를 넣는다.)

- be동사 과거형 의문문의 대답이 긍정이면 「Yes, 주어+be동사의 과거형.」, 부정이면 「No, 주어+be동사의 과거형 +not.」으로 한다. 부정의 대답에서 「be동사+not」은 축약형으로 쓴다.

의문문의 형태	Be동사의 과거형+주어 ~?	Was she busy yesterday?
대답(긍정)	Yes, 주어+be동사의 과거형.	Yes, she was.
대답(부정)	No, 주어+be동사의 과거형+not.	No, she wasn't.

Practice

A. 다음 괄호 안의 단어를 배열하여 의문문을 만드시오.

1. (he, was, an actor)?　→ _____
2. (were, sleepy, you)?　→ _____
3. (it, good news, was)?　→ _____

B. 다음 문장을 의문문으로 바꿔 쓰시오.

1. The water was very cold.
   → _____

2. They were thirsty then.
   → _____

3. He was in the bookstore yesterday.
   → _____

4. You were at the party.
   → _____

C. 다음 대화의 빈칸에 알맞은 말을 쓰시오.

1. A: Was the box heavy?
   B: No, _____.

2. A: Were Dan and Tom very close?
   B: Yes, _____.

3. A: Were they in the office at that time?
   B: No, _____.

4. A: Was your brother a good player?
   B: No, _____.

Unit 24 일반동사의 과거형 1(규칙 변화)

- 과거에 발생한 일을 나타낼 때에는 일반동사의 과거형을 사용하여 나타낸다.
- 일반동사의 과거형은 인칭과 수에 관계없이 일반적으로 동사원형에 -ed를 붙여서 만든다.
  She **cleans** the room. (현재형)
  She **cleaned** the room yesterday. (과거형)

대부분의 동사	동사원형+-ed	watched, wanted, worked
-e로 끝나는 동사	동사원형+-d	liked, loved, moved
「자음+y」로 끝나는 동사	y를 i로 고치고+-ed	tried, cried, studied
「모음+y」로 끝나는 동사	동사원형+-ed	played, enjoyed, stayed
「단모음+단자음」으로 끝나는 1음절 동사	마지막 자음을 한 번 더 쓰고+-ed	stopped, dropped, planned

 Practice

A. 다음 괄호 안에서 알맞은 것을 고르시오.

1. He (washes, washed) his car yesterday.
2. Tom and Ann (move, moved) to Chicago then.
3. Daniel (fixes, fixed) his gate last Friday.
4. I (visit, visited) my grandfather last month.
5. You (carry, carried) the luggage a few hours ago.

B. 다음 밑줄 친 부분을 과거형으로 바꿔 쓰시오.

1. I watch TV with them last night.
2. We play basketball in the afternoon.
3. The students study history then.
4. She lives in England two years ago.
5. They stop their fight at that time.

C. 다음 빈칸에 알맞은 말을 〈보기〉에서 골라 알맞게 쓰시오.

〈보기〉 love work walk finish stay

1. The man _____ for a bank two years ago.
2. We _____ at the hotel last year.
3. A prince _____ a princess at that time.
4. He _____ his homework last night.
5. They _____ to the market then.

Grammar Tip

과거의 일은 과거형으로 나타내며 일반동사 과거형은 일반적으로 동사원형에 -(e)d를 붙여서 나타낸다.

A. move 이사하다
luggage 짐

B. England 영국
fight 싸움

C. princess 공주
homework 숙제

25 일반동사의 과거형 2(불규칙 변화)

• 일반동사의 과거형은 일반적으로 -(e)d를 붙여서 나타내지만, 불규칙적으로 변하는 것들도 있다.

My mother **bought** clothes yesterday.

Emily **put** the notebook on the desk.

현재형과 과거형이 다른 동사			현재형과 과거형이 같은 동사
begin – began	give – gave	see – saw	cut – cut
buy – bought	go – went	sing – sang	hit – hit
come – came	have – had	sit – sat	hurt – hurt
do – did	lose – lost	swim – swam	put – put
eat – ate	make – made	take – took	read – read
get – got	run – ran	write – wrote	shut – shut

Practice

A. 다음 동사의 과거형을 쓰시오.

1. see   – _____
2. write   – _____
3. run   – _____
4. cut   – _____
5. eat   – _____
6. give   – _____
7. hurt   – _____
8. leave – _____

B. 다음 밑줄 친 부분을 바르게 고치시오.

1. She <u>comes</u> to the meeting late yesterday.
2. The concert <u>begins</u> at that time.
3. I <u>find</u> my ring under the bed then.
4. Alice <u>taked</u> a piano lesson last weekend.
5. Harry <u>does</u> his work last night.

C. 다음 괄호 안의 단어를 과거형으로 바꿔 쓰시오.

1. We _____ to the zoo last Sunday. (go)
2. He _____ toy cars for the kids. (make)
3. I _____ up early in the morning. (get)
4. Billy _____ the vegetables on the table. (put)
5. She _____ many pets in the house. (have)
6. My mother _____ the newspaper. (read)
7. They _____ him in the post office. (meet)
8. Brian _____ new clothes yesterday. (buy)

Grammar Tip

일반동사의 과거형이 불규칙적으로 변하는 동사 중에 cut, hit, hurt, put과 같은 동사는 현재형과 과거형이 같은 동사들이다.

B. concert 콘서트
lesson 수업, 강습

동사 read는 현재형과 과거형의 형태는 같지만 발음은 다르다.
read[ri:d](현재), read[red](과거)

C. zoo 동물원
vegetable 야채
newspaper 신문

 **Review Test**

A. 다음 빈칸에 알맞은 be동사를 쓰시오.

1. They _____ in France in 2015.

2. She _____ in the sixth grade last year.

3. You _____ late for the meeting yesterday.

4. I _____ in the library last Sunday.

B. 다음 괄호 안의 단어를 바르게 배열하여 문장을 완성하시오.

1. (not, I, was) a farmer. → _____

2. It (was, beautiful, not). → _____

3. The test (was, not, easy). → _____

4. (They, were, not) dentists. → _____

C. 다음 문장을 의문문으로 바꿔 쓰시오.

1. He was Mr. Smith. → _____

2. They were close friends. → _____

3. Kate was a good chef. → _____

D. 다음 괄호 안에서 알맞은 것을 고르시오.

1. A singer (visit / visits / visited) Seoul last month.

2. My sister (go / goes / went) to the movies yesterday.

3. The man (help / helps / helped) a lady a few days ago.

4. He (meet / meets / met) his friends last weekend.

E. 다음 괄호 안의 단어를 알맞은 형태로 바꿔 빈칸에 쓰시오.

1. He _____ a letter to her last night. (write)

2. Sue _____ the dress yesterday. (buy)

3. They _____ the new dance at that time. (learn)

4. We _____ dinner in a restaurant then. (eat)

F. 다음 밑줄 친 부분 중 어법상 어색한 것은?

I ①had a special vacation last summer. I ②spent a week with my cousins. We ③swimmed in the pool and ④went to the concert.

Grammar Tip

be동사 am과 is의 과거형은 was 이고 are의 과거형은 were이다.

A. France 프랑스
grade 등급, 학년

B. farmer 농부
dentist 치과 의사

be동사 과거형의 의문문은 주어와 be동사의 위치를 바꾸고 문장 끝에 물음표를 붙인다.

C. chef 요리사

일반동사의 과거형은 동사원형에 -(e)d를 붙여서 나타내며 불규칙적으로 변하는 동사도 있다.

E. letter 편지
restaurant 식당

F. special 특별한
cousin 사촌

26 일반동사 과거형의 부정문

· 일반동사 과거형의 부정문은 주어의 인칭과 수에 관계없이 「주어+did not[didn't]+동사원형 ~.」의 형태로 쓰며 '~하지 않았다'의 의미이다.

형태	예문
주어+did not+동사원형 ~. (did not = didn't)	I got up early yesterday. → I **didn't** get up early yesterday. She visited her uncle. → She **didn't** visit her uncle.

 Practice

A. 다음 괄호 안에서 알맞은 것을 고르시오.

1. He (doesn't / didn't) buy a purse yesterday.

2. They (don't / didn't) have dinner then.

3. She didn't (come / came) home late last night.

B. 다음 밑줄 친 부분을 바르게 고치시오.

1. My father didn't <u>fixed</u> the radio.

2. She <u>doesn't</u> go to school yesterday.

3. We didn't <u>caught</u> many fish last Sunday.

4. Jimmy <u>don't</u> read a magazine a few days ago.

5. I didn't <u>met</u> many people in the park.

C. 다음 문장을 부정문으로 바꿔 쓰시오.

1. The train stopped at this station.

   → _____

2. I went to the amusement park then.

   → _____

3. The child made a paper airplane.

   → _____

4. He saw the movie at the theater.

   → _____

5. Lisa helped his son with his homework.

   → _____

Grammar Tip

A. purse 지갑

일반동사 과거형의 부정문은 주어의 인칭과 수에 상관없이 did not을 사용하여 나타낸다.

B. catch 잡다
magazine 잡지

C. amusement park 놀이동산
paper 종이
theater 극장

Unit

27 | 일반동사 과거형의 의문문

· 일반동사 과거형의 의문문은 「Did+주어+동사원형 ~?」의 형태로 쓰며, '~했니?'의 의미이다.
· Did 뒤에 오는 동사는 반드시 동사원형으로 쓰며, 대답은 Yes나 No를 이용하여 나타낸다.

형태	예문
Did+주어+동사원형 ~? 대답 : Yes, 주어+did. 〈긍정〉 No, 주어+didn't. 〈부정〉	You met Laura at the park. → **Did** you meet Laura at the park? – Yes, I did. / No, I didn't. He played computer games. → **Did** he play computer games? – Yes, he did. / No, he didn't.

Practice

A. 다음 괄호 안에서 알맞은 것을 고르시오.

1. Did she (have / had) a terrible headache?

2. (Did / Does) Laura go on a trip alone then?

3. Did they (like / liked) my presents yesterday?

B. 다음 대화의 빈칸에 알맞은 말을 쓰시오.

1. A: _____ she live in Paris?
   B: No, she didn't.

2. A: Did the girls go to the concert?
   B: Yes, _____ _____.

3. A: Did Susan draw this picture?
   B: No, _____ _____.

C. 다음 문장을 의문문으로 바꿔 쓰시오.

1. She bought an expensive dress.
   → _____

2. They did many good things there.
   → _____

3. Jane read the novel again.
   → _____

4. My sister played tennis after dinner.
   → _____

Grammar Tip

A. terrible 끔찍한
   headache 두통
   alone 홀로

의문문의 주어가 단수명사나 복수명사일 때, 대답에서는 인칭대명사 he, she, it, they를 사용하여 나타낸다.

B. concert 콘서트
   draw 그리다

C. expensive 비싼
   thing 일
   novel 소설
   again 다시

Unit 28 진행형의 의미와 형태

· 동작이 특정 시점에 진행 중임을 나타낼 때 진행형을 쓰며, 「be동사+동사원형-ing」의 형태로 '~하고 있(었)다, ~ 하는 중이(었)다'라는 의미이다.

He **is going** to the park. (현재진행형)　　He **was going** to the park. (과거진행형)

· 동사의 -ing형 만드는 방법

대부분의 동사	동사원형+-ing	eat → eating, read → reading
-e로 끝나는 동사	e를 빼고+-ing	come → coming, make → making
「단모음+단자음」으로 끝나는 1음절 동사	자음을 한 번 더 쓰고+-ing	run → running, swim → swimming
-ie로 끝나는 동사	ie를 y로 고치고+-ing	lie → lying, die → dying

Practice

A. 다음 동사의 진행형을 쓰시오.

1. wait　　– _____
2. run　　– _____
3. sit　　– _____
4. buy　　– _____
5. carry　　– _____
6. drive　　– _____
7. play　　– _____
8. have　　– _____
9. cut　　– _____
10. tie　　– _____

B. 다음 괄호 안에서 알맞은 것을 고르시오.

1. I (am going / am go) to the bakery.
2. It (raining / is raining) outside now.
3. She is (rideing / riding) the bike.
4. They are (lieing / lying) to their teacher.
5. Mike (is looking / are looking) at the painting.

C. 다음 괄호 안의 동사를 빈칸에 알맞은 형태로 쓰시오.

1. She is _____ a birthday card. (make)
2. The boys are _____ in the pool now. (swim)
3. The man is _____ too fast. (walk)
4. My mother is _____ the cookies. (bake)
5. Jake and I are _____ the flowers. (water)

Grammar Tip

동사의 -ing형을 만들 때 -y로 끝나는 동사는 바로 앞 철자가 자음이나 모음과 상관없이 -ing만 붙인다.

A. tie 묶다, 매다

B. bakery 빵집
painting 그림

C. bake 굽다
water 물을 주다

Unit 29 현재진행형과 과거진행형

· 현재진행형은 현재 진행 중인 동작을 나타내고, 과거진행형은 과거 한 시점에서 진행 중인 동작을 나타낸다.

	현재진행형	과거진행형
형태	am, are, is+동사원형-ing	was, were+동사원형-ing
의미	~하는 중이다, ~하고 있다 (현재 진행 중인 동작)	~하는 중이었다, ~하고 있었다 (과거의 한 시점에서 진행 중인 동작)
예문	He **is swimming** now. She **is cleaning** in the room.	He **was swimming** at that time. We **were playing** computer games.
비고	**진행형으로 쓸 수 없는 동사** → 소유나 상태를 나타내는 동사(want, like, have, know), 감각동사(taste, hear) *have는 '먹다, (시간을) 보내다'라는 뜻일 때는 진행형으로 쓸 수 있다. I am having the ball. (×) / I am having lunch. (○)	

Practice

A. 다음 괄호 안의 동사를 알맞은 형태로 바꿔 쓰시오.

1. Sally is _____ in the kitchen. (cook)

2. Jim was _____ at that time. (sing)

3. They were _____ pictures. (take)

B. 다음 밑줄 친 부분을 바르게 고치시오.

1. I <u>was</u> listening to music now.

2. The woman <u>are writeing</u> a letter.

3. They <u>was</u> sleeping at that time.

4. People <u>are knowing</u> the greedy man.

5. She <u>were</u> standing behind the gate then.

C. 다음 괄호 안의 동사를 이용하여 빈칸에 알맞은 말을 쓰시오.

1. 그는 지금 샤워를 하고 있다. (take)
   → _____ a shower now.

2. 그 소년은 피아노를 치고 있었다. (play)
   → _____ the piano.

3. 그들은 정오에 점심을 먹고 있었다. (eat)
   → _____ lunch at noon.

4. 우리는 그 책들을 가지고 있다. (have)
   → _____ the books.

Grammar Tip

A. kitchen 부엌

소유나 상태, 감각동사는 진행의 의미를 가지고 있으며 진행형으로 쓸 수 없다.

B. greedy 욕심 많은
behind ~ 뒤에

C. shower 샤워
noon 정오

30 진행형의 부정문과 의문문

• 진행형의 부정문은 be동사 뒤에 not을 넣어 만들며, 의문문은 주어와 be동사의 위치를 바꾸고 문장 끝에 물음표를 붙인다.

부정문	주어+be동사+not+동사원형-ing ～.	I **am not** listening to music. We **were not** talking about you.
의문문	Be동사+주어+동사원형-ing ～? – Yes, 주어+be동사. 〈긍정〉 / 　No, 주어+be동사+not. 〈부정〉	**Are** you going to the hospital? – Yes, I am. / No, I'm not. **Was** she watching a movie? – Yes, she was. / No, she wasn't.

Practice

A. 다음 밑줄 친 부분을 바르게 고치시오.

1. They <u>not are</u> playing soccer there.

2. Many students <u>wasn't</u> studying math.

3. <u>Was</u> Kate and you eating some bread?

4. <u>It is</u> snowing in Seoul in the afternoon?

5. <u>Were</u> she tying the blue ribbons yesterday?

B. 다음 괄호 안의 지시대로 문장을 바꿔 쓰시오.

1. The train was arriving at that time. (부정문으로)
   → _____

2. He is waiting for him at the bookstore. (의문문으로)
   → _____

3. I'm doing my homework now. (부정문으로)
   → _____

4. Her father was finding the treasure map. (의문문으로)
   → _____

C. 다음 우리말과 같은 뜻이 되도록 문장을 완성하시오.

1. A: What was Roy doing last evening?
   B: _____
   (그는 축구를 하고 있었어요.)

2. A: Is your sister playing the violin?
   B: No, she isn't. _____
   (그녀는 음악을 듣고 있어요.)

Grammar Tip

A. bread 빵
　ribbon 리본

진행형의 부정문과 의문문은 be동사의 부정문과 의문문 만드는 방법과 같다.

B. arrive 도착하다
　treasure 보물
　map 지도

C. evening 저녁
　violin 바이올린

A. 다음 문장에서 <u>잘못된</u> 부분을 찾아 고치시오.

1. Alice didn't looked sleepy.

2. Did he told the students a story?

3. Jane not took a piano lesson.

4. He doesn't wash the car yesterday.

5. Was she come to the party early?

B. 다음 괄호 안의 지시대로 바꿔 쓰시오.

1. The woman put on a hat at that time. (부정문으로)

   → _____

2. She carried the baby in her arm. (의문문으로)

   → _____

3. You read the comic books last night. (부정문으로)

   → _____

C. 다음 밑줄 친 동사에 유의하여 진행형으로 바꿔 쓰시오.

1. It <u>snowed</u> a lot last night.

   → _____

2. My daughter <u>studies</u> English hard.

   → _____

3. I <u>drink</u> a glass of milk.

   → _____

4. They <u>lived</u> in the apartment.

   → _____

D. 다음 우리말과 같도록 빈칸에 알맞은 말을 쓰시오.

1. Tony는 그의 친구들과 이야기를 하고 있다.
   → Tony _____ _____ with his friends.

2. 그녀는 지금 그 말을 타고 있지 않다.
   → She _____ _____ the horse now.

3. 그 승무원은 여행용 가방을 나르고 있었다.
   → The attendant _____ _____ a suitcase.

4. 그 새들은 남쪽으로 날아가고 있니?
   → _____ the birds _____ to the south?

1. 다음 두 단어의 관계가 <u>다른</u> 것은?
① take – took   ② know – knew
③ run – run   ④ buy – bought
⑤ work – worked

2. 다음 중 동사의 과거형 변화가 나머지 넷과 <u>다른</u> 것은?
① watch   ② show
③ need   ④ catch
⑤ look

3. 다음 중 동사의 -ing형이 바르게 짝지어지지 <u>않은</u> 것은?
① bake – baking   ② eat – eatting
③ die – dying   ④ listen – listening
⑤ hit – hitting

4. 다음 빈칸에 Was가 들어갈 수 있는 것은?
① _____ they very hungry?
② _____ the game interesting?
③ _____ he and his wife in the park?
④ _____ these girls in the same class?
⑤ _____ you happy at that time?

5. 다음 빈칸에 공통으로 알맞은 것은?

> · Dan _____ his homework yesterday.
> · The girl _____ not buy anything.

① was   ② do
③ does   ④ didn't
⑤ did

6. 다음 빈칸에 들어갈 말이 나머지와 <u>다른</u> 것은?
① My mother _____ sick yesterday.
② I _____ at the party last weekend.
③ He _____ in the kitchen then.
④ Her brother _____ very tired now.
⑤ The old man _____ a cook in 2014.

7. 다음 빈칸에 알맞은 것은?

> He _____ a comic book now.

① read   ② readed
③ reading   ④ is reading
⑤ was reading

8. 다음 빈칸에 공통으로 알맞은 것은?

> · The room _____ clean. It was dirty.
> · Jenny _____ short. She was tall.

① isn't   ② aren't
③ wasn't   ④ weren't
⑤ didn't

9. 다음 문장 중 부정문으로 <u>잘못</u> 바꾼 것은?
① The boy ran to the park.
   → The boy didn't ran to the park.
② Mike finished his homework.
   → Mike didn't finish his homework.
③ We watched a movie last night.
   → We didn't watch a movie last night.
④ My sister read newspaper.
   → My sister didn't read newspaper.
⑤ He and she sat on the grass.
   → He and she didn't sit on the grass.

[10-11] 다음 빈칸에 알맞지 <u>않은</u> 것을 고르시오.

10.

> Amy was in the hospital _____.

① yesterday   ② last week

③ two days ago   ④ last year

⑤ tomorrow

11.

> He _____ last Friday.

① met Julie   ② helped the man

③ walked his dog   ④ visits his uncle

⑤ rode his bike

12. 다음 문장을 <보기>와 같이 바꿔 쓰시오.

> <보기> Mike is in his room.
> → Is Mike in his room?

The concert was very exciting.

→ _____

13. 다음 중 밑줄 친 부분의 쓰임이 <u>잘못된</u> 것은?

① <u>Are</u> your mom and dad sad?

② She <u>is</u> a teacher at that time.

③ We <u>were</u> late for the meeting.

④ <u>Were</u> they at the library?

⑤ Bob <u>was</u> fourteen years old.

14. 다음 문장을 의문문으로 바꿀 때, 빈칸에 들어갈 말이 바르게 짝지어진 것은?

> Sue cleaned her room then.
> → _____ Sue _____ her room then?

① Was – clean   ② Is – clean

③ Does – clean   ④ Did – clean

⑤ Did – cleaned

15. 다음 대화의 빈칸에 알맞은 대답은?

> A: Did Jim help your work?
> B: _____ He was busy.

① Yes, he did.   ② No, he didn't.

③ Yes, he does.   ④ No, he doesn't.

⑤ No, he wasn't.

16. 다음 문장을 부정문으로 만들 때 빈칸에 알맞은 말을 쓰시오.

> We had a great time at the party.
> → We _____ _____ have
> a great time at the party.
> = We _____ have a great
> time at the party.

17. 다음 빈칸에 들어갈 말이 순서대로 짝지어진 것은?

> A: Did you _____ at home yesterday?
> B: No, I didn't. I _____ to the theater.

① stay – go   ② stay – went

③ stayed – go   ④ stayed – went

⑤ stays – went

18. 다음 중 밑줄 친 동사의 과거형이 잘못된 것은?

① My dad <u>made</u> spaghetti.

② She <u>sang</u> a song loudly.

③ I <u>lost</u> my bag on the subway.

④ Eric <u>put</u> his coat on the sofa.

⑤ He <u>readed</u> books in the library.

19. 다음 대화의 빈칸에 공통으로 알맞은 것은?

> A: Sam, _____ you sleep well last night?
> B: Yes, I _____.

① do   ② does

③ did   ④ don't

⑤ didn't

20. 다음 밑줄 친 부분 중 어법상 옳은 것은?

① I didn't <u>wanted</u> an umbrella.

② Did she <u>saw</u> the man again?

③ Julie didn't <u>answers</u> the question.

④ <u>Does</u> he find his bag yesterday?

⑤ They <u>didn't</u> go on a trip then.

21. 다음 밑줄 친 부분 중 어법상 어색한 것은?

> I ①<u>got up</u> late in the morning, so I ②<u>don't</u> ③<u>have</u> breakfast. I ④<u>am</u> very hungry ⑤<u>now</u>.

22. 다음 빈칸에 Were가 올 수 있는 것은?

① _____ you very happy?

② _____ she a singer then?

③ _____ Tom play the drums?

④ _____ you studying now?

⑤ _____ you draw the picture?

[23-24] 다음 중 어법상 어색한 것을 고르시오.

23. ① They come back early.

② They didn't finish their homework.

③ Does Lucy call you last night?

④ Was your father building a house?

⑤ My sister wasn't driving at that time.

24. ① He is having the blue ball.

② My mother didn't drink coffee.

③ We are having lunch at home.

④ Jack didn't work at a hospital then.

⑤ The woman was standing by the door.

25. 다음 우리말과 같은 뜻이 되도록 할 때, 빈칸에 알맞은 것은?

> 우리는 어제 TV를 보지 않았다.
> → We _____ TV yesterday.

① don't watch   ② doesn't watch

③ didn't watched   ④ didn't watch

⑤ watched not

26. 다음 빈칸에 공통으로 알맞은 말을 쓰시오.

> · The children _____ sick yesterday.
> · We _____ going to the museum.

27. 다음 대화의 빈칸에 알맞은 대답은?

> *A*: Is she cooking in the kitchen?
> *B*: _____ She is making salad.

① Yes, she was.　② Yes, she is.
③ Yes, she does.　④ No, she wasn't.
⑤ No, she isn't.

28. 다음 밑줄 친 부분의 쓰임이 바르지 않은 것은?
① Our parents are knowing her.
② Are you listening to music?
③ The sun rises in the east.
④ She put her gloves on the bag.
⑤ They are meeting their teacher.

29. 다음 빈칸에 알맞은 말이 순서대로 짝지어진 것은?

> · She _____ coffee every morning.
> (그녀는 매일 아침 커피를 마신다.)
> · She _____ coffee this morning.
> (그녀는 오늘 아침에 커피를 마셨다.)

① drinks – drinks　② drank – drinks
③ drinks – drank　④ drink – drank
⑤ drank – drank

30. 다음 문장을 진행형으로 바꿀 때, 빈칸에 알맞은 것은?

> We didn't study math at that time.
> → We _____ math at that time.

① don't study　② didn't studying
③ aren't studying　④ weren't studying
⑤ wasn't studying

31. 다음 질문에 어울리는 대답은?

> Is it snowing outside?

① No, it's sunny.
② Yes, I like summer.
③ No, it will be fine.
④ Yes, it's very hot outside.
⑤ No, I can't go there.

32. 다음 우리말을 영어로 바르게 바꾼 것은?

> Ann은 나에게 생일 선물을 주었다.

① Ann gived me a birthday present.
② Ann gives me a birthday present.
③ Ann gave me a birthday present.
④ Ann was give me a birthday present.
⑤ Ann didn't give me a birthday present.

33. 다음 밑줄 친 부분이 어법상 어색한 것은?
① She's taking a picture.
② They're loving each other.
③ I'm looking for a shirt.
④ We're going to the bank.
⑤ He's helping his father.

34. 다음 중 어법상 옳은 것은?

① I not tired last Sunday.

② She is practice the piano.

③ People was in the store now.

④ They haved a great time there.

⑤ My mother was preparing dinner.

35. 다음 빈칸에 들어갈 말을 <보기>에서 골라 알맞은 형태로 바꿔 쓰시오.

<보기>	see	hurt	write

(1) Sue and I _____ a movie yesterday.

(2) I was ____ letters to my friends then.

(3) My brother _____ his leg last week.

<서술형 문제>

36. 다음 주어진 단어를 참고하여 우리말과 같도록 빈칸에 알맞은 말을 쓰시오.

(1) Jessica는 안경을 쓰니? (wear)

= _____ Jessica _____ glasses?

(2) 그들은 창문들을 열지 않았다. (open)

= They _____ _____ windows.

37. 다음 괄호 안의 단어를 어법에 맞게 고쳐 문장을 다시 쓰시오.

(1) I _____ a cold last week. (catch)

→ _____

(2) He _____ lunch at noon at that time. (have)

→ _____

38. 다음 <보기>와 같이 괄호 안의 어구를 넣어 문장을 다시 쓰시오.

<보기> They have fun at the party. (then)
→ They had fun at the party then.

She goes on a picnic. (last month)

→ _____

39. 다음 괄호 안에 주어진 말을 알맞은 형태로 바꾸어 빈칸에 쓰시오.

(1) Cindy _____ (play) the guitar very well. She _____ (learn) it from her uncle two years ago. He _____ (like) a famous guitarist at that time.

(2) Susan _____ (go) to the swimming pool every Saturday. Yesterday _____ (be) Saturday. So she went to the swimming pool and _____ (swim) for two hours.

40. 다음 Bill의 오후 일과표를 보고, 빈칸에 알맞은 말을 쓰시오.

4:30~5:30	play with his friends
5:30~6:30	do his homework
6:30~7:30	have dinner
7:30~8:30	read books

(1) At 5:10, he _____.

(2) At 6:20, he _____.

(3) At 7:10, he _____.

(4) At 7:50, he _____.

의문사란 무엇인가?

의문사는 특정한 정보를 묻기 위해 사용하는 말로 who, what, when, where, why, how 등이 있다. 의문사 의문문을 만들 때는 의문사를 문장 맨 앞에 쓰고 be동사나 일반동사 의문문의 순서로 쓴다.

What is your name?

Where do you meet him?

How does she go to the theater?

Chapter 6. 의문사

31 | who, whose

· who는 '누구, 누가'라는 뜻으로 사람의 이름이나 사람과의 관계를 물을 때 쓴다. whose는 '누구의, 누구의 것'이라는 뜻으로 소유를 물을 때 쓴다.

주격	누구	Who is she? – She is my sister.
	누가	Who cooks dinner? – My father does.
목적격	누구를	Who(m) do you meet? – I meet my cousin.
소유격	누구의	Whose bag is this? – It's mine.
소유대명사	누구의 것	Whose is this book? – It's my brother's.

＊who가 의문문에서 주어 역할을 하기도 하는데, 3인칭 단수 취급하여 동사는 3인칭 단수형으로 쓰며 의문문을 만들 때 do/does does를 사용하지 않는다.

 ## Practice

 Grammar Tip

A. 다음 괄호 안에서 알맞은 것을 고르시오.

1. (Who / Whose) is the handsome man?

2. (Who / Whose) sneakers are these?

3. (Who / Whose) lives in London?

4. (Whom / Who) is your favorite actor?

B. 다음 의문문에서 밑줄 친 부분을 바르게 고쳐 쓰시오.

1. <u>Whom</u> are these glasses? – They are his.

2. <u>Whose</u> do you like? – I like Bean.

3. Who <u>does teach</u> them history? – Mr. Jason.

4. <u>Who</u> purse is that? – It's my sister's.

C. 다음 우리말과 같도록 괄호 안의 단어를 바르게 배열하시오.

1. 그 예쁜 소녀는 누구니? (the pretty girl, is, who)

→ _____

2. 누가 그 꽃병을 깼니? (broke, who, the vase)

→ _____

3. 저 차는 누구의 것이니? (whose, that car, is)

→ _____

4. 그녀는 누구를 만났니? (who, she, meet, did)

→ _____

5. 이것은 누구의 개니? (this, is, whose, dog)

→ _____

A. handsome 잘생긴
actor 배우

의문사 Who가 의문문의 주어인 경우에는 3인칭 단수로 취급한다.

B. glasses 안경
history 역사

C. pretty 예쁜
vase 꽃병

Unit 32 | what, which

- what은 '무엇'이라는 뜻으로 사물의 이름이나 사람의 직업, 역할 등을 물을 때 쓴다.

무엇	**What** is his job?(What does he do?) – He is a baker.
무엇이(주격)	**What** makes him happy? – His baby.
무슨(어떤)+명사	**What** sport do you like? – I like soccer.

* what이 주격으로 의문문의 주어로 쓰인 경우에는 3인칭 단수 취급한다.

- which는 '어느 것'이라는 뜻으로 정해진 대상 중에서 선택을 물을 때 쓴다.

어느 것	**Which** do you want, coffee or tea? – I want some coffee.
어느+명사	**Which** bag is yours, this or that? – This one.

Practice

A. 다음 괄호 안에서 알맞은 것을 고르시오.

1. A: (What / Which) do you do?
   B: I'm a baker.

2. A: (What / Which) car is yours, this or that?
   B: That one.

3. A: (What / Which) do you like better, blue or red?
   B: I like blue better.

B. 다음 대화의 빈칸에 알맞은 의문사를 쓰시오.

1. A: _____ do you need?
   B: I need a black hat.

2. A: _____ ring do you like better, this or that?
   B: That one is better.

3. A: _____ do you want for your birthday?
   B: I want a new bike.

C. 다음 괄호 안의 단어를 이용하여 우리말과 같도록 완성하시오.

1. 너의 남동생은 어떤 과목을 좋아하니? (subject)
   → _____ _____ _____ your brother like?

2. 너는 여름과 겨울 중 어느 계절을 좋아하니? (season)
   → _____ _____ _____ you like, summer or winter?

3. 너는 피자와 스파게티 중 어느 것을 더 원하니? (better)
   → _____ do you want _____, pizza _____ spaghetti?

Grammar Tip

정해지지 않은 대상을 물을 때는 what을 쓰고, 정해진 어떤 것을 물을 때는 which를 쓴다.

A. baker 제빵사
better 더 좋은

B. ring 반지
birthday 생일

C. subject 과목
season 계절
spaghetti 스파게티

33 | when, where

- when은 '언제'라는 뜻으로 시간이나 날짜, 때를 물을 때 쓴다.

언제	**When** is your birthday? – It's November 24th.
	When do you have lunch? – I have lunch at 12:30.

＊when으로 시작하는 의문문에 대한 대답은 시간의 전치사 at, in, on을 이용한다.

- where는 '어디에, 어디서'라는 뜻으로 위치, 장소나 출신을 물을 때 쓴다.

어디에	**Where** is the bank? – It's across the street.
어디서	**Where** did you meet Tim? – I met him in the park.

＊where로 시작하는 의문문에 대한 대답은 장소, 위치, 방향을 나타내는 전치사를 이용한다.
＊장소, 위치, 방향을 나타내는 전치사에는 in, at, on, under, across, next to 등이 있다.

Practice

A. 다음 괄호 안에서 알맞은 것을 고르시오.

1. (What / When) do you come home?
2. (Where / When) does she live?
3. (Where / When) is Arbor Day in Korea?
4. (What / Where) is the bus stop?

B. 다음 빈칸에 알맞은 의문사를 쓰시오.

1. _____ are they from?
2. _____ do you go to the library?
3. _____ is the final test?
4. _____ does he go on Sunday?

C. 다음 문장에서 <u>잘못된</u> 부분을 찾아 바르게 고쳐 쓰시오.

1. What does the class start? – It starts at nine.
   _____ → _____

2. When are my gloves? – They are under the chair.
   _____ → _____

3. Who are you going? – I am going to the market.
   _____ → _____

4. Which did she call him? – She called him at noon.
   _____ → _____

5. What is the hospital? – It's next to the bakery.
   _____ → _____

Grammar Tip

시간을 물을 때는 when을 사용하고 장소를 물을 때는 where를 사용한다.

A. bus stop 버스 정류장

B. final 마지막의

C. market 시장
hospital 병원
bakery 빵집

34 why, how

- why는 '왜'라는 뜻으로 이유나 원인을 물을 때 쓴다. why로 시작하는 의문문에 대한 대답은 because(왜냐하면)로 시작하는데 because는 생략할 수 있다.

왜(이유, 원인)	**Why** is he in a hurry? – Because he is late for school.
	Why do you like this movie? – It's very interesting.

- how는 '어떤, 어떻게'라는 뜻으로 상태나 방법, 교통수단을 물을 때 쓴다.

상태	**How** is the weather? – It's very cloudy.
방법	**How** can I get in? – Just push the door.
교통수단	**How** do you go to school? – I go to school by bike.

Practice

A. 다음 질문에 알맞은 대답을 〈보기〉에서 골라 기호를 쓰시오.

〈보기〉 ⓐ Because he likes them.　ⓑ I'm a little tired.
　　　ⓒ Because she broke his toys.　ⓓ He goes there by bus.

1. Why is he so angry?　　　–　_____
2. How are you today?　　　–　_____
3. Why does he grow vegetables?　–　_____
4. How does he go to the station?　–　_____

B. 다음 대화의 빈칸에 알맞은 의문사를 쓰시오.

> *A*: _____ are you so happy?
> *B*: Because I got a new bike for my birthday.

C. 다음 우리말과 같도록 빈칸에 알맞은 말을 쓰시오.

1. 너는 왜 그 가방을 선택했니?
　→ _____ _____ you choose the bag?

2. 제주도의 날씨는 어떠니?
　→ _____ _____ the weather in Jeju-do?

3. 너는 왜 학교에 결석했니?
　→ _____ _____ you absent from school?

4. 우리는 공항에 어떻게 가니?
　→ _____ _____ _____ go to the airport?

Grammar Tip

교통수단을 나타낼 때는 「by+교통수단」으로 나타내며 걸어서 가는 경우는 on foot이라고 한다.

A. tired 피곤한
　vegetable 야채

C. choose 선택하다, 고르다
　absent 결석의
　airport 공항

Unit 35 how + 형용사/부사

- 「How+형용사/부사 ~?」의 형태로 쓰여 수나 양, 정도를 물을 때 쓴다.

How many ~?	~ 얼마나 많니?(수)	How many sisters do you have? – I have two sisters.
How much ~?	~ 얼마니?(양, 가격)	How much milk do you want? – I want a glass of milk.
How old ~?	~ 몇 살이니?(나이)	How old is your daughter? – She is three years old.
How often ~?	얼마나 자주 ~하니?(빈도)	How often do you go to the gym? – Every day.
How long ~?	~ 길이가 얼마니?(길이), 얼마나 오래 ~하니?(기간)	How long did you live in New York? – I lived there for ten years.
How tall ~?	~ 얼마나 크니?(키, 높이)	How tall are you? – I'm 170 centimeters tall.
How far ~?	~ 얼마나 멀리 있니?(거리)	How far is the zoo from here? – It is about one kilometer.

Practice

A. 다음 괄호 안에서 알맞은 것을 고르시오.

1. How (many / much) is this jacket? – It's 25 dollars.
2. How (long / far) is the snake? – It's two meters long.
3. How (tall / often) do you come here? – Once a month.

B. 다음 빈칸에 알맞은 말을 〈보기〉에서 골라 쓰시오.

| 〈보기〉 tall long much far many |

1. How _____ hairpins do you have?
2. How _____ is he?
3. How _____ is the station from here?
4. How _____ did you stay in New York?

C. 다음 괄호 안의 단어를 이용하여 우리말을 영어로 쓰시오.

1. 너의 여동생은 몇 살이니? (how old, your sister)
   → _____

2. 이 스웨터는 얼마입니까? (how much, this sweater)
   → _____

3. 저 다리는 얼마나 깁니까? (how long, that bridge)
   → _____

Grammar Tip

A. jacket 재킷
snake 뱀

How many 뒤에는 셀 수 있는 명사의 복수형이 오고 How much 뒤에는 셀 수 없는 명사가 온다.

B. hairpin 헤어핀
stay 머물다

C. sweater 스웨터
bridge 다리

A. 다음 빈칸에 알맞은 말을 <보기>에서 골라 쓰시오.

<보기> How	Whose	When	Which

1. _____ car is that?

2. _____ many onions do you want?

3. _____ do you like better, skiing or skating?

4. _____ does your class finish?

B. 다음 우리말과 같도록 빈칸에 알맞은 말을 쓰시오.
1. 네가 가장 좋아하는 가수는 누구니?
   → _____ _____ your favorite singer?

2. 그녀는 왜 그렇게 늦게 도착했니?
   → _____ _____ she arrive so late?

3. 그는 그의 개를 어디서 잃어버렸니?
   → _____ _____ he lose his dog?

4. 이 절은 얼마나 오래됐니?
   → _____ _____ _____ this temple?

C. 다음 대화의 빈칸에 알맞은 의문사를 쓰시오.
1. A: _____ did you have dinner last Sunday?
   B: I had dinner at the Japanese restaurant.

2. A: _____ wrote the letter to him?
   B: Tina wrote the letter to him.

3. A: _____ bus goes to your house?
   B: Bus No. 61.

4. A: _____ were you late for the meeting?
   B: Because there is a lot of traffic.

D. 다음 대답의 밑줄 친 부분을 참고하여 알맞은 질문을 쓰시오.
1. A: _____
   B: I clean my room <u>once a week</u>.

2. A: _____
   B: She is <u>165 centimeters</u>.

3. A: _____
   B: I get up <u>at seven o'clock</u>.

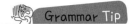
75

1. 다음 중 밑줄 친 부분의 쓰임이 잘못된 것은?

   ① <u>When</u> is your birthday?
   ② <u>Where</u> does Lisa live?
   ③ <u>Whose</u> shoes are they?
   ④ <u>Why</u> are you so angry?
   ⑤ <u>Who</u> are your hobbies?

[2-3] 다음 빈칸에 알맞은 것을 고르시오.

2.
   A: _____ was the festival?
   B: It was fun.

   ① Where   ② How
   ③ When   ④ Why
   ⑤ Which

3.
   A: _____ is faster, a taxi or a train?
   B: A train.

   ① What   ② Which
   ③ How   ④ Why
   ⑤ Where

4. 다음 빈칸에 Whose를 쓸 수 <u>없는</u> 것은?

   ① _____ is that necklace?
   ② _____ bags are these?
   ③ _____ are those big gloves?
   ④ _____ is this honest boy?
   ⑤ _____ watch is this?

[5-6] 다음 중 어법상 <u>어색한</u> 것을 고르시오.

5. ① How old is that tree?
   ② How often do you visit them?
   ③ How much are these pants?
   ④ How long is your sister?
   ⑤ How far is the store from here?

6. ① How is it going?
   ② Where are you, Ashley?
   ③ What season do you like?
   ④ Who is your favorite subject?
   ⑤ Why do the people like Mike?

7. 다음 빈칸에 공통으로 알맞은 것은?

   · _____ did you buy this hat?
   · _____ were you at that time?

   ① Where   ② How
   ③ Who   ④ When
   ⑤ Which

8. 다음 대화의 괄호 안에서 알맞은 것을 고르시오.

   A: How (many / much) desks are there in your class?
   B: There are thirty desks in my class.

9. 다음 빈칸에 공통으로 알맞은 의문사를 쓰시오.

> · _____ likes hot soup?
>
> · _____ teaches you English?

10. 다음 대화의 빈칸에 들어갈 말이 순서대로 짝지어진 것은?

> A: _____ do you go to school?
> B: I go to school by bus.
> A: How _____ does it take?
> B: It takes about 20 minutes.

① Where – long　② How – far
③ How – long　④ Why – often
⑤ When – far

11. 다음 빈칸에 When을 쓸 수 있는 것은?
① _____ is Christmas Eve?
② _____ is her job?
③ _____ is your office?
④ _____ fruit do you like?
⑤ _____ did you stay last Sunday?

12. 다음 질문에 대한 대답으로 알맞은 것은?

> How long is the concert?

① It's 32 years old.
② It's five kilometers.
③ It's about two hours.
④ It's 145 centimeters long.
⑤ It's nine thousand won.

13. 다음 대화의 밑줄 친 ①~⑤ 중 어법상 어색한 것은?

> A: ① How ② old do horses ③ live?
> B: They live ④ for about 30 ⑤ years.

14. 다음 대화의 빈칸에 알맞지 않은 것은?

> A: Whose sweater is this?
> B: It's _____.

① mine　　　　② Julia
③ his　　　　④ hers
⑤ my mother's

15. 다음 질문의 답에 해당하는 숫자를 모두 더하면?

> · How many legs does a cat have?
> · How many days are there in a week?
> · How many fingers do you have?

① 19　　　　　② 20
③ 21　　　　　④ 22
⑤ 23

16. 다음 빈칸에 들어갈 말이 나머지와 다른 것은?
① _____ gave you this doll?
② _____ knows Sarah?
③ _____ is your best friend?
④ _____ did the dishes yesterday?
⑤ _____ is your first class today?

[17-18] 다음 대답에 대한 알맞은 질문을 〈보기〉에서 고르시오.

> 〈보기〉 ⓐ How much is the doll?
> ⓑ Where are you going?
> ⓒ Where did you meet Bean?
> ⓓ How long does it take?

17. It's five thousand won.　　　　(　)

18. I met him at the station.　　　　(　)

[19-20] 다음 대화 중 <u>어색한</u> 것을 고르시오.

19. ① A: When does the train start?
　　 B: It starts at 4:10.
② A: Where did you put the book?
　　 B: I put it on the desk.
③ A: How often do you wash your hair?
　　 B: Every day.
④ A: Whose bike is that?
　　 B: It's mine.
⑤ A: Who do you like?
　　 B: Everyone likes me.

20. ① A: What does Emily do?
　　 B: Because she works at a bank.
② A: How do you go to City Hall?
　　 B: By subway.
③ A: Why are you nervous?
　　 B: Because I have a test today.
④ A: How was the movie?
　　 B: It was really great.
⑤ A: Where is my cell phone?
　　 B: I saw it on the table.

〈서술형 문제〉

[21-22] 다음 우리말과 같도록 괄호 안의 단어를 배열하여 문장을 완성하시오.

21. 그는 집에서 언제 피아노를 연주하니?
→ _____
the piano at home? (he, when, does, play)

22. 너는 월요일에 얼마나 많은 수업이 있니?
→ _____
on Monday? (classes, do, many, you, how, have)

23. 다음 대화에서 어법상 <u>어색한</u> 것을 찾아 바르게 고치시오.

> A: Kate, where are you going?
> B: I'm going to the hospital.
> A: How are you going there?
> B: Because I have a fever.

_____ → _____

24. 다음 대화의 빈칸에 알맞은 말을 각각 쓰시오.

> A: _____ do you go to the library?
> B: I go there three times a week.
> A: _____ do you study?
> B: I usually read books for two hours.

25. 다음 대화의 내용과 일치하도록 빈칸에 알맞은 질문을 쓰시오.

> A: Is Max ten years old?
> B: No, he was ten years old last year.

→ Q: _____
A: Max is eleven years old.

조동사란 무엇인가?

조동사는 동사를 도와주는 말로 미래, 가능, 추측, 의무 등을 나타낸다. 영어에서는 동사만으로 의미를 정확하게 전달할 수 없을 때 조동사를 사용하여 의미를 정확하게 전달할 수 있다.

I **can** pass the exam.

조동사의 특징은 무엇인가?

– 조동사 뒤에는 항상 동사원형을 쓰며, 조동사는 인칭과 수에 따라 형태가 변하지 않는다.

– 조동사는 두 개 이상 연속으로 사용할 수 없으며 하나는 바꾸어 쓸 수 있는 말로 바꾸어야 한다.

– 조동사의 부정문은 조동사 뒤에 not을 붙이며 의문문은 조동사를 맨 앞에 쓰고 의문문의 형태로 쓴다.

Chapter 7. 조동사

Unit

36 | will, be going to

· will은 미래나 의지를 나타낼 때 사용하며 미래의 의미를 나타낼 때는 be going to로 바꿔 쓸 수 있다.

조동사 will	'~할 것이다, ~일 것이다'라는 뜻으로 미래에 일어날 일이나 의지를 나타낸다.
	My sister **will** be five years old next month. He **will** finish the work by two o'clock.
be going to+동사원형	'~할 것이다, ~할 예정이다'의 뜻으로 가까운 미래의 일이나 계획을 나타낸다.
	We**'re going to** take the train to Busan. I**'m going to** clean my room today.

＊인칭대명사 다음에 나오는 will은 'll로 줄여 쓸 수 있다.
Are you hungry? I'll make a sandwich for you.

Practice

A. 다음 밑줄 친 부분을 바르게 고치시오.

1. Anna will <u>calls</u> you tonight.

2. My grandmother will <u>is</u> sixty years old next year.

3. He <u>wills</u> leave tomorrow.

4. She <u>are</u> going to visit her uncle.

B. 다음 괄호 안에 주어진 말을 넣어 문장을 다시 쓰시오.

1. She is here. (will, in five minutes)
→ _____

2. He learns Chinese. (will, this year)
→ _____

3. Sally buys a bike. (be going to, next week)
→ _____

4. You go to the library. (be going to, tomorrow)
→ _____

C. 다음 빈칸에 이어질 말을 〈보기〉에서 골라 기호를 쓰시오.

〈보기〉 ⓐ I'll put on a jacket.   ⓑ We're going to be late.
ⓒ I'll eat two hamburgers.   ⓓ It's going to rain soon.

1. I'm hungry. _____   2. Let's hurry. _____

3. It's cold. _____   4. Bring your umbrella. _____

Grammar Tip

조동사 뒤에는 항상 동사원형이 오며 주어가 3인칭 단수라도 -s를 붙이지 않는다.

A. tonight 오늘밤
tomorrow 내일

미래시제는 미래를 나타내는 부사(구)와 쓰이는 경우가 많다.
tomorrow(내일), next month(다음 달), this week(이번 주)

B. in five minutes 5분 뒤에
learn 배우다

37 will의 부정문과 의문문

- will의 부정문은 「주어+will not+동사원형~.」으로 나타내고 '~하지 않을 것이다'의 뜻이다.
  I **will not** eat lunch today.　She **won't** be at home. (won't = will not)
- will의 의문문은 「Will+주어+동사원형~?」으로 나타내고 '~할 거니?'의 뜻이다.
  A: **Will** they win the game?　*B:* Yes, they will. / No, they won't.
  A: **Will** you help me with my work? (요청의 뜻인 경우)　*B:* Sure. / Sorry, I can't.
  ＊will 의문문의 대답은 Yes나 No를 사용하여 답하며 부정의 대답은 축약형 won't가 쓰인다.
- be going to의 부정문은 be동사 다음에 not을, 의문문은 be동사를 주어 앞에 써서 표현한다.
  He **is not going to** work.
  A: **Are** you **going to** buy a new bicycle?　*B:* Yes, I am. / No, I'm not.

 ## Practice

A. 다음 괄호 안의 단어를 바르게 배열하여 문장을 다시 쓰시오.

1. (going, he, not, is, to) arrive there.
   → _____

2. (will, join, she) our team this week?
   → _____

3. (open, you, will) the window?
   → _____

4. (be, won't, she, late) for school again.
   → _____

5. (to, go, they, are, going) camping this weekend?
   → _____

B. 다음 괄호 안의 지시대로 문장을 바꿔 쓰시오.

1. He is going to see a doctor. (부정문으로)
   → _____

2. You will visit Janet in hospital. (의문문으로)
   → _____

3. The lady will meet the man. (부정문으로)
   → _____

4. You are going to play soccer after school. (의문문으로)
   → _____

5. You will play baseball with them tomorrow. (의문문으로)
   → _____

Grammar Tip

A. go camping 캠핑가다
　　weekend 주말

Will you ~? 의문문은 상대방에게 요청이나 부탁을 할 때 사용하기도 한다.

B. see a doctor 병원에 가다
　　in hospital 입원해 있는

Will 의문문에 대한 부정의 대답에는 주로 축약형 won't가 쓰인다.

Unit 38 | can, be able to

· can은 '~할 수 있다'의 뜻으로 능력을 나타내며 be able to로 바꾸어 쓸 수 있다. 또한 '~해도 좋다, ~해도 된다'의 뜻으로 허락을 나타낸다.

능력, 가능	~할 수 있다 (= be able to)	I **can** play the piano. She **can** speak four languages.
		My brother **can** swim. = My brother **is able to** swim.
허락	~해도 좋다, ~해도 된다	You **can** come in. You **can** use my umbrella.

· 과거의 능력은 can의 과거형 could나 「was/were able to+동사원형」으로 표현한다.

Einstein **could** answer difficult questions.

He **was able to** get the concert tickets.

Practice

A. 다음 우리말과 같도록 〈보기〉의 단어들을 이용하여 빈칸에 쓰시오.

| 〈보기〉 | find | ride | see | solve |

1. 내 여동생은 자전거를 탈 수 있다.
   → My sister _____ _____ a bike.
2. 그는 그 문제를 풀 수 있었다.
   → He _____ _____ the problem.
3. 고양이들은 어두운 곳에서도 볼 수 있다.
   → Cats _____ _____ in the dark.
4. 나는 드디어 내 안경을 찾을 수 있었다.
   → I finally _____ _____ my glasses.

B. 다음 문장을 be able to를 이용하여 바꿔 쓰시오.

1. He can speak Chinese.
   → _____
2. I can run 100 meters in 14 seconds.
   → _____
3. Judy could ski when she was young.
   → _____

C. 다음 can의 의미를 '능력'과 '허가' 중에서 골라 쓰시오.

1. You <u>can</u> use my computer.
2. She <u>can</u> finish the work on time.
3. We <u>can</u> change the world.

39 can의 부정문과 의문문

· can의 부정문은 cannot으로 표현하며 '~하지 못한다, ~할 줄 모른다'의 뜻이다.

The boy **cannot** walk.   She **couldn't** sleep last night.

  * 축약형은 can't이고 과거시제에는 could not 또는 couldn't를 쓴다.

· can의 의문문은 can을 주어 앞에 써서 표현한다.

A: **Can** you jump over this puddle?   *B*: Yes, I can. / No, I can't.

  * Can you ~?는 '~ 좀 해 줄 수 있니?'의 요청의 의미로도 많이 쓴다.

A: **Can you** help me?   *B*: Sure. / Sorry, I can't.

· be able to의 부정문은 be동사 다음에 not을, 의문문은 be동사를 주어 앞에 써서 표현한다.

We **are not able to** live without water.

A: **Was** he **able to** come to your party?   *B*: Yes, he was. / No, he wasn't.

Practice

A. 다음 우리말과 같도록 빈칸에 알맞은 말을 쓰시오.

1. 내 아들은 피아노를 연주할 수 있다.
   → My son _____ play the piano.

2. 그녀는 그녀의 개를 찾을 수가 없다.
   → She _____ find her dog.

3. 그 남자는 운전을 잘 할 수 있니?
   → _____ the man drive a car well?

B. 다음 빈칸에 Can I와 Can you 중 알맞은 것을 쓰시오.

1. 너는 연 날릴 줄 아니?   → _____ fly a kite?

2. 질문해도 돼요?   → _____ ask you a question?

3. 잠깐만 기다려 주겠니?   → _____ wait a moment, please?

C. 다음 괄호 안의 지시대로 문장을 바꿔 쓰시오.

1. She is able to understand the book. (can, 부정문으로)
   → _____

2. Is he able to make spaghetti? (can, 의문문으로)
   → _____

3. Mark can drive a car. (be able to, 의문문으로)
   → _____

4. We couldn't count to ten. (be able to, 부정문으로)
   → _____

Grammar Tip

A. drive 운전하다

Can I ~?는 '~해도 되나요?'의 뜻으로 허가를 구할 때 쓴다.

B. question 질문
 a moment 잠시, 잠깐

C. understand 이해하다
 count (순서, 숫자를) 세다

40 | may

- may는 추측이나 허락 등을 나타낼 때 사용한다.
  (1) '~일지도 모른다'의 뜻으로 추측을 나타낸다.

    It **may** rain tonight.   Alex **may** know her real name.

  (2) '~해도 좋다'의 뜻으로 허락을 나타내며 can과 바꿔 쓸 수 있다.

    You **may** use my pen. = You can use my pen.

- may의 부정문은 may not으로 표현하며 '~이 아닐지도 모른다(추측), ~하면 안 된다(금지)'의 뜻이다.

  He **may not** be Chinese.   You **may** not take pictures in the hall.

- may의 의문문은 May I ~?의 형태이며 '~해도 되나요?'의 뜻으로 허락을 물을 때 쓴다.

  A: **May** I try this shirt on?   *B*: Yes, you may. / No, you may not.

Practice

A. 다음 문장의 의미가 '추측'인지, '허락'인지 고르시오.

1. You may watch TV after eight. (추측 / 허락)

2. I might be a little late. (추측 / 허락)

3. May I have another piece of cake? (추측 / 허락)

B. 다음 문장에 괄호 안에 주어진 말을 넣어 문장을 완성하시오.

1. You catch a cold. (may)

   → _____

2. She sings the song on the stage. (may)

   → _____

3. They don't believe your story. (may)

   → _____

C. 다음 우리말과 같도록 괄호 안의 말을 알맞게 배열하시오.

1. 밖은 추울지 몰라. (be, outside, it, may, cold)

   → _____

2. 그는 그 모임에 안 올지 몰라. (not, the meeting, to, may, he, come)

   → _____

3. 너는 나의 사전을 사용해도 돼. (my, may, use, dictionary, you)

   → _____

4. 네 우산 좀 빌려도 되니? (your, may, borrow, umbrella, I)

   → _____

41 must, have to, should

- must는 '~해야 한다'의 뜻으로 강한 의무나 '~임에 틀림없다'의 뜻으로 강한 추측을 나타낸다.

  You **must** follow the rules. (의무, must＝have to)

  That girl **must** be Olivia's sister. (강한 추측)

  *의무를 나타내는 must는 have to로 바꿀 수 있다.

- have to는 '~해야 한다'의 뜻으로 의무나 필요를 나타내며 주어가 3인칭 단수이면 has to를 쓰고, 과거이면 had to를 쓴다.

  You **have to** swim here.   He **has to** do the work before dinner.

- should는 '~해야 한다, ~하는 게 좋다'의 뜻으로 의무나 충고 또는 조언을 나타낸다.

  You **should** keep milk in the refrigerator. (의무, 충고)

Practice

A. 다음 두 문장의 의미가 같도록 빈칸에 알맞은 말을 쓰시오.

1. The child must do it right now.
   = The child _____ _____ do it right now.

2. You must practice the piano there.
   = You _____ _____ practice the piano there.

B. 다음 우리말과 같도록 빈칸에 알맞은 말을 쓰시오.

1. 그는 정직한 게 틀림없다.
   → He _____ be honest.

2. 우리는 불쌍한 사람들을 도와주는 것이 좋다.
   → We _____ _____ poor people.

3. 너는 일찍 일어나야만 한다.
   → You _____ _____ get up early.

4. Ben은 따뜻한 옷을 입어야 한다.
   → Ben _____ _____ on warm clothes.

C. 다음 문장에서 잘못된 부분을 고쳐 다시 바르게 쓰시오.

1. She should saves her money.
   → _____

2. You have to go home yesterday.
   → _____

3. They should are quiet in the gallery.
   → _____

4. Tom have to wear his school uniform.
   → _____

Grammar Tip

의무의 must는 have to로 바꾸어 쓸 수 있다. 주어가 3인칭 단수일 경우에는 has to로 쓴다.

A. right now 당장

must는 강제적으로 반드시 해야만 하는 의무에 쓰고, should는 도덕적 의무나 권고에 쓴다.

B. honest 정직한
   put on 입다

C. save 절약하다
   school uniform 교복

42 must, have to, should의 부정문과 의문문

- must의 부정문은 must not으로 표현하며 '~해서는 안 된다'의 뜻으로 강한 금지를 나타낸다. 의문문은 「Must＋주어＋동사원형 ~?」으로 쓴다.

  You **must not** take pictures here. (금지)

  A: **Must** he stay there?　*B*: Yes, he must. / No, he doesn't have to.

- have to의 부정문과 의문문은 일반동사와 같은 방법으로 do, does, did를 써서 표현한다. 부정문에서 don't have to는 '~할 필요가 없다'의 뜻이므로 주의해야 한다.

  We **don't have to** wear school uniforms. (불필요)　　Do you **have to** walk your dog?

- should의 부정문은 should not[shouldn't]로 나타내며 '~하면 안 된다'의 뜻이다. 의문문은 「Should＋주어＋동사원형 ~?」으로 쓴다.

  You **should not[shouldn't]** talk in the library.

Practice

A. 다음 우리말과 같도록 빈칸에 알맞은 말을 쓰시오.

1. 사람들은 불량 식품을 먹으면 안 된다.
   → People _____ _____ eat junk food.

2. 저는 약을 먹어야 하나요?
   → _____ I _____ _____ take medicine?

3. 우리는 그를 잊으면 안 됩니다.
   → We _____ _____ forget him.

B. 다음 괄호 안에서 알맞은 것을 고르시오.

1. You (must not, don't have) to hurry.

2. We (should, have to) not make noise here.

3. She (don't have, doesn't have) to cut in line.

C. 다음 문장을 밑줄 친 부분에 주의하여 우리말로 옮기시오.

1. We <u>shouldn't</u> be late.
   → _____

2. You <u>must not</u> run in the museum.
   → _____

3. She <u>should not</u> drink too much Coke.
   → _____

4. You <u>don't have to</u> bring your lunch.
   → _____

Grammar Tip

A. junk food 불량 식품
   medicine 약

must의 과거(~해야 했다)는 had to, 미래(~해야 할 것이다)는 will have to로 표현한다.

B. noise 소음
   cut in 끼어들다

C. Coke 콜라
   bring 가지고 오다

Grammar Tip

A. crosswalk 횡단보도
   puzzle 퍼즐

don't have to는 '~할 필요가 없
다'는 뜻으로 쓰인다.

B. park 주차하다

D. stranger 낯선 사람

A. 다음 문장에서 밑줄 친 부분 대신 바꿔 쓸 수 있는 말을 쓰시오.

1. You <u>must</u> stop on the crosswalk.

2. <u>Can he</u> solve the puzzle?

3. He <u>must</u> wait for his parents.

4. You <u>will</u> tell her about the truth.

B. 다음 우리말과 같도록 빈칸에 알맞은 말을 쓰시오.

1. 우리 개는 다음 달에 12살이 돼.
   → My dog _____ _____ twelve next month.

2. 그는 피곤한 게 틀림없어.
   → He _____ _____ tired.

3. 우리는 달걀과 우유를 좀 사야 해.
   → We _____ buy some eggs and milk.

4. 그녀는 일찍 일어날 필요가 없어.
   → She _____ _____ _____ get up early.

5. 여기는 주차가 안 됩니다.
   → You _____ park here.

C. 다음 문장의 밑줄 친 부분을 바르게 고치시오.

1. Mike <u>doesn't can</u> dance very well.

2. He may <u>wants</u> some bread and milk.

3. They <u>have</u> to study for the exam last night.

4. She <u>not may</u> call you.

D. 다음 문장을 괄호 안의 지시대로 바꾸시오.

1. I will be there tomorrow. (부정문으로)
   → _____

2. You must talk to strangers. (부정문으로)
   → _____

3. She is going to change her mind. (의문문으로)
   → _____

4. He is able to speak Korean. (과거시제로)
   → _____

87

[1-2] 다음 빈칸에 알맞은 것을 고르시오.

1.
> Everyone is wearing a coat. It _____ be cold.

① is able to   ② must
③ shouldn't   ④ can't
⑤ won't

2.
> She _____ play the piano. She is a very good pianist.

① can't   ② may not
③ can   ④ won't
⑤ doesn't have to

3. 다음 대화의 빈칸에 알맞은 것은?

> A: Where is my cell phone?
> B: It _____ in your bag.

① be   ② has to
③ may be   ④ should
⑤ are going to be

4. 다음 중 어법상 옳은 것은?

① You may be watch TV tonight.
② Children must to go to bed early.
③ She must does her homework every day.
④ You shouldn't have to eat too fast.
⑤ I will not tell him about the surprise party.

5. 다음 빈칸에 공통으로 알맞은 말을 쓰시오.

> · The sun _____ rise at seven.
> · He _____ be a good police officer.

6. 다음 문장의 밑줄 친 말과 바꿔 쓸 수 있는 말이 <u>잘못</u> 연결된 것은?

① I'm going to work hard this year. → will
② She can't swim here. → isn't able to
③ You must eat more vegetables. → have to
④ Can I go to the bathroom? → Must
⑤ He will follow the rule. → is going to

[7-8] 다음 밑줄 친 부분의 의미가 나머지와 <u>다른</u> 것을 고르시오.

7. ① May I come in?
② It may rain this afternoon.
③ He may not remember you.
④ She may go shopping today.
⑤ We may be late for the meeting.

8. ① I must call my mother tomorrow.
② They must be at school now.
③ The men must finish their work.
④ You must not smoke inside the building.
⑤ You must arrive on time.

9. 다음 빈칸에 can이 들어가기에 어색한 것은?

① _____ I have a glass of water?
② Where is he? I _____ not see him.
③ You _____ leave now.
④ _____ you show me your puppy?
⑤ They _____ be kind to people.

10. 다음 대화의 빈칸에 알맞지 <u>않은</u> 것은?

> *A*: _____
> *B*: Yes, she is.

① Is your mother able to speak English?
② Is she your math teacher?
③ Is Emily going to meet her friends?
④ Does she have to return the book?
⑤ Is Ms. Brown working in the garden?

11. 다음 대화의 우리말과 같은 뜻이 되도록 빈칸에 알맞은 말을 쓰시오.

> *A*: Do I have to buy the book?
> *B*: _____
> (아니, 그럴 필요 없어.)

12. 다음 중 어법상 <u>어색한</u> 것은?

① Everything is going to be fine.
② You should not drive too fast.
③ Did he can fix the computer?
④ She doesn't have to come early.
⑤ Will you be here tonight?

[13-14] 다음 문장의 밑줄 친 부분과 바꿔 쓸 수 있는 것을 고르시오.

13.
> You <u>may</u> sit next to me.

① can
② will
③ have to
④ are able to
⑤ should

14.
> John <u>must</u> tell the truth.

① have to
② may
③ can
④ will
⑤ has to

15. 다음 밑줄 친 must의 의미가 <보기>와 같은 것은?

> <보기> He worked hard all day.
>   He <u>must</u> be tired.

① You <u>must</u> go there in ten minutes.
② Students <u>must</u> not ride bicycles here.
③ The car <u>must</u> be expensive.
④ You <u>must</u> not tell about it.
⑤ You <u>must</u> pass the exam.

16. 다음 문장의 밑줄 친 부분이 <u>어색한</u> 것은?

① It's 8:30! You're <u>going to</u> be late!
② You <u>must not</u> touch the pan. It's too hot.
③ He is sick. He <u>may not</u> come to school.
④ I <u>can't</u> hear you. Will you speak loudly?
⑤ She <u>don't have to</u> drive me to the bank.

[17-18] 다음 대화의 빈칸에 알맞은 말을 고르시오.

17.
> A: Will you clean the board for me?
> B: _____

① No, I don't.　② Sure.
③ Yes, you have to.　④ Sounds good.
⑤ Sorry, I may not.

18.
> A: I'm cold.
> B: OK. _____

① I'll close the window.
② You may open the window.
③ I'm able to open the window.
④ I won't close the window.
⑤ I can't open the window.

19. 다음 대화의 빈칸에 들어갈 말이 순서대로 짝지어진 것은?

> A: Hello. _____ I speak to Jenny?
> B: Sorry, she's out now. Will you leave a message?
> A: No, I _____ call again.

① Can – should　② May – will
③ Must – will　④ May – must
⑤ Will – have to

20. 다음 빈칸에 알맞지 <u>않은</u> 것은?

> We're going to play soccer _____.

① tomorrow　② this weekend
③ next Friday　④ last week
⑤ after lunch

〈서술형 문제〉

[21-22] 다음 괄호 안의 지시대로 바꿔 쓰시오.

21. Pass me the butter.
→ _____
(상대방에게 부탁하는 말로)

22. It's a nice day today.
→ _____
(today를 tomorrow로 바꿔서)

[23-24] 다음 빈칸에 알맞은 말을 괄호 안에 주어진 말을 이용하여 쓰시오.

23. (can, come, birthday party)
→ She is busy, so _____.
(그녀는 바빠. 그래서 내 생일 파티에 못 와.)

24. (have to, get up, early)
→ _____ It's a holiday.
(내일 넌 일찍 일어날 필요가 없어. 휴일이야.)

25. 다음 밑줄 친 부분에서 어색한 것을 찾아 바르게 고치시오.

> A: Eric, you <u>should</u> play basketball today.
> B: Mom, but I <u>am going to</u> have a game this weekend. I <u>have to</u> practice.
> A: You have a fever. I'm afraid you <u>may</u> catch a cold. You <u>must</u> stay home and take a rest.

_____ → _____

형용사란 무엇인가?

형용사는 명사나 대명사를 수식하는 말로 문장에서 명사나 대명사의 앞이나 뒤에서 꾸미는 역할을 하거나 be동사 뒤에서 주어의 성격을 나타낸다.

This is a **green** apple.

The old man is **kind**.

부사란 무엇인가?

부사는 동사, 형용사, 다른 부사나 문장을 수식하거나 동작이나 상태에 대한 정보를 구체적으로 나타낸다. 또한 빈도부사는 동사를 수식하여 행동이나 사건이 얼마나 자주 일어나는지 빈도를 나타낸다.

The tall woman walked **slowly**.

I **always** go to bed at ten.

Chapter 8. 형용사와 부사

43 형용사의 역할

- 형용사는 사람이나 물건의 상태, 성질 등을 설명해 준다.
  (1) 명사 앞에 들어가 그 명사를 직접 수식한다.

  This is an **interesting** story.   He is a **rich** man.

  (2) 동사 다음에 들어가 주어의 상태, 성질 등을 설명한다.

  The story is **interesting**.

  She feels **cold**.

Practice

A. 다음 문장에서 형용사를 골라 동그라미 하시오.

1. There is a bag of red apples.
2. You look tired and hungry.
3. The sandwiches are delicious.
4. We bought a new table.
5. Hamburgers are not healthy food.
6. She has brown hair.
7. They have two cute puppies.

B. 다음 빈칸에 알맞은 형용사를 〈보기〉에서 골라 쓰시오.

〈보기〉 different   easy   Japanese   old   wonderful

1. She has an _____ painting. (오래된)
2. The test was not _____. (쉬운)
3. They had dinner in a _____ restaurant. (일본의)
4. The students come from _____ countries. (다른)
5. You built a _____ tower. (멋진)

C. 다음 두 문장이 같은 뜻이 되도록 빈칸에 알맞은 말을 쓰시오.

1. Kevin is smart. → Kevin is a _____ boy.
2. The song was _____. → It was a beautiful song.
3. This house is empty. → This is an _____ house.
4. The road is wide. → It is a _____ road.
5. The movic was scary. → It was a _____ movie.

Grammar Tip

형용사는 색, 키, 크기, 나이, 맛, 감정, 국적 등 명사의 다양한 성질이나 상태를 나타내 준다.

A. a bag of ~ 한 봉지
brown 갈색의

B. painting 그림
restaurant 식당
come from ~ 출신이다

C. empty 비어 있는
wide 넓은
road 길, 도로
scary 무서운

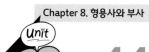

44 | some, any

- some과 any는 '약간의, 조금의'라는 뜻으로 명사 앞에 쓴다. 셀 수 있는 명사와 셀 수 없는 명사 앞에 모두 쓸 수 있으며 정해지지 않은 수나 양을 나타낸다.

some	긍정문	There are **some** people in the park. He gave me **some** money.
	권유, 부탁	Would you like **some** cookies? (권유) Can I have **some** milk? (부탁)
any	부정문, 의문문	There isn't **any** milk in the bottle. Do you have **any** brothers?

＊some과 any 다음에 셀 수 있는 명사가 올 때는 복수형으로 쓴다.

Practice

A. 다음 빈칸에 some과 any 중 알맞은 것을 쓰시오.

1. I need a hammer and _____ nails.
2. Do you want _____ tea?
3. There aren't _____ tomatoes in the fridge.
4. You should put _____ flowers on the table.
5. Did the teacher give _____ homework?

B. 다음 우리말과 같도록 빈칸에 알맞은 말을 쓰시오.

1. 그는 크리스마스 선물을 몇 개 받았다. (present)
   → He got _____ _____ for Christmas.

2. 하늘에 새들을 조금도 볼 수가 없다. (bird)
   → I can't see _____ _____ in the sky.

3. 너는 유명한 사람을 좀 알고 있니? (famous)
   → Do you know _____ _____ people?

C. 다음 괄호 안의 지시대로 문장을 바꿔 쓰시오.

1. We need some help. (부정문으로)
   → _____

2. He caught some fish. (의문문으로)
   → _____

3. Robert doesn't have any pets. (긍정문으로)
   → _____

4. I made some mistakes on the exam. (부정문으로)
   → _____

Grammar Tip

some과 any 다음에 셀 수 있는 명사는 복수형으로 온다.

A. hammer 망치
   nail 못
   fridge 냉장고

B. Christmas 크리스마스
   know 알다

any가 긍정문에 쓰이면 '어떤 ~라도'의 의미가 된다.
Any boy can do it.
어떤 소년이라도 그것을 할 수 있다.

C. help 도움
   catch 잡다
   make a mistake 실수하다

45 | many, much, a lot of

· many, much는 '많은'이라는 뜻으로 many는 셀 수 있는 명사의 복수형 앞에, much는 셀 수 없는 명사 앞에 쓰인다.

many+셀 수 있는 명사(복수형)	She **has many** friends. Are there **many** cars on the street?
much+셀 수 없는 명사	He doesn't drink **much** coffee. Do you have **much** cheese?

· many와 much는 a lot of, lots of로 바꿔 쓸 수 있다.

A lot of people work here.   We had **lots of** fun at his birthday party.

＊much는 주로 부정문과 의문문에 사용되며 긍정문에는 a lot of나 lots of를 사용한다.

Practice

A. 다음 빈칸에 many와 much 중 알맞은 깃올 쓰시오.

1. _____ children
2. _____ letters
3. _____ time
4. _____ heat
5. _____ pictures
6. _____ numbers
7. _____ cheese
8. _____ plates

B. 다음 괄호 안에서 쓸 수 없는 것을 고르시오.

1. I found (some, much, any) money in my pocket.
2. There aren't (some, any, many) chairs in the room.
3. This plant needs (lots of, much, many) sunlight.
4. Does he have (any, many, a lot of) homework today?
5. How many (pens, juice, apples) did he buy?

C. 다음 우리말과 같도록 빈칸에 알맞은 말을 쓰시오.

1. There are _____ _____ poor people in the world.
   세상에는 가난한 사람들이 많이 있다.

2. I can see _____ _____ _____ stars in the sky tonight.
   오늘밤 하늘에는 별이 많이 보인다.

3. How _____ milk does your son drink in the morning?
   너의 아들은 아침에 얼마나 많은 우유를 마시니?

4. We didn't spend _____ money this week.
   우리는 이번 주에 돈을 많이 쓰지 않았다.

5. How _____ eggs do we have?
   우리는 딜갈이 얼마나 많이 있니?

Grammar Tip

A. heat 열, 열기
   plate 접시

much는 주로 부정문, 의문문에 쓰는 경우가 많다. 또한 물건의 개수가 몇 개인지 물을 때는 How many를, 양이 얼마나 되는지 물을 때는 How much를 쓴다.

B. pocket 주머니
   sunlight 햇볕

C. poor 가난한
   spend (돈, 시간을) 쓰다

Unit 46 (a) few, (a) little

- a few와 a little은 모두 '조금의, 약간의'라는 뜻으로 a few 다음에는 셀 수 있는 명사의 복수형이 오고, a little 다음에는 셀 수 없는 명사가 온다.
- few와 little은 모두 '거의 없는'의 뜻으로 부정의 의미를 가진다. few 다음에는 셀 수 있는 명사의 복수형이, little 다음에는 셀 수 없는 명사가 온다.

a few+셀 수 있는 명사(복수형)	There are **a few** bananas on the table.
a little+셀 수 없는 명사	She drank some coffee and ate **a little** bread.
few+셀 수 있는 명사(복수형)	There were **few** people on the bus.
little+셀 수 없는 명사	**Little** food is in the refrigerator.

*a few와 a little은 긍정문에서는 some, 부정문과 의문문에서는 any와 바꿔 쓸 수 있다.

Practice

Grammar Tip

few와 little는 '거의 없는'의 뜻으로 부정의 뜻을 가지고 있지만, 완전히 없다는 의미는 아니다. 완전 부정은 not ~ any로 표현한다.

A. 다음 우리말과 같도록 〈보기〉에서 알맞은 것을 골라 쓰시오.

> 〈보기〉 a few   few   a little   little

1. Put _____ cooking oil in the pan.
   팬에 식용유를 좀 넣어라.
2. _____ friends visited me yesterday.
   어제 친구 몇 명이 나를 찾아왔다.
3. He knows _____ about Chinese culture.
   그는 중국 문화에 대해서는 아는 게 거의 없다.
4. There were _____ people at the concert.
   콘서트에는 사람들이 거의 없었다.

A. cooking oil 식용유
    culture 문화

B. 다음 괄호 안에서 알맞은 것을 고르시오.

1. There is little (water, fish) in the pond.
2. I can see few (snow, cars) on the road.
3. You need a few (eggs, milk) and a little flour.
4. Give him a little (cookies, cheese), please.

B. pond 연못
    flour 밀가루

C. 다음 우리말과 같도록 밑줄 친 부분을 바르게 고치시오.

1. It will be <u>little</u> rain this week.
   이번 주는 비가 조금 올 거야.
2. He got very <u>few</u> sleep last night.
   그는 어젯밤에 잠을 거의 못 잤다.
3. Can you buy <u>a little</u> bottles of water for me?
   물 몇 병 좀 사주겠니?
4. <u>A few</u> people were interested in the exhibition.
   그 전시에 관심 있는 사람들은 거의 없었다.

C. sleep 잠, 수면
    bottle 병
    exhibition 전시

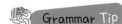

A. 다음 두 문장을 한 문장으로 쓸 때 빈칸에 알맞은 말을 쓰시오.

1. She is wearing a dress. The dress is beautiful.
   → She is wearing _____.

2. They live in a city. The city is big.
   → They live in _____.

3. Sam has a bicycle. The bicycle is blue.
   → Sam has _____.

4. They sell vegetables. The vegetables are fresh.
   → They sell _____.

B. 다음 괄호 안의 단어를 바르게 배열하여 문장을 완성하시오.

1. We visited _____. (the, library, new)

2. She's _____. (a, kind, very, person)

3. He gave me _____ _____. (answer, wrong, the)

4. This castle has _____. (history, an, interesting)

C. 다음 괄호 안에서 알맞은 것을 고르시오.

1. Does he have (much / many) pencils?

2. There are (much / a lot of) potatoes in the basket.

3. She didn't spend (much / many) money on clothes.

4. I need (a few / a little) help from my friends.

D. 다음 우리말과 같도록 <보기>에서 알맞은 것을 골라 쓰시오.

<보기>	a few	any	few	little	lots of

1. 그는 돈이 거의 없다.
   → He has _____ money.

2. 그들은 몇 가지 실수를 했다.
   → They made _____ mistakes.

3. 그녀는 과일을 많이 먹는다.
   → She eats _____ fruit.

4. 기차 시간에 대한 정보 좀 있니?
   → Do you have _____ information about train times?

5. 회의에 참석한 사람들은 거의 없었다.
   → _____ people were at the meeting.

47 부사의 역할과 형태

· 부사는 '어떻게' 또는 '얼마나'에 대한 답이 되는 말로 문장에서 동사, 형용사, 부사를 꾸며준다.

He drives **carefully**. (동사인 drive 수식)   They were **really** happy. (형용사인 happy 수식)

She walks **very** slowly. (부사인 slowly 수식)

· 부사의 형태 : 부사는 주로 형용사 뒤에 -ly를 붙여서 만든다.

대부분의 경우	형용사+-ly	beautiful → beautifully, slow → slowly, nice → nicely, loud → loudly
자음+y로 끝나는 경우	y를 i로 고치고+-ly	happy → happily, easy → easily, lucky → luckily, angry → angrily
-le, -ue로 끝나는 경우	e를 빼고+-y	simple → simply, true → truly
형용사와 부사의 형태가 같은 경우		fast, late, early, near, far, high, low, much, enough, long, hard, …
형용사와 부사의 형태가 다른 경우		good – well

It was an **early** morning. (형용사)   He got up **early**. (부사)

 Practice

A. 다음 문장에서 부사를 모두 찾아 동그라미 하시오.

1. It's a really good movie.

2. We found the house easily.

3. He shook his head slowly.

4. You are walking too carefully.

5. She plays the guitar quite well.

B. 다음 밑줄 친 말이 형용사이면 '형', 부사이면 '부'라고 쓰시오.

1. We had an <u>early</u> dinner on Sunday.

2. We met a <u>wise</u> girl.

3. It was raining <u>hard</u>.

4. That clock is five minutes <u>fast</u>.

5. It's <u>pretty</u> cold outside.

C. 다음 괄호 안에 주어진 말의 부사형을 빈칸에 쓰시오.

1. They went to bed _____. (late)

2. Kids grew up _____. (strong)

3. She wrote a novel very _____. (clear)

4. The story ended _____. (happy)

Grammar Tip

y로 끝나는 형용사는 y를 빼고 -ily 를 붙인다.
easy – easily
happy – happily

A. shook shake (흔들다)의 과거형
quite 꽤, 몹시

pretty는 형용사일 때는 '예쁜', 부사 일 때는 '꽤, 몹시'의 뜻이다. hardly 는 '거의 ~하지 않다'의 뜻이다.
I can hardly believe it.
나는 그것을 좀처럼 믿을 수가 없다.

C. grow up 자라다

Unit 48 빈도부사

- 빈도부사는 어떤 일이 얼마나 자주 일어나는지를 나타내 주는 부사이다.

| always(항상, 늘) > usually(주로, 보통) > often(자주, 종종) > sometimes(때때로, 가끔) > never(결코 ~아닌) |

- 빈도부사는 문장에서 일반동사 앞이나 be동사나 조동사 뒤에 위치한다.

I **sometimes** have lots of homework.

He is **never** late for school.

What time do you **usually** wake up on weekends?

Practice

A. 다음 우리말과 같도록 빈칸에 알맞은 말을 쓰시오.

1. You should _____ do your homework.
   너는 항상 숙제를 해야 힌다.

2. She is _____ worried about her health.
   그녀는 자주 건강에 대해 걱정한다.

3. He _____ forgets his wife's birthday.
   그는 가끔 아내의 생일을 잊어버린다.

4. He _____ eats vegetables.
   그는 야채를 절대 먹지 않는다.

B. 다음 괄호 안의 빈도부사가 들어갈 알맞은 곳을 고르시오.

1. She ① eats ② a ③ big breakfast ④. (never)

2. He ① listens ② to ③ classical music ④. (always)

3. Do ① you ② go ③ to school ④ by bike? (usually)

4. I ① am ② busy ③ on ④ Monday. (often)

C. 다음 괄호 안의 말을 넣어 문장을 다시 쓰시오.

1. I will forget his smile. (never)
   → _____

2. We go shopping on Saturday. (often)
   → _____

3. He walks his dog in the evening. (sometimes)
   → _____

4. What does he do in the evening? (usually)
   → _____

Grammar Tip

문장에 조동사와 일반동사가 있을 때 또는 조동사와 be동사가 있을 때 빈도부사는 그 사이에 들어간다.
You should always be on time.
너는 항상 시간에 맞게 와야 한다.

A. worried 걱정하는
    forget 잊다

B. classical music 고전 음악

빈도부사 often과 sometimes는 문장의 맨 앞 또는 맨 뒤에 오기도 한다. 또한 어떤 일을 얼마나 자주 하는지 빈도를 물을 때는 How often을 사용한다.
How often do you go to the movies? 영화 보러 얼마나 자주 가니?

C. smile 미소, 미소 짓다

Unit 49 | 비교급, 최상급

- 비교급과 최상급은 형용사나 부사의 변화형으로 어떤 대상과 서로 비교할 때 사용한다.
  (1) 비교급은 비교 대상이 둘인 경우에 사용하는데, '더 ~한'이라는 뜻이다.
  (2) 최상급은 셋 이상을 놓고 서로 비교할 때 사용하는데, '가장 ~한'이라는 뜻이다.
- 비교급과 최상급의 형태 : 대부분의 경우, 비교급은 -er, 최상급은 -est를 붙인다.

대부분의 형용사나 부사	「원급+er/est」	tall – taller – tallest, old – older – oldest
-e로 끝나는 경우	「원급+r/st」	large – larger – largest, nice – nicer – nicest
「자음+-y」로 끝나는 경우	y를 i로 고치고 er/est	happy – happier – happiest, early – earlier – earliest
「단모음+단자음」으로 끝나는 1음절의 경우	마지막 자음 한번 더 쓰고 er/est	big – bigger – biggest, sad – sadder – saddest
-ed, -ing, -ful, -less, -ous, -ly로 끝나거나 3음절 이상인 경우	「more/most+원급」	beautiful – more beautiful – most beautiful, famous – more famous – most famous

불규칙 변화	good/well – better – best, bad/badly – worse – worst, many/much – more – most, little – less – least

Practice

A. 다음 주어진 단어의 비교급과 최상급을 쓰시오.

원급	비교급	최상급
1. short	_____	_____
2. wide	_____	_____
3. small	_____	_____
4. difficult	_____	_____
5. busy	_____	_____
6. thin	_____	_____
7. cute	_____	_____
8. young	_____	_____

B. 다음 우리말을 참고하여 빈칸에 알맞은 말을 쓰시오.

1. Max is _____ than his sister. (더 키가 큰, tall)

2. A melon is _____ than an apple. (더 큰, big)

3. This ruler is the _____ of the three. (가장 긴, long)

4. August is the _____ month in Korea. (가장 더운, hot)

5. Today is _____ than yesterday. (더 추운, cold)

Grammar Tip

비교급, 최상급은 형용사와 부사에만 있으며, 형용사와 부사의 원래 형태를 원급이라고 한다.

A. difficult 어려운
   busy 바쁜

B. melon 멜론
   ruler 자

50 비교 구문

- 원급 문장 : 「as+형용사/부사의 원급+as」의 형태로 '~만큼 …한(하게)'이라는 뜻으로 비교하는 대상의 정도가 같음을 나타낸다.

  I'm **as tall as** my brother.   She is **not as[so] fast as** her sister.

- 비교급 문장 : 두 대상을 비교하여 '~보다 더 …하다'라는 뜻으로 「비교급+than」으로 표현한다.

  It's **colder** today **than** yesterday.   This computer is **better than** that one.

- 최상급 문장 : 셋 이상을 비교하여 '~ 중에서 가장 …하다'라는 뜻으로 「최상급+in/of」로 표현한다.

  My sister is **the tallest in** our family.   She is the youngest **of** all the students.

  *최상급 문장에서 in 뒤에는 범위나 소속이 오고 of 뒤에는 대상이 온다.

 ## Practice

A. 다음 괄호 안에서 알맞은 것을 고르시오.

1. I am (older / oldest) than Tim.

2. Matt is the (heavier / heaviest) boy of all.

3. Andrew is as (popular / more popular) as James.

4. Monkeys are (smarter / more smart) than horses.

5. He is the most famous singer (in / of) Korea.

B. 다음 밑줄 친 부분을 알맞게 고치시오.

1. Kevin is not as <u>strongest</u> as David.

2. Your dog runs <u>fast</u> than Jim's dog.

3. It was the <u>happy</u> day of my life.

4. This apple is as <u>sweeter</u> as this orange.

C. 다음 우리말과 같도록 빈칸에 알맞은 말을 쓰시오.

1. 버스는 지하철만큼 혼잡하다. (crowded)

   → The bus is _____ _____ _____ the subway.

2. 이번 시험은 지난번만큼 어렵지 않았다. (difficult)

   → This test was not _____ _____ _____ the last one.

3. 러시아는 세계에서 가장 큰 나라이다. (big)

   → Russia is _____ _____ country in the world.

4. 이 스웨터가 저 재킷보다 더 비싸다. (expensive)

   → This sweater is _____ _____ _____ that jacket.

Grammar Tip

「as+원급+as」다음에 인칭대명사는 주로 주격이 오지만 목적격이 오기도 한다.
My brother is as tall as I(me).

A. heavy
　무거운, 몸무게가 많이 나가는
　popular 인기 있는

최상급 앞에는 the를 쓰지만 부사의 최상급에는 생략할 수 있다.

C. crowded 복잡한, 혼잡한
　Russia 러시아
　expensive 비싼

A. 다음 우리말과 같도록 <u>틀린</u> 부분을 찾아 바르게 고치시오.

1. I went to bed lately last night. _____ → _____
   나는 어젯밤에 늦게 잤다.

2. We solved the problem easy. _____ → _____
   우리는 그 문제를 쉽게 풀었다.

3. The old woman speaks slow. _____ → _____
   그 할머니는 천천히 말씀하신다.

4. It was raining heavy. _____ → _____
   비가 세차게 내리고 있었다.

B. 다음 괄호 안에서 알맞은 것을 고르시오.

1. She sings very (good / well).

2. The seats were really (hard / hardly).

3. The television is too (loud / loudly).

4. You are a (fast / fastly) runner.

C. 다음 괄호 안의 단어를 넣어 문장을 다시 쓰시오.

1. He goes to the movies. (often)
   → _____

2. She could find her ring. (never)
   → _____

3. I have toast for breakfast. (usually)
   → _____

4. We will remember that day. (always)
   → _____

D. 다음 우리말과 같도록 주어진 단어를 이용하여 문장을 완성하시오.

1. 그 빨간 풍선이 그 파란 풍선보다 더 크다.
   → The red balloon is _____ _____ the blue one. (big)

2. 이 컴퓨터는 저것보다 더 좋다.
   → This computer is _____ _____ that one. (good)

3. 어제는 일년 중 가장 추웠다.
   → Yesterday was _____ _____ day of the year. (cold)

4. 이 책은 지난번 책보다 재미가 없다.
   → This book is not _____ _____ as the last one. (exciting)

1. 다음 빈칸에 알맞지 <u>않은</u> 것은?

> Jane is _____.

① a cute girl ② kind
③ lately ④ a nice student
⑤ very smart

[2-3] 다음 빈칸에 공통으로 알맞은 것을 고르시오.

2.
> · There isn't _____ water in the glass.
> · Do you have _____ good ideas?

① a ② some
③ any ④ many
⑤ much

3.
> · The English test was very _____.
> · She practices the violin very _____.

① well ② hard
③ much ④ easy
⑤ difficult

4. 다음 두 단어의 관계가 나머지와 <u>다른</u> 하나는?
① true – truly ② bad – badly
③ much – more ④ good – well
⑤ careful – carefully

5. 다음 괄호 안의 단어를 넣어 문장을 다시 쓰시오.

> It is cold today. (really)
>
> → _____

6. 다음 중 밑줄 친 부분이 어법상 <u>어색한</u> 것은?
① They lived <u>happily</u>.
② The baby slept <u>good</u> last night.
③ She got up <u>early</u> this morning.
④ My brother speaks English <u>quite</u> well.
⑤ The boys ran <u>fast</u> to the post office.

7. 다음 우리말을 바르게 영작한 것은?

> 나는 공원에서 많은 사람들을 보았다.

① I saw much people in the park.
② I saw many people in the park.
③ I saw any people in the park.
④ I saw lot of people in the park.
⑤ I saw some people in the park.

8. 다음 중 표의 내용과 일치하지 <u>않는</u> 것은?

Name	David	Matthew	Jason
Height(cm)	163	170	165
Weight(kg)	49	54	52

① Jason is taller than David.
② Matthew is heavier than Jason.
③ Jason is not as tall as David.
④ David is the shortest of the three.
⑤ Matthew is the heaviest of the three.

9. 다음 중 빈칸에 들어갈 말이 나머지와 <u>다른</u> 것은?
① My hair is longer _____ yours.
② She feels better _____ yesterday.
③ Seoul is bigger _____ Busan.
④ He is the best student _____ my class.
⑤ She walks more slowly _____ I.

10. 다음 빈칸에 들어갈 말이 바르게 짝지어진 것은?

> · Would you like _____ cookies?
> · There aren't _____ cars on the street.

① any – some
② many – any
③ much – some
④ some – much
⑤ some – many

11. 다음 중 어법상 알맞은 것은?

① There are little flowers in the garden.
② They sang few songs together.
③ Let's go outside for a few fresh air.
④ They made little mistakes.
⑤ Can I have a few sugar for my coffee?

12. 다음 중 밑줄 친 부사의 위치가 바르지 <u>않은</u> 것은?

① I am <u>usually</u> sad on rainy days.
② He <u>often</u> makes dinner on weekends.
③ Does he <u>sometimes</u> worry about his health?
④ My brother is <u>always</u> happy.
⑤ She <u>never</u> will change her mind.

13. 다음 두 문장이 같은 뜻이 되도록 빈칸에 알맞은 말을 쓰시오.

> A doll is 8 dollars. A robot is 10 dollars.
> → A robot is _____ than a doll.

14. 다음 문장에서 어법상 <u>어색한</u> 곳을 찾아 바르게 고치시오.

> My brother is not as taller as my father.

_____ → _____

15. 다음 중 내용이 일치하는 것은?

> A – The pencil is 12 centimeters.
> B – The ruler is 10 centimeters.
> C – The eraser is 5 centimeters.

① A is longer than B.
② B is as long as C.
③ C is longer than A.
④ B is the shortest of the three.
⑤ C is the longest of the three.

16. 다음 세 사람 중 지각을 자주 하는 순서대로 나열한 것은?

> Mike: I am sometimes late for school.
> Alex: I am often late for school.
> John: I am never late for school.

① Mike > Alex > John
② Mike > John > Alex
③ Alex > Mike > John
④ Alex > John > Mike
⑤ John > Alex > Mike

17. 다음 밑줄 친 fast의 쓰임이 나머지와 <u>다른</u> 것은?

① My dog runs <u>fast</u>.
② James walked <u>fast</u> with her.
③ My brother rides a bike <u>fast</u>.
④ The baby is growing <u>fast</u>.
⑤ She is a <u>fast</u> swimmer.

18. 다음 빈칸에 many가 들어갈 수 없는 것은?

① _____ children are on the playground.

② Does she have _____ cats and dogs?

③ How _____ people at the party?

④ He doesn't have _____ time now.

⑤ Are there _____ parks in your town?

[19-20] 다음 중 어법상 어색한 것을 고르시오.

19. ① The game was a lot of fun.

② I have lots of questions.

③ We didn't have many snow last winter.

④ I met my friend a few days ago.

⑤ She puts a little milk in her coffee.

20. ① Thomas is smarter than his brother.

② He climbed the ladder slowly.

③ Apples are not as cheap as oranges.

④ Health is importanter than money.

⑤ Matthew came earlier than his friends.

21. 다음 중 주어진 문장과 의미가 같은 것은?

> James is older than Peter.

① James is as old as Peter.

② James is not as old as Peter.

③ Peter is younger than James.

④ Peter is as young as James.

⑤ James is Peter's younger brother.

〈서술형 문제〉

22. 다음 표를 보고 문장을 완성하시오.

Name	Age	Height	Weight
Emily	10	135	28
Jane	9	139	25
Olivia	9	135	34

(1) Emily is _____ Jane and Olivia.

(2) Olivia is _____ tall _____ Emily.

(3) Olivia is _____ of all.

[23-24] 다음 주어진 문장과 뜻이 같도록 빈칸에 알맞은 말을 쓰시오.

23.

> We saw a movie yesterday. The movie was exciting.

→ We saw _____ yesterday.

24.

> Daniel plays baseball. He is a good baseball player.

→ Daniel plays _____.

25. 다음 대화의 밑줄 친 부분 중 어법상 어색한 것을 찾아 바르게 고쳐 다시 쓰시오.

> A: What do usually you do on Sundays?
> B: I usually play badminton with my friends, but I'll go swimming this weekend.
> A: Sounds fun! Can I go with you?
> B: Sure.

→ _____

명령문이란 무엇인가?

명령문은 지시나 명령, 금지, 제안을 나타내는 문장으로 일반 명령문, 부정명령문, 청유문이 있다.

Open the door.   **Don't** go outside now.

Let's go on a picnic.

감탄문이란 무엇인가?

기쁨, 슬픔, 놀람 등 감정을 나타낼 때 사용하며 문장은 What이나 How로 시작하고 문장 끝에 느낌표를 붙인다.

What a pretty girl she is!   **How** nice the house is!

의문문에는 어떤 것이 있는가?

무엇인가를 확인하거나 부탁, 권유를 나타낼 때 의문문을 사용하며 의문문에는 일반적인 형태의 의문문 외에도 부가의문문, 선택의문문, 부정의문문이 있다.

He was a good singer, **wasn't he**?

Which do you want, **chicken or pizza**?

Don't they play soccer in the park?

Chapter 9. 문장의 종류

51 명령문

- 명령문은 '~해라, ~하세요'라는 뜻으로 상대방에게 명령, 지시, 요청 등을 할 때 쓰며 동사원형으로 시작한다.

  Close the window.   **Be** careful.

- 부정명령문은 '~하지 마라, ~하지 마세요'라는 뜻으로 상대방에게 명령, 지시, 요청하는 내용이 부정이나 금지일 때 쓰며 「Don't+동사원형~.」으로 나타낸다.

  Don't touch the picture.   **Don't be** sad.

- 명령문 앞이나 뒤에 please를 넣어 좀 더 공손하게 명령을 전달할 수 있다.

  Close the window, **please**.   **Please** don't be late.

 ## Practice

A. 다음 괄호 안에서 알맞은 것을 고르시오.

1. (Wash / Washes) your hands.

2. (Don't be / Don't are) sad.

3. (Don't / Doesn't) go to bed late.

4. (Turn / Turns) off your cell phones.

B. 다음 괄호 안의 지시대로 문장을 바꿔 쓰시오.

1. You are quiet in the library. (명령문으로)

   → _____

2. You tell a lie. (부정명령문으로)

   → _____

3. You are noisy. (부정명령문으로)

   → _____

4. You pass me the salt. (명령문으로)

   → _____

C. 다음 우리말과 같도록 빈칸에 알맞은 말을 쓰시오.

1. 착한 아이가 되어라.

   → Please _____ _____ nice boy.

2. 시간 낭비하지 마세요.

   → _____ _____ your time.

3. 그 개를 무서워하지 마.

   → _____ _____ afraid of the dog.

4. 앉으세요.

   → _____ _____, please.

Grammar Tip

명령문은 상대방에게 하는 말이므로 명령문의 생략된 주어는 You이다.

A. turn off 끄다
cell phone 핸드폰

B. tell a lie 거짓말하다
noisy 시끄러운
pass 건네주다
salt 소금

C. waste 낭비하다
afraid 두려운, 무서워하는

52 청유문

- 청유문은 '~하자'라는 뜻으로 제안할 때 써서 제안문이라고도 하며 「Let's+동사원형 ~.」으로 나타낸다.
  Let's play soccer after school.
- '~하지 말자'라는 뜻으로 부정을 나타낼 때는 「Let's not+동사원형 ~.」으로 나타낸다.
  Let's not buy the oranges.
- 청유문에 대한 대답으로 수락할 때는 Yes, let's. / Okay. / Sure. / Why not? / That's a good idea. (그러자. / 좋아.) 등으로 하고, 거절할 때는 No, let's not. / I'm sorry, I can't. / I'm afraid I can't. (그러지 말자. / 미안하지만 안 돼.) 등으로 한다.
  A: Let's go swimming.   *B:* Okay. / I'm sorry, I can't.

 Practice

A. 다음 괄호 안에서 알맞은 것을 고르시오.

1. Let's (go / goes) to a movie.
2. (Not let's / Let's not) open the box.
3. (Let / Let's) change the subject.
4. (Let's not / Don't let's) wear a jacket.
5. Let's (not throw / don't throw) away the clothes.

B. 다음 빈칸에 Let's와 Let's not 중에서 알맞은 것을 쓰시오.

1. It will rain. _____ take an umbrella.
2. He's in trouble. _____ help him.
3. The English test is tomorrow. _____ study together.
4. I am tired today. _____ go shopping.
5. _____ take the subway. It will be faster.
6. _____ play outside. It's very cold.

C. 다음 밑줄 친 말과 바꿔 쓸 수 있는 것을 두 개 이상 쓰시오.

1. *A:* Let's go to the park.
   B: <u>Okay.</u>

2. *A:* Let's meet tomorrow.
   B: <u>I'm sorry, I can't.</u>

Grammar Tip

명령문은 상대방에게 그 행동을 지시, 요청하는 의미가 있고, 청유문은 우리가 함께 하자는 의미가 있다.

A. change 바꾸다
subject 주제
throw away 버리다

'~하지 말자'라는 뜻으로 제안하는 부정청유문은 「Let's not+동사원형 ~.」으로 나타낸다.

B. in trouble 어려움에 빠진
subway 지하철

unit 53 | 명령문 + and/or

- 「명령문, and」는 '~해라, 그러면 …할 것이다'라는 뜻으로, 접속사 if(~한다면)를 써서 문장을 바꿔 쓸 수 있다.
  Take some rest, **and** you will feel better.
  = If you **take** some rest, you will feel better.

- 「명령문, or」는 '~해라, 그렇지 않으면 …할 것이다'라는 뜻으로 or는 부정의 의미를 가지고 있으며, 접속사 if와 not(~하지 않는다면)을 써서 문장을 바꿔 쓸 수 있다.
  Go to bed early, **or** you will be tired tomorrow.
  = If you **don't go** to bed early, you will be tired tomorrow.

Practice

A. 다음 우리말과 같도록 빈칸에 알맞은 말을 쓰시오.

1. 왼쪽으로 도세요, 그러면 버스 정류장이 보일 거예요.
   → _____ left, _____ you'll find the bus stop.

2. 서두르세요, 그렇지 않으면 우리는 비행기를 놓칠 거예요.
   → _____ up, _____ we'll miss our flight.

3. 눈을 떠 보세요, 그러면 깜짝 놀랄 거예요.
   → _____ your eyes, _____ you'll be surprised.

4. 조용히 하세요, 그렇지 않으면 아기가 잠을 잘 못 자요.
   → _____ quiet, _____ the baby can't sleep well.

B. 다음 빈칸에 and와 or 중 알맞은 것을 쓰시오.

1. Study hard, _____ you'll pass the exam.
2. Tell him the truth, _____ he'll get angry.
3. Do your best, _____ you'll lose the game.
4. Exercise regularly, _____ you'll be healthy.
5. Get up now, _____ you'll be late for school.

C. 다음 문장과 뜻이 같도록 빈칸에 알맞은 말을 쓰시오.

1. If you push the button, the door will open.
   → _____ the button, _____ the door will open.

2. If you don't start now, you'll miss the train.
   → _____ now, _____ you'll miss the train.

3. If you don't stop crying, you won't get a present.
   → _____ crying, _____ you won't get a present.

4. If you come to the party, you'll see him.
   → _____ to the party, _____ you'll see him.

Grammar Tip

「명령문, and」와 「명령문, or」를 「접속사 if+주어+동사」로 바꿔 쓸 수 있다. and는 '그러면'의 의미이므로 if 문장이 긍정문, or는 '그렇지 않으면'의 의미이므로 if 문장이 부정으로 표현된다.

A. miss 놓치다
　　flight 비행, 항공편

B. truth 사실, 진실
　　exercise 운동하다
　　regularly 규칙적으로

C. push 누르다
　　button 단추

54 감탄문

• 감탄문은 놀람이나 기쁨, 슬픔 등의 감정을 나타내는 문장이다. What이나 How로 시작하고 문장의 마지막에 !(느낌표)를 쓴다.

What으로 시작하는 감탄문	형태 : 「What+a(an)+형용사+명사+(주어+동사)!」
	「주어+동사」는 생략할 수 있다. 복수명사이거나 셀 수 없는 명사의 경우에는 a나 an을 쓰지 않는다.
	What a good **idea** (it is)! = It's a very good idea. **What** nice **shoes** (they are)! = They are very nice shoes.
How로 시작하는 감탄문	형태 : 「How+형용사(부사)+(주어+동사)!」
	감정을 강조하여 표현하고 싶은 말이 형용사나 부사일 때 사용한다.
	How beautiful she is! = She is very beautiful. **How quickly** he speaks! = He speaks very quickly.

Practice

A. 다음 괄호 안에서 알맞은 것을 고르시오.

1. (What / How) a pretty bird it is!
2. What kind (boy / people) they are!
3. (What / How) exciting the game is!
4. How big (are the animals / the animals are)!

B. 다음 빈칸에 How 또는 What을 쓰시오.

1. _____ tall the tree is!
2. _____ a scary movie it is!
3. _____ fast he runs!
4. _____ brave children they are!
5. _____ a huge building it is!

C. 다음 괄호 안의 단어를 배열하여 감탄문을 완성하시오.

1. (the bridge, long, is, how)
   → _____

2. (it, a lovely dress, what, is)
   → _____

3. (how, are, the problems, easy)
   → _____

4. (what, stories, are, they, amazing)
   → _____

Grammar Tip

감탄문을 평서문으로 바꾸면 감정을 강조하는 뜻으로 very가 들어간다.

A. exciting 신나는
　　animal 동물

How로 시작하는 감탄문에는 a(n)이 없다.

B. scary 무서운
　　brave 용감한

C. bridge 다리
　　amazing 놀라운

Unit 55 부가의문문

- 부가의문문은 '그렇지?, 그렇지 않니?'라는 뜻으로 상대방의 동의를 구하거나 사실을 확인하기 위해 평서문 끝에 「동사+주어(인칭대명사)?」의 형태로 짧게 붙인다.

  Sally is pretty, **isn't she**?

- 부가의문문 만드는 방법

  (1) 긍정문이면 부정형으로, 부정문이면 긍정형으로 부가의문문을 만든다.

  (2) 문장에 be동사와 조동사가 쓰였으면 그대로 쓰고, 일반동사가 쓰였으면 do, does, did를 사용하여 부가의문문을 만든다. 또한 주어가 명사이면 부가의문문에서는 인칭대명사로 쓴다.

  She is over seventy, **isn't she**?　　**Alex can** dive, **can't he**?

  They passed the exam, **didn't they**?

- 부가의문문에 대한 대답은 대답하는 내용이 긍정이면 Yes로, 부정이면 No로 답한다.

  A: You don't like tomatoes, do you?

  B: Yes, I do. (좋아할 경우) / No, I don't. (좋아하지 않을 경우)

 Practice

A. 다음 괄호 안에서 알맞은 부가의문문을 고르시오.

1. You are bored, (don't you / aren't you)?
2. They will go camping, (will they / won't they)?
3. Jane can't ride a bike, (can she / can't she)?
4. Tony comes from Canada, (does he / doesn't he)?
5. You ate the cake, (didn't you / weren't you)?
6. Jason is a lawyer, (is he / isn't he)?
7. They won't go swimming, (will they / won't they)?

B. 다음 빈칸에 알맞은 부가의문문을 쓰시오.

1. The movie was good, _____ _____?
2. She wants to be a singer, _____ _____?
3. They weren't at the party, _____ _____?
4. James lost his cell phone, _____ _____?
5. They don't live in Seoul, _____ _____?
6. The men are very diligent, _____ _____?
7. You didn't watch the movie, _____ _____?

C. 다음 대화의 빈칸에 알맞은 말을 쓰시오.

A: He doesn't have any brothers, _____ _____?

B: Yes, _____ _____. He has two brothers.

Grammar Tip

부정형 부가의문문은 반드시 축약형을 쓴다.

A. bored 지루한
　　lawyer 변호사

명령문의 부가의문문은 모두 will you ?이고, 청유문의 부가의문문은 shall we?이다.
Open the door, will you?
Let's play soccer, shall we?

B. diligent 부지런한, 근면한

56 선택의문문

- 선택의문문은 or를 써서, 둘 중 하나를 선택하도록 하는 의문문이다.

  A: Do you go to school by bus **or** by bike?

  B: I go to school by bike.

- 선택의문문은 대답을 Yes나 No로 하지 않고, 둘 중 선택한 하나로 대답한다. which나 who 등을 써서 선택을 물을 수도 있다.

  A: **Which** do you want, milk **or** juice?　　*A*: **Who** is taller, Tom **or** David?

  B: I want juice.　　　　　　　　　　　　*B*: Tom is taller.

A. 다음 우리말과 같도록 빈칸에 알맞은 말을 쓰시오.

1. 그는 일본 사람이니, 아니면 중국 사람이니?

   → Is he Japanese _____ Chinese?

2. 너는 축구와 야구 중 어느 것을 더 좋아하니?

   → _____ do you like better, soccer _____ baseball?

3. Tom과 Mike 중 누가 이겼니?

   → _____ is the winner, Tom _____ Mike?

4. 너는 그를 어제 만났니, 아니면 지난 주에 만났니?

   → Did you meet him yesterday _____ last week?

5. 이 가방은 네 거니, 아니면 민수 거니?

   → Is this bag yours _____ Minsu's?

B. 다음 괄호 안의 말을 이용하여 질문에 대한 대답을 완전한 문장으로 쓰시오.

1. Do you go to school by bike or by bus? (by bus)

   → _____

2. Did you order pizza or sandwiches? (sandwiches)

   → _____

3. Which coat is yours, this one or that one? (that one)

   → _____

4. Which do you want, ice cream or yogurt? (yogurt)

   → _____

5. Who sings better, you or your sister? (my sister)

   → _____

Grammar Tip

'또는, 아니면'의 뜻을 가진 or는 접속사로 둘, 또는 그 이상 있는 것들 중에서 하나를 가리킨다.
and는 '~와'의 뜻으로 둘, 또는 그 이상 있는 것들을 모두 가리킨다.

coffee or tea 커피 또는 차
coffee and tea 커피와 차

B. order 주문하다
coat 코트

111

Unit 57 부정의문문

• 부정의문문은 의문문에 not이 들어 있어 부정의 뜻을 갖는 의문문으로 '~이지(하지) 않니?'라는 뜻으로 「〈be동사/do동사/조동사+not〉의 축약형+주어 ~?」의 형태로 쓴다.

be동사	**Isn't** it cold there? – Yes, it is.　　– No, it isn't.	*대답 내용이 긍정이면 Yes, 부정이면 No로 답한다. 이 때, Yes는 '아니오', No는 '예'의 의미이다.
일반동사	**Doesn't** he like apples? – Yes, he does.　– No, he doesn't.	
조동사	**Won't** you go to the park? – Yes, I will.　　– No, I won't.	

Practice

A. 다음 문장을 부정의문문으로 바꾸어 쓰시오.

1. You saw a ghost yesterday.

   → _____

2. She is a great musician.

   → _____

3. The soccer player was famous.

   → _____

4. They will wait for her at the bus stop.

   → _____

5. Sally can arrive here soon.

   → _____

B. 다음 부정의문문과 응답의 빈칸에 알맞은 말을 쓰시오.

1. A: _____ you meet Matt in the library?

   B: _____, I didn't. I met Billy there.

2. A: Didn't he have lunch at noon?

   B: _____ He had lunch at twelve.

3. A: Isn't this shirt too tight on me?

   B: _____ Buy a larger size.

4. A: Doesn't your father wear glasses?

   B: _____ He has good sight.

5. A: _____ frogs jump high?

   B: _____, they can. They can jump high.

A. 다음 우리말을 참고하여 <u>틀린</u> 부분을 찾아 바르게 고쳐 쓰시오.

1. Opens your eyes. (눈 떠.)

2. I'm so hungry. Let's not eat something. (배가 많이 고파. 뭔가 좀 먹자.)

3. Not be so nervous. (너무 긴장하지 마.)

4. Wear glasses, or you'll see better. (안경을 써, 그러면 더 잘 보일 거야.)

B. 다음 <보기>에서 알맞은 부가의문문을 골라 빈칸에 쓰시오.

<보기> did he? won't they? isn't it? do you?

1. You don't remember his name, _____

2. He didn't read the book, _____

3. Ken and Max will go swimming, _____

4. It's a wonderful day today, _____

C. 다음 문장과 뜻이 같도록 빈칸에 알맞은 말을 쓰시오.

1. This is a very exciting game.
→ _____ _____ _____ game this is!

2. She dances very beautifully.
→ _____ _____ she dances!

3. If you drink some hot tea, you'll feel better.
→ _____ some hot tea, _____ you'll feel better.

4. If you don't invite him, he'll be upset.
→ _____ him, _____ he'll be upset.

D. 다음 대화의 빈칸에 알맞은 말을 쓰시오.

1. A: Amy likes junk food, doesn't she?
B: No, _____. She never eats junk food.

2. A: He will go hiking this weekend, won't he?
B: Yes, _____. He goes hiking every weekend.

3. A: Which do you want for lunch, pizza or spaghetti?
B: _____ pizza.

4. A: Do you take a shower in the morning or before bed?
B: _____ in the morning.

Grammar Tip

A. nervous 긴장하는
glasses 안경

B. remember 기억하다

if ~ not의 의미로 unless를 쓸 수 있다.
If you don't invite him, ~
= Unless you invite him, ~
= Invite him, or ~

C. tea 차
invite 초대하다

D. junk food 정크 푸드 (건강에 좋지 못한 것으로 여겨지는 인스턴트 음식이나 패스트푸드)
take a shower 샤워하다

113

[1-2] 다음 빈칸에 알맞은 것을 고르시오.

1.
> _____ a wonderful story it is!

① How   ② must
③ What   ④ Why
⑤ That

2.
> Do you live in a house _____ in an apartment?

① and   ② but
③ so   ④ if
⑤ or

[3-4] 다음 대화의 빈칸에 알맞은 것을 고르시오.

3.
> A: Which do you need, cheese or butter?
> B: _____

① Yes, I need some.
② No, I need cheese.
③ I need some butter.
④ I don't like cheese.
⑤ I need a cheese cake.

4.
> A: Brian and Carol were busy yesterday, _____?
> B: Yes, they were.

① was she   ② were they
③ weren't they   ④ aren't they
⑤ arc they

5. 다음 빈칸에 들어갈 말이 나머지와 <u>다른</u> 것은?

① _____ a sunny day it is!
② _____ cute the baby is!
③ _____ sweet strawberries they are!
④ _____ a good question it is!
⑤ _____ wonderful dinner it is!

6. 다음 빈칸에 알맞지 <u>않은</u> 것은?

> Don't _____ here.

① plays   ② swim
③ run   ④ eat
⑤ talk

7. 다음 빈칸에 Be(be)가 들어갈 수 <u>없는</u> 것은?

① _____ kind to other people.
② Don't _____ afraid.
③ _____ happy.
④ Please _____ quiet.
⑤ _____ take pictures.

8. 다음 우리말을 영어로 바르게 옮긴 것은?

> 그것은 정말 영리한 개이구나!

① What a smart dog it is!
② How a smart dog it is!
③ How smart is the dog!
④ What smart the dog is!
⑤ What smart a dog it is!

9. 다음 중 어법상 어색한 문장은?

① Is Emily at home or at school?

② What a fast swimmers they are!

③ How tall the building is!

④ You have a new computer, don't you?

⑤ It's cold outside. Let's not go outside.

10. 다음 짝지어진 대화 중 어색한 것은?

① A: Let's play basketball this afternoon.
   B: That's a good idea.

② A: Don't eat before you go to bed.
   B: Okay.

③ A: Which do you have, a dog or a cat?
   B: No, I don't have a dog.

④ A: Amy hurt her arm, didn't she?
   B: Yes, she did.

⑤ A: Your friends are watching a movie, aren't they?
   B: No, they are studying now.

11. 다음 빈칸에 들어갈 말이 바르게 짝지어진 것은?

> · _____ eat cookies in the museum.
> · _____ on your jacket.

① Be – Be   ② Don't – Put
③ Be – Puts   ④ Be – Put
⑤ Being – Be put

12. 다음 밑줄 친 ①~⑤ 중 어법상 어색한 것은?

> ①How ②a ③lazy ④man ⑤he is!

[13-14] 다음 밑줄 친 부분이 어법상 어색한 것을 고르시오.

13. ① Please listen to me carefully.

② She doesn't live with them, does she?

③ Which is your ball, this one or that one?

④ Let's take not a taxi here.

⑤ What a nice pen you have!

14. ① It is a nice gift, isn't it?

② Grace doesn't like cats, does she?

③ They will go shopping, don't they?

④ Tony can speak Chinese, can't he?

⑤ You didn't read this book, did you?

15. 다음 중 문장의 의미가 나머지와 다른 것은?

① What a great dancer she is!

② She is a really great dancer.

③ How great the dancer is!

④ Be a great dancer.

⑤ What a great dancer!

16. 다음 주어진 문장과 뜻이 같도록 빈칸에 알맞은 말을 쓰시오.

> This is a very big city.

= _____ _____ _____ city this is!

= _____ _____ this city is!

17. 다음 밑줄 친 부분을 바르게 고쳐 쓰시오.

> <u>Not</u> be worried. Everything will be fine.

_____

18. 다음 문장에 대한 대답으로 알맞은 것을 <u>모두</u> 고르면?

> Let's join the soccer team.

① Yes, I do.
② No, let's.
③ That's a good idea.
④ I'm sorry, I can't.
⑤ Yes, I like tennis.

19. 다음 빈칸에 Do(do)가 들어갈 수 없는 것은?

① _____ you get up early or late?
② Girls don't like sports, _____ they?
③ _____ your homework first.
④ They speak English, _____ they?
⑤ The men don't watch TV, _____ they?

20. 다음 빈칸에 들어갈 말로 and가 알맞은 것은?

① Take your umbrella, _____ you'll get wet.
② Be on time, _____ you can't get the tickets.
③ Do your homework, _____ you can't go out.
④ Run to school now, _____ you'll be late again.
⑤ Wait for a few minutes, _____ the bus will arrive soon.

〈서술형 문제〉

21. 다음 대화에서 어법상 어색한 것을 모두 찾아 동그라미하고 바르게 고치시오.

> A: Mike went to the beach last week, didn't Mike?
> B: Yes, he does. He had a great time.

→ _____, _____

[22-23] 다음 〈보기〉에서 가장 알맞은 것을 골라 Let's 또는 Let's not으로 시작하는 문장을 완성하시오.

> 〈보기〉 go to the movies
> open the window

22. We need some fresh air.
→ _____

23. We have to finish our homework.
→ _____

[24-25] 다음 카드를 보고 〈보기〉와 같이 질문에 대한 대답을 쓰시오.

> Name: Paul Green
> Age: 33
> From: Canada
> Job: Math teacher
>
> 〈보기〉
> A: His name is Paul, isn't it?
> B: Yes, it is.

24. Paul comes from Canada, doesn't he?
→ _____

25. What subject does Paul teach?
→ _____

Go! Go!

to부정사란 무엇인가?
to부정사는 문장에서 「to+동사원형」의 형태로 동사가 명사, 형용사,
부사의 역할을 하며 '~하기, ~하는 것' 등으로 해석한다.
I like **to watch** movies.

동명사란 무엇인가?
동명사는 「동사원형+-ing」의 형태로 동사가 명사처럼 쓰이기 때문
에 동명사라고 하며 문장에서 명사 역할인 주어, 목적어, 보어로 쓸
수 있다.
Swimming is very fun.

Chapter 10. **to부정사와 동명사**

Unit 58 to부정사의 명사적 용법

- to부정사가 명사처럼 사용되는 경우로 문장 안에서 주어, 목적어, 보어 역할을 하며, '~하기, ~하는 것'의 뜻으로 쓰인다.

주어 역할	「to부정사+동사」	~하는 것은, ~하기는	To play soccer is fun. To speak English is not easy.
보어 역할	「동사(be동사, seem 등)+ to부정사」	~하는 것(이다)	My dream is to become a singer. His plan is to travel around the world.
목적어 역할	「동사(like, want 등)+ to부정사」	~하는 것을, ~하기를	I want to eat some bread. I like to take a walk after dinner.

- to부정사가 주어 역할을 할 때는 보통 가주어 it을 to부정사 자리에 놓고 to부정사를 문장 뒤로 보낸다.

  To get up early is not easy. = It is not easy **to get** up early.

 Practice

A. 다음 괄호 안에서 알맞은 것을 고르시오.

1. I want (visit / to visit) Europe someday.

2. Her hobby is (collects / to collect) stamps.

3. (Play / To play) the guitar is interesting.

4. I hope (to see / to seeing) my uncle soon.

B. 다음 밑줄 친 부분의 to부정사의 역할을 고르시오.

1. My hope is to be 180 cm tall. (주어 / 보어 / 목적어)

2. I like to draw pictures. (주어 / 보어 / 목적어)

3. To stay healthy is very important. (주어 / 보어 / 목적어)

4. The teacher started to talk to me. (주어 / 보어 / 목적어)

5. It is hard to walk all day long. (주어 / 보어 / 목적어)

C. 다음 빈칸에 알맞은 말을 〈보기〉에서 골라 to부정사 형태로 쓰시오.

〈보기〉	swim	play	teach	be	buy

1. My new job is _____ Chinese.

2. They like _____ basketball after school.

3. _____ in a deep river is dangerous.

4. Her dream is _____ a famous actress.

5. I want _____ an expensive car.

Grammar Tip

A. Europe 유럽
 hobby 취미
 stamp 우표

to부정사는 「to+동사원형」의 형태로 문장 안에서 명사, 형용사, 부사의 역할을 한다.

B. healthy 건강한
 important 중요한

C. job 직업, 일
 deep 깊은
 dangerous 위험한

59 | to부정사의 형용사적 용법

· to부정사가 형용사처럼 사용되는 경우로 '~할, ~하는'의 뜻으로 명사나 대명사 뒤에서 수식하는 역할을 한다.

명사(구)/대명사+to부정사	~할, ~하는	I have a lot of <u>things</u> **to do** today. (앞의 명사 things 수식)
		Please give me <u>something</u> **to drink**. (앞의 대명사 something 수식)

· to부정사의 꾸밈을 받는 명사가 전치사의 목적어인 경우, to부정사 뒤에 있는 전치사를 생략해서는 안 된다.

I need <u>a piece of paper</u> **to write on**. (→ write on a piece of paper)

They look for <u>a house</u> **to live in**. (→ live in a house)

Practice

A. 다음 밑줄 친 to부정사가 수식하는 것을 쓰시오.

1. Please give me something <u>to eat</u>.

2. She buys a dress <u>to wear</u> for the party.

3. There are palaces <u>to visit</u> in Seoul.

B. 다음 우리말과 같도록 빈칸에 알맞은 말을 쓰시오.

1. Green 씨는 읽을 책 몇 권을 원한다.
   → Mr. Green wants some books _____ _____.

2. 마실 뭔가가 있나요?
   → Is there anything _____ _____?

3. 학교에 갈 시간이다.
   → It's time _____ _____ to school.

4. 그녀는 이 문을 열 열쇠가 필요하다.
   → She needs a key _____ _____ this door.

5. 나는 나를 도와줄 누군가가 필요하다.
   → I need someone _____ _____ me.

C. 다음 괄호 안에서 알맞은 전치사를 고르시오.

1. She doesn't have a pen to write (on / with).

2. Carol has no one to live (in / with).

3. There is no chair to sit (on / in).

4. Judy has many friends to play (with / for).

5. They have something to talk (about / with).

Grammar Tip

to부정사의 형용사적 용법은 앞에 있는 명사나 대명사를 수식한다.

A. palace 궁궐, 궁전

B. anything 어떤 것
someone 누군가

to부정사 다음에 전치사가 오는 경우에는 to부정사가 수식하는 명사나 대명사가 전치사의 목적어 역할을 한다.
→ write with a pen 펜으로 쓰다

Unit 60 | to부정사의 부사적 용법

· to부정사가 부사처럼 사용되는 경우로 문장 안에서 형용사, 동사, 다른 부사를 수식하며 목적, 감정의 원인, 결과 등을 나타낸다.

목적	「형용사, 동사, 부사 +to부정사」	~하기 위해서	I studied hard **to pass** the test. He saved money **to buy** a bike.
감정의 원인		~해서	I'm very glad **to see** you again. They were sad **to hear** the news.
결과		~해서 (결국) …하다	Harry grew up **to be** a doctor. The woman lived **to be** ninety.

· 감정의 원인으로 쓰인 경우에는 to부정사 앞에 감정을 나타내는 형용사가 오며, 결과로 쓰인 경우에는 grow, live 등의 동사와 함께 쓰인다.

Practice

A. 다음 밑줄 친 부분을 우리말로 옮기시오.

1. I was happy <u>to find my necklace</u>. _____

2. Lucy <u>grew up to be a cook</u>. _____

3. He went to the park <u>to meet them</u>. _____

4. We tuned off the light <u>to save energy</u>. _____

B. 다음 밑줄 친 부분과 서로 관계있는 것끼리 연결하시오.

1. He lived <u>to be eighty-five</u>. •   • ⓐ 감정의 원인

2. Sue was shocked <u>to hear that</u>. •   • ⓑ 결과

3. We went out <u>to eat lunch</u>. •   • ⓒ 목적

C. 다음 두 문장을 to부정사를 이용하여 한 문장으로 쓰시오.

1. He went out. He wanted to play with his friends.
   → He went out _____.

2. Isabell grew up. She became a famous model.
   → Isabell grew up _____.

3. They were sad. They lost their dog.
   → They were sad _____.

4. I practice the piano. I want to be a pianist.
   → I _____.

Grammar Tip

A. necklace 목걸이
cook 요리사
save 절약하다

to부정사가 문장 안에서 부사처럼 쓰이는 경우, 앞에 있는 형용사, 동사, 부사를 수식한다.

C. model 모델
lose 잃어버리다
pianist 피아니스트

A. 다음 밑줄 친 to부정사가 명사, 형용사, 부사 중 어떤 역할을 하는지 쓰시오.

1. I have something <u>to tell</u> you. _____

2. Jimmy is surprised <u>to win</u> the race. _____

3. She likes <u>to watch</u> movies at night. _____

4. We bought some bananas <u>to make</u> dessert. _____

B. 다음 두 문장의 의미가 같도록 빈칸에 알맞은 말을 쓰시오.

1. To visit a new place is exciting.
   → _____ is exciting _____ _____ a new place.

2. I was happy because I passed the exam.
   → I was _____ _____ _____ the exam.

C. 다음 문장의 밑줄 친 부분을 바르게 고치시오.

1. My dream is <u>to being</u> an architect.

2. He is sad <u>to has</u> a lot of homework.

3. Amy is looking for a house <u>to live</u>.

D. 다음 우리말과 같도록 괄호 안의 단어들을 알맞게 배열하시오.

1. 그녀는 지갑을 잃어버려 슬펐다. (lose, her, to, wallet)
   → She was sad _____.

2. 헤어질 시간이다. (say, to, goodbye)
   → It is time _____.

3. 그는 여기에 머물 시간이 없다. (stay, here, to)
   → He doesn't have time _____.

4. 그 학생들은 잡지 읽는 것을 좋아한다. (to, magazines, read)
   → The students like _____.

E. 다음 밑줄 친 부분 중 어법상 어색한 것을 고르시오.

1. He <u>doesn't</u> <u>have</u> a pen <u>to write</u>. He needs a <u>new pen</u>.
          ①   ②   ③   ④

2. I want <u>to baked</u> cookies <u>this evening</u>. <u>Can</u> you <u>help</u> me?
          ①   ②   ③   ④

Grammar Tip

A. race 경주
   dessert 디저트, 후식

to부정사의 꾸밈을 받는 명사가 전치사의 목적어인 경우에는 전치사를 생략해서는 안 된다.

C. architect 건축가

D. wallet 지갑
   magazine 잡지

to부정사는 「to+동사원형」의 형태로 인칭이나 시제, 수에 영향을 받지 않는다.

61 동명사의 용법

· 동명사는 「동사원형+-ing」의 형태로 명사처럼 쓰이며 문장에서 주어, 보어, 목적어의 역할을 한다.

주어 역할	~하는 것은, ~하기는	Eating vegetables is good for your health. Doing your best is very important.
보어 역할	~하는 것(이다)	My hobby is **collecting** stamps. Mark's job is **selling** cars.
목적어 역할	~하는 것을, ~하기를	I enjoy **cooking** for my family. Susie likes **meeting** new friends.

· 동명사는 전치사의 목적어로 쓰이기도 하는데, 전치사의 목적어 자리에 동사가 올 경우에는 동명사의 형태로 쓴다.

I am good at **playing** the guitar.

＊동명사는 to부정사의 명사적 용법과 같은 의미로 바꾸어 쓸 수 있지만, to부정사에는 없는 전치사의 목적어로도 쓰인다.

Practice

A. 다음 괄호 안에서 알맞은 것을 고르시오.

1. I'm interested in (take / taking) pictures.

2. (Get up / Getting up) early is not easy for me.

3. They started (swim / swimming) an hour ago.

4. Thank you for (helping / to help) me.

B. 다음 밑줄 친 동명사의 역할을 고르시오.

1. My job is <u>writing</u> novels. (주어 / 보어 / 목적어)

2. <u>Driving</u> fast is very dangerous. (주어 / 보어 / 목적어)

3. She likes <u>watering</u> the plants. (주어 / 보어 / 목적어)

4. My brother hates <u>taking</u> a shower. (주어 / 보어 / 목적어)

5. <u>Learning</u> Chinese is not difficult. (주어 / 보어 / 목적어)

C. 다음 빈칸에 알맞은 말을 〈보기〉에서 골라 동명사 형태로 쓰시오.

〈보기〉 watch	play	write	tell	bake

1. John is good at _____ soccer.

2. Emily finished _____ a letter to him.

3. They enjoy _____ movies at home.

4. The man avoids _____ the truth.

5. My hobby is _____ cookies.

Grammar Tip

동명사는 to부정사의 명사적 용법과 같은 의미이며 바꾸어 쓸 수 있지만, 전치사의 목적어로 쓰인 경우는 동명사로 써야 한다.

B. novel 소설
   water 물을 주다
   plant 식물

C. avoid 피하다
   truth 진실

Unit 62 동명사와 to부정사

· 동사에 따라 동명사나 to부정사를 목적어로 쓴다. 동명사와 to부정사를 모두 목적어로 쓸 수 있는 동사도 있다.

동명사를 목적어로 쓰는 동사	enjoy, finish, avoid, give up, mind, stop, keep, postpone 등 I finished **doing** my homework.
to부정사를 목적어로 쓰는 동사	want, wish, hope, decide, plan, learn, promise, fail 등 He decides **to visit** the old man.
동명사와 to부정사 둘 다 목적어로 쓰는 동사	like, love, hate, start, begin, continue 등 The baby began **crying**. ＝ The baby began **to cry**.

· stop 뒤에는 동명사나 to부정사가 올 수 있는데, 「stop+동명사」는 '～하는 것을 멈추다'라는 뜻이고 「stop+to부정사」는 부사적 역할로 '～하기 위해 멈추다'라는 뜻이다.

She stopped **dancing**. (동명사는 stop의 목적어)　　She stopped **to dance**. (to부정사는 부사적 역할)

Practice

A. 다음 괄호 안에서 알맞은 것을 고르시오.

1. I like (watch / watching) TV in the evening.

2. Bill avoids (answering / to answer) the question.

3. Kate wants (reading / to read) books on weekends.

4. They planned (having / to have) a birthday party.

B. 다음 두 문장이 같도록 빈칸에 알맞은 말을 쓰시오.

1. He began working at a bank.
   = He began _____ at a bank.

2. Ann loves to have dinner with her friends.
   = Ann loves _____ dinner with her friends.

3. They don't like to clean the house.
   = They don't like _____ the house.

C. 다음 우리말과 같도록 괄호 안의 말을 이용하여 완성하시오.

1. 나는 말 타는 것을 즐긴다. (ride a horse)
   → I enjoy _____.

2. 나는 당근 먹는 것을 꺼리지 않는다. (eat carrots)
   → I don't mind _____.

3. 그는 살을 빼기를 원했다. (lose weight)
   → He wanted _____.

4. 그녀는 설거지하는 것을 끝냈다. (wash the dishes)
   → She finished _____.

63 동명사와 현재분사

- 동명사와 현재분사는 「동사원형+-ing」로 형태는 같지만, 동명사는 문장에서 명사의 역할을 하고 현재분사는 형용사 역할로 명사를 수식하거나 진행형을 나타낸다.

	동명사	현재분사
역할	명사 역할(주어, 보어, 목적어)	형용사 역할(명사 수식, 진행형)
의미	~하는 것, ~하기	~하는, ~하고 있는
예문	Sleeping on the bed is comfortable. His hobby is **taking** pictures.	The **sleeping** baby is very cute. He is **taking** pictures in the park.

* 동명사와 현재분사는 형태는 같지만 문장에서 역할이 달라 문장에서의 쓰임으로 구분해야 한다.
→ 주어, 보어, 목적어로 쓰이면 동명사, 명사 앞이나 뒤에서 수식하거나 진행형으로 쓰이면 현재분사

Practice

A. 다음 괄호 안의 동사를 알맞은 형태로 바꿔 쓰시오.

1. It was _____ cold. (get)

2. Susan likes _____ songs. (sing)

3. Thank you for _____ me. (call)

4. _____ with him was so boring. (talk)

5. She is _____ a car in the town. (drive)

6. The _____ woman is my aunt. (laugh)

7. Adam gave up _____ a big kite. (make)

8. My favorite activity is _____ pictures. (draw)

B. 다음 괄호 안의 동사를 이용하여 빈칸에 알맞은 말을 쓰시오.

1. 그 어린이는 우는 것을 멈추었다. (cry)
   → The child stopped _____.

2. 그 앉아 있는 소년은 나의 남동생이다. (sit)
   → The _____ boy is my brother.

3. 그들은 공원에서 축구를 하고 있다. (play)
   → They _____ soccer in the park.

4. 그는 그 산을 오르는 것을 즐긴다. (climb)
   → He enjoys _____ the mountain.

5. 나의 여동생은 그 멋진 정장을 입고 있다. (wear)
   → My sister _____ the nice suit.

124

A. 다음 괄호 안의 단어를 알맞은 형태로 바꿔 빈칸에 쓰시오.

1. He enjoyed _____ skiing last winter. (go)

2. I'm interested in _____ Korean food. (cook)

3. Ashley wants _____ her old friends. (meet)

4. They decided _____ a new camera. (buy)

5. Her pleasure is _____ foreign coins. (collect)

B. 다음 빈칸에 알맞은 말을 <보기>에서 골라 쓰시오.

<보기>	telling the truth	to become a great artist
	to hear the news	breaking your window

1. Brian was surprised _____.

2. I'm sorry for _____.

3. The boy grew up _____.

4. My sister avoided _____.

C. 다음 문장에서 어법상 <u>어색한</u> 부분을 바르게 고치시오.

1. They hope meet their grandparents. _____

2. Sam was glad to got a letter from her. _____

3. He decided changing his hair style. _____

4. Would you mind to lend me your bike? _____

5. I got up early taking a walk in the park. _____

D. 다음 밑줄 친 부분이 동명사인지, 현재분사인지 구분하시오.

1. His job is <u>building</u> houses in the city. (   )

2. He is <u>building</u> houses in the city. (   )

3. Thank you for <u>saving</u> her life. (   )

4. The students are <u>waiting</u> for me. (   )

5. We are <u>having</u> fun at the camp. (   )

6. <u>Eating</u> junk food is unhealthy for you. (   )

7. Julia is good at <u>playing</u> the violin. (   )

8. The <u>sitting</u> woman is my teacher. (   )

125

1. 다음 빈칸에 알맞지 <u>않은</u> 것은?

> Lucy _____ to go hiking with friends.

① decided   ② wants
③ planned   ④ finishes
⑤ hopes

2. 다음 빈칸에 알맞은 것은?

> Do you enjoy _____ a bike?

① ride   ② to ride
③ riding   ④ to riding
⑤ rode

3. 다음 밑줄 친 부분을 바르게 고친 것은?

> Susan went to the grocery store <u>buy</u> some vegetables.

① buys   ② bought
③ buying   ④ will buy
⑤ to buy

4. 다음 빈칸에 들어갈 말이 바르게 짝지어진 것은?

> · I hope _____ Paris someday.
> · I'm worried about _____ a test next week.

① visit – take   ② visiting – taking
③ to visit – taking   ④ visiting – to take
⑤ to visit – take

5. 다음 밑줄 친 부분이 어법상 옳은 것은?

① They <u>like playing</u> baseball.
② She <u>gave up to study</u> math yesterday.
③ He <u>planned going</u> to the zoo tomorrow.
④ Tom is <u>interested in speak</u> English.
⑤ I <u>postpone go</u> shopping on weekends.

6. 다음 밑줄 친 부분의 용법과 같은 것은?

> I'm looking for something <u>to drink</u>.

① He wants <u>to be</u> an actor.
② My sister has many books <u>to read</u>.
③ She got up early <u>to go</u> jogging.
④ I like <u>to watch</u> TV at home.
⑤ His job is <u>to teach</u> math at school.

7. 다음 빈칸에 공통으로 들어갈 말로 알맞지 <u>않은</u> 것은?

> · The children _____ playing soccer.
> · They _____ to read comic books.

① love   ② started
③ like   ④ avoid
⑤ began

8. 다음 to부정사의 용법이 나머지와 <u>다른</u> 것은?

① Her dream is to be a dentist.
② I need a chair to sit on.
③ I hope to travel around the world.
④ They decided to learn French.
⑤ To keep a diary is a good habit.

9. 다음 밑줄 친 ①~⑤ 중 어법상 어색한 것은?

> *A*: ①Did you finish ②to clean your room?
> *B*: ③Not yet. But I ④will ⑤finish it before lunch.

10. 다음 밑줄 친 부분의 역할을 <보기>에서 골라 쓰시오.

> <보기> 주어   목적어   보어

(1) I like drawing pictures in the park.

(2) Walking fast is good for your health.

(3) Her job is helping sick people.

11. 다음 중 어법상 어색한 것은?
① It's time to have lunch.
② I'm afraid of swimming.
③ My brother loves going fishing.
④ Joe grew up being a firefighter.
⑤ We talked about having the party.

12. 다음 빈칸에 공통으로 알맞은 것은?

> Kate's hobby is _____ cake. She really enjoys _____ delicious cake for her family.

① making   ② to make
③ make   ④ makes
⑤ will make

13. 다음 빈칸에 들어갈 말이 바르게 짝지어진 것을 고르시오.

> · He began _____ the car.
> · My sister is good at _____ tennis.
> · Cindy went out _____ her friends.

① to fix – to play – to meet
② to fix – playing – meeting
③ fixing – playing – to meet
④ fixing – playing – meeting
⑤ fixing – to play – to meet

14. 다음 빈칸에 공통으로 알맞은 말을 쓰시오.

> · He decided _____ eat some fruit.
> · Dona is going _____ visit them.

15. 다음 밑줄 친 부분의 쓰임이 나머지와 다른 것은?
① They started playing the piano.
② Joan likes talking with her parents.
③ I give up watching scary movies.
④ She finished writing the letter.
⑤ My sister is singing songs happily.

16. 다음 중 어법상 옳은 것은?
① It began snow at that time.
② How about saving the money?
③ She planned leaving at 2:00.
④ He doesn't mind to eat alone.
⑤ They were shocked hearing the news.

17. 다음 우리말과 같도록 빈칸에 알맞은 것을 <u>모두</u> 고르시오.

> Nick은 말을 타는 것을 매우 좋아한다.
> → Nick loves _____ a horse.

① ride   ② riding

③ to ride   ④ rides

⑤ rode

18. 다음 두 문장을 하나로 연결할 때 빈칸에 알맞은 말을 쓰시오.

> He went to the bookstore. He bought a magazine.
> = He went to the bookstore _____ a magazine.

19. 다음 밑줄 친 부분을 동명사로 바꿔 쓸 수 있는 것은?

① Do you like <u>to cook the food</u>?

② We need water <u>to drink</u>.

③ I was surprised <u>to see</u> him again.

④ Jason ran fast <u>to catch</u> the last train.

⑤ He doesn't have money <u>to buy</u> a car.

20. 다음 우리말을 영어로 바르게 옮긴 것은?

> 영어를 말하는 것은 나에게 쉽지 않다.

① Speaking English is not easy for me.

② To speak English not is easy for me.

③ Speak English is not easy for me.

④ Speaks English is not easy for me.

⑤ To spoke English is not easy for me.

〈서술형 문제〉

21. 다음 문장에서 어법상 어색한 것을 찾아 바르게 고쳐 쓰시오.

> Would you mind to open the window?

_____ → _____

22. 다음 괄호 안의 단어를 포함하여 빈칸에 알맞은 말을 쓰시오.

> My favorite subject is music. I like to sing songs. I _____ in the future.

(hope, famous singer)

→ _____

[23-24] 다음 표를 보고 빈칸에 알맞은 말을 쓰시오.

	이번 주 계획	싫어하는 것
Sue	read books	clean her room
Mike	visit the museum	play soccer

23. Sue's plan is _____ this week.
She hates _____.

24. Mike decided _____ this week.
He doesn't like _____.

25. 다음 메시지를 읽고, 밑줄 친 부분을 바르게 고치시오.

> I'm going to the department store
> (1) <u>buy</u> a gift for my sister. I want
> (2) <u>giving</u> her clothes but I can't choose
> anything. I need your help (3) <u>choose</u> a
> good thing. Please come to me.

(1) _____   (2) _____

(3) _____

문장의 형식이란 무엇인가?
문장을 이루는 중심 구성 요소인 주어, 동사, 목적어, 보어의 구성에 따라 문장의 형식을 구분하여 분류한 것으로 1~5형식이 있다.

문장의 형식은 어떻게 구분하는가?
1형식 :「주어+동사」로 이루어진 문장
2형식 :「주어+동사+보어」로 이루어진 문장
3형식 :「주어+동사+목적어」로 이루어진 문장
4형식 :「주어+동사+간접목적어+직접목적어」로 이루어진 문장
5형식 :「주어+동사+목적어+목적격보어」로 이루어진 문장

Chapter 11. 문장의 형식

64 1형식 문장과 There is/are

- 「주어+동사」로 이루어진 의미가 완전한 문장을 1형식 문장이라고 한다. 부사(구)는 문장 형식에 영향을 주지 않는다.
  James studies.　　　James studies hard.　　　James studies hard in the room.

- There is/are 구문은 '~이 있다'라는 뜻으로 is/are 다음에 오는 말이 주어이며, 1형식 문장이다.

긍정문	「There is+단수명사 ~.」 「There are+복수명사 ~.」	There **is** a dog on the mat. There **are** some apples in the basket.
부정문	「There is[are]+not ~.」	There is **not**[**isn't**] much money in the wallet. There are **not**[**aren't**] any books on the desk.
의문문	Is[Are] there ~? – Yes, there is[are]. / 　No, there isn't[aren't].	**Is there** a bank near here? – Yes, there is. / No, there isn't.

＊셀 수 없는 명사는 단수 취급하므로 There is로 쓴다.
There is some water in the bottle.

Practice

A. 다음 문장에서 주어와 동사를 찾아 쓰시오.

1. Tigers run fast.　　　　　주어 : _____　　동사 : _____

2. We go to bed at ten.　　　주어 : _____　　동사 : _____

3. She sings on the stage.　　주어 : _____　　동사 : _____

4. The sun sets in the west.　주어 : _____　　동사 : _____

B. 다음 괄호 안에서 알맞은 것을 고르시오.

1. There (is / are) two balls on the playground.

2. There (isn't / aren't) any pencils in the bag.

3. Is there any (milk / oranges) in the glass?

4. There (is / are) some money in my pocket.

5. There (is / are) many children in the hall.

C. 다음 문장을 괄호 안의 지시대로 바꾸시오.

1. There is a doll on the sofa. (a lot of dolls)
   → _____

2. There are many caps on the shelf. (부정문으로)
   → _____

3. There is a blue house on the hill. (의문문으로)
   → _____

Grammar Tip

A. stage 무대
　　set 지다, 저물다

There is/are 구문에서 is/are 다음에 오는 말이 주어이며 셀 수 없는 명사는 단수 취급한다.

B. playground 운동장
　　pocket 주머니

C. shelf 선반
　　hill 언덕

65 2형식 문장과 감각동사

- 「주어+동사+보어」로 이루어진 문장을 2형식 문장이라고 하며, 보어 자리에는 명사나 형용사가 온다.

  She is **a famous singer**.　　　The man is **rich**.

- look, sound, feel, smell, taste 등과 같이 사람의 감각을 표현하는 동사를 감각동사라고 한다. 감각동사 뒤에는 형용사가 오며 주어의 상태나 성질을 보충 설명한다.

look 보이다	He **looks** happy today.	feel 느끼다	I **feel** hungry.
sound 들리다	Her voice **sounds** sweet.	smell 냄새가 나다	This soup **smells** good.
taste 맛이 나다	The pizza **tasted** great.	보어가 부사처럼 해석되지만 형용사가 온다.	

* 감각동사 뒤에 명사가 올 경우, 「감각동사+like+명사」의 형태로 쓴다.

He looks **like** a bear.

 Practice

A. 다음 괄호 안에서 알맞은 것을 고르시오.

1. This blouse feels (soft / softly).
2. You look very (angry / angrily).
3. The chocolate tastes (sweet / sweetly).
4. Betty swims very (good / well).
5. Her idea sounds (great / greatly).
6. The woman is (sad / sadly).
7. The soup smells (delicious / deliciously).
8. He looks (with / like) a doctor.

B. 다음 괄호 안의 동사를 이용하여 문장을 바꿔 쓰시오.

1. The clothes are smooth. (feel)

   → _____

2. The girls are beautiful. (look)

   → _____

3. This lemon is sour and sweet. (taste)

   → _____

C. 다음 대화의 밑줄 친 부분 중 어색한 것을 고르시오.

> A: You look ①excited today.
> B: I feel ②good. I'm ③planning ④to go skating.
> A: That sounds ⑤greatly.

Grammar Tip

look, feel, smell과 같은 감각동사 뒤에 오는 보어는 부사처럼 해석되지만 형용사가 와야 한다.

A. soft 부드러운
　　delicious 맛있는

B. smooth 매끄러운
　　sour 신

C. excited 흥분한

131

66 3형식 문장과 4형식 문장

- 「주어+동사+목적어」로 이루어진 문장을 3형식 문장이라고 하며 목적어 자리에는 명사나 대명사가 온다.

3형식 문장	「주어+동사+목적어」: 주어가 ~을(를) 하다
	We played **soccer** in the park.

* 목적어 자리에는 to부정사나 동명사도 올 수 있다.　He likes **to play[playing]** soccer.

- 「주어+동사+간접목적어+직접목적어」로 이루어진 문장을 4형식 문장이라고 한다. 4형식 문장에 쓰이는 동사를 수여동사라고 하며 주로 간접목적어에는 사람이, 직접목적어에는 사물이 온다.

4형식 문장	「주어+동사+간접목적어(~에게)+직접목적어(~을)」
	My father gave **me a doll**.

* 수여동사 : give, make, buy, send, tell, find, teach, show, ask 등

 Practice

A. 다음 괄호 안의 문장 요소에 해당하는 것에 밑줄 그으시오.

1. The birds begin to sing in the tree. (목적어)

2. He told me an exciting story. (간접목적어)

3. My mother makes me cookies. (직접목적어)

B. 다음 문장의 형식을 쓰시오.

1. He bought a black bag.　　　　(　　　)형식 문장

2. Sarah wrote her a postcard.　　(　　　)형식 문장

3. Leo lost his purse yesterday.　(　　　)형식 문장

C. 다음 괄호 안의 단어를 바르게 배열하여 문장을 완성하시오.

1. (teaches, science, us, he)

　→ _____

2. (she, spaghetti, me, made)

　→ _____

3. (him, passed, a ball, I)

　→ _____

4. (good advice, can, she, them, give)

　→ _____

5. (will, you, they, send, a gift)

　→ _____

Grammar Tip

목적어 자리에는 명사, 대명사, to부정사, 동명사가 올 수 있다.

B. postcard 엽서
　　purse 지갑

C. pass 건네주다
　　advice 충고

Unit 67 4형식 문장의 3형식 전환

- 4형식 문장은 간접목적어와 직접목적어의 어순을 바꾸고 간접목적어 앞에 전치사를 써서 3형식 문장으로 나타낼 수 있다.

  He gave his son a bike. → He gave a bike **to his son**.

  She bought me a new shirt. → She bought a new shirt **for me**.

- 4형식 문장을 3형식 문장으로 바꿀 때 간접목적어 앞에 전치사를 붙이는데, 이때 전치사는 동사에 따라 달라진다.

to를 쓰는 동사	give, send, bring, teach, show, tell, write, lend 등
for를 쓰는 동사	make, buy, cook, find 등
of를 쓰는 동사	ask

Practice

A. 다음 괄호 안에서 알맞은 것을 고르시오.

1. Alice sent a letter (to / for) her friend.

2. They will buy pants (for / of) their father.

3. I asked a question (to / of) Eric.

4. The girl told her name (to / for) me.

B. 다음 빈칸에 알맞은 것을 고르시오.

1. Susan cooked dinner _____ me.
   ① to   ② for   ③ of   ④ by

2. Tom's brother _____ many questions of her.
   ① asked   ② told   ③ showed   ④ sent

3. He _____ a beautiful scarf to Susan.
   ① found   ② gave   ③ made   ④ bought

C. 다음 4형식 문장을 3형식 문장으로 바꿔 쓰시오.

1. My uncle showed me a camera.
   → _____

2. She bought her daughter a new bike.
   → _____

3. They told him interesting stories.
   → _____

4. Can you bring me some juice?
   → _____

Grammar Tip

4형식 문장을 3형식 문장으로 바꿀 때 간접목적어 앞에 전치사를 붙이는데 동사에 따라서 달라진다.

B. cook 요리하다
scarf 스카프, 목도리

C. daughter 딸
bring 가져오다

Unit 68 | 5형식 문장

· 「주어＋동사＋목적어＋목적격보어」로 이루어진 문장을 5형식 문장이라고 한다. 5형식 문장에는 make, call, name, keep, find 등의 동사가 쓰이며 이런 동사 뒤에는 명사나 형용사가 목적격보어로 온다.

They **named** their baby Paul. (명사)　　The news **made** me **happy**. (형용사)

· want, tell, ask, allow, advise, expect 등의 동사는 목적격보어로 to부정사가 온다.

I **want** you **to go** with me.　　　　He **advised** **to exercise** every day.

5형식 문장의 목적격보어의 형태	명사	목적어와 동일 대상
	형용사	목적어의 상태 설명
	to부정사	목적어의 행동이나 상태

Practice

A. 다음 괄호 안에서 알맞은 것을 골라 빈칸에 쓰시오.

1. This movie made _____ happy. (I / me)

2. I _____ the luggage heavy. (gave / found)

3. We expects Jason _____ the game. (win / to win)

4. Please _____ me Cindy. (call / say)

5. Tom wanted him _____ the books. (read / to read)

B. 다음 밑줄 친 부분을 바르게 고치시오.

1. We should keep our body <u>cleanly</u>.　→ _____

2. He told me <u>brush</u> my teeth.　→ _____

3. The book made him <u>sadly</u>.　→ _____

4. She didn't allow him <u>plays</u> soccer.　→ _____

C. 다음 우리말과 같도록 빈칸에 알맞은 말을 쓰시오.

1. 사람들은 그를 Jack이라고 부른다.
   → People call _____ _____.

2. 그녀는 내게 물을 많이 마시라고 충고했다.
   → She advised me _____ _____ lots of water.

3. 그는 그 시험이 쉽다는 것을 알았다.
   → He found _____ _____ _____.

4. 나는 그녀가 곧 돌아오기를 기대한다.
   → I expect _____ _____ _____ back soon.

Grammar Tip

A. luggage 짐
expect 기대하다

5형식 문장의 목적격보어에는 명사나 형용사, to부정사가 올 수 있다.

B. body 몸
allow 허락하다

C. exam 시험
soon 곧

A. 다음 밑줄 친 부분의 문장 요소를 <보기>에서 골라 쓰시오.

> <보기>   간접목적어   직접목적어   주격보어   목적격보어

1. Carol sent <u>Laura</u> a gift.　　　→ _____
2. Mr. Smith looked <u>worried</u>.　　→ _____
3. She bought me <u>a cheese cake</u>.　→ _____
4. She found the problem <u>difficult</u>.　→ _____

B. 다음 괄호 안에서 알맞은 것을 고르시오.

1. Amy wants me (go / to go) hiking with her.
2. Will you buy a sweater (for / to) me?
3. This soup smells (good / well).
4. (Is / Are) there any cheese in the store?

C. 다음 우리말과 같도록 괄호 안의 단어를 이용하여 쓰시오.
1. 이 초콜릿은 쓰고 단맛이 난다. (bitter, sweet)
   → This chocolate tastes _____.
2. 하늘에 많은 별이 있다. (many, stars)
   → _____ in the sky.
3. 그는 나에게 파이를 만들어 주었다. (a pie, for me)
   → He _____.

D. 다음 괄호 안에서 알맞은 것을 고르시오.
1. He asked me (help / to help) with his work.
2. My mother told me (cleans / to clean) my room.
3. I want you (come / to come) to my party.

E. 다음 문장에서 어색한 곳을 찾아 밑줄 긋고 바르게 고치시오.
1. Our teacher told us study hard.　　→ _____
2. There are some juice in the glass.　→ _____
3. Jim felt very tiredly, so he took a rest.　→ _____
4. The man gave a ring for the woman.　→ _____

[1-2] 다음 빈칸에 알맞지 **않은** 것을 고르시오.

1.
> Andrew and Nick look _____.

① happy   ② well
③ tired   ④ sad
⑤ nice

2.
> She _____ me to help with her work.

① asked   ② told
③ made   ④ wanted
⑤ expected

[3-4] 다음 빈칸에 알맞은 것을 고르시오.

3.
> Peter showed _____.

① us his album   ② his album us
③ his album for us   ④ our his album
⑤ us to his album

4.
> There is _____ on the table.

① three cups   ② fresh apples
③ lots of keys   ④ Jimmy's glasses
⑤ some bread

5. 다음 밑줄 친 ①~⑤ 중 어법상 어색한 것은?

> He ① made ② for ③ me ④ delicious ⑤ soup.

6. 다음 밑줄 친 부분의 문장 요소가 나머지와 **다른** 것은?
① They called the dog <u>Cutie</u>.
② The movie made me <u>happy</u>.
③ She expects me <u>to pass the exam</u>.
④ We should keep our room <u>clean</u>.
⑤ His voice sounded very <u>sweet</u>.

7. 다음 대화의 빈칸에 들어갈 말이 바르게 짝지어진 것은?

> A: _____ there any milk in the bottle?
> B: _____ We have to buy some milk.

① Is - Yes, there are.
② Is - No, there isn't.
③ Is - Yes, it is.
④ Are - Yes, there are.
⑤ Are - No, there aren't.

8. 다음 괄호 안에서 알맞은 것을 고르시오.

> This spaghetti smells (good / well), but it tastes (bad / badly).

9. 다음 중 빈칸에 들어갈 말이 나머지와 <u>다른</u> 것은?

① She bought a toy _____ her son.
② Please give a pencil _____ me.
③ Julia made food _____ them.
④ My mom cooked lunch _____ me.
⑤ He found a map _____ the kids.

10. 다음 중 3형식 문장으로 <u>잘못</u> 바꾼 것은?

① He passed me a book.
  → He passed a book to me.
② She asked me easy questions.
  → She asked easy questions of me.
③ Can you make me sandwiches?
  → Can you make sandwiches for me?
④ Please send Bill this letter.
  → Please send this letter for Bill.
⑤ He bought her parents flowers.
  → He bought flowers for her parents.

[11-12] 다음 두 문장이 같은 뜻이 되도록 빈칸에 알맞은 말을 쓰시오.

11.
Tony teaches the students English.
= Tony teaches English _____.

12.
Ann has lots of juice in her bag.
= _____ lots of juice in Ann's bag.

13. 다음 중 어법상 <u>어색한</u> 것은?

① He found the news terrible.
② His music made her comfortable.
③ I want you to have dinner with me.
④ We call him "Walking Dictionary."
⑤ Michelle allowed him watching TV.

14. 다음 대화의 빈칸에 알맞은 것은?

A: Is there a bakery near your house?
B: _____

① Yes, there is.   ② Yes, there are.
③ No, there aren't.   ④ No, it isn't.
⑤ Yes, there isn't.

15. 다음 빈칸에 알맞은 것은?

This coat will _____.

① keep you warm   ② keep you warmly
③ keep warm you   ④ keep warmly
⑤ you to keep warm

16. 다음 우리말을 영어로 바르게 옮긴 것을 두 개 고르면?

Linda는 그에게 자전거를 주었다.

① Linda gave a bike him.
② Linda gave him a bike.
③ Linda gave to him a bike.
④ Linda gave a bike for him.
⑤ Linda gave a bike to him.

137

17. 다음 빈칸에 공통으로 들어갈 말을 쓰시오.

> · He taught Japanese _____ me.
> · She showed her coins _____ us.

18. 다음 빈칸에 들어갈 말이 바르게 짝지어진 것은?

> · May I ask a favor _____ you?
> · He made a toy car _____ his son.

① of – for
② of – to
③ to – to
④ for – for
⑤ to – of

19. 다음 두 문장이 같도록 빈칸에 들어갈 말이 바르게 짝지어진 것은?

> I watched the movie. It was exciting.
> = I _____ the movie _____.

① found – exciting
② found – excited
③ watched – excited
④ watched – exciting
⑤ told – excited

20. 다음 중 <보기>의 밑줄 친 부분과 쓰임이 다른 것은?

> <보기> He made me upset.

① The music made the woman sad.
② She made me a good actor.
③ This medicine made me sleepy.
④ Tony made his son special dinner.
⑤ Having breakfast made us healthy.

<서술형 문제>

21. 다음 우리말과 같도록 괄호 안의 단어를 이용하여 문장을 완성하시오.

> 너의 목소리는 이상하게 들려. (strange)
> → Your voice _____.

22. 다음 글에서 어법상 어색한 곳을 찾아 바르게 고치시오.

> I was taking a walk by the lake yesterday. Two girls came to me and they asked me take pictures.

_____ → _____

23. 다음 괄호 안의 단어를 알맞은 형태로 바꿔 문장을 완성하시오.

(1)
> I talked with Lisa in the library. A man told us _____ quiet. (be)

(2)
> This road looks _____.
> Be careful. (danger)

24. 다음 괄호 안의 단어들을 바르게 배열하여 대화를 완성하시오.

> A: _____
> (my watch, is, on the table, there)?
> B: Yes, there is.

→ _____

25. 다음 우리말과 같도록 괄호 안의 단어를 바르게 배열하시오.

> 그들은 내가 많은 책을 읽기를 원하신다.
> (want, many, read, to, they, me, books)

→ _____

전치사란 무엇인가?

전치사는 문장에서 시간, 장소, 위치, 방향, 방법 등을 자세하게 나타내 주는 말로 전치사 다음에는 명사가 오며 동사가 올 경우에는 동명사의 형태로 쓴다.

I meet her in the park at noon.

전치사에는 어떤 것들이 있는가?

전치사는 명사와 함께 쓰여 시간, 장소, 위치, 방향, 방법 등을 나타내 주는데 시간의 전치사, 장소의 전치사 외에도 다양한 전치사가 있다.

Chapter 12. 전치사

Unit 69 시간의 전치사 1

· 전치사를 이용하여 시간을 나타낼 수 있는데, 시간을 나타내는 전치사에는 at, in, on이 있다.

at	+구체적인 시각, 특정한 시점 (정오, 자정, 밤)	at 8:40, at night, at that time, ⋯ I usually get up at seven. Don't stay up late at night.
in	+월, 연도, 계절, 시기 (오전, 오후, 저녁)	in the afternoon, in 2015, in July, in winter, ⋯ He reads the newspaper in the morning. The weather is too hot in August.
on	+요일, 날짜, 특정한 날	on Sunday, on July 8th, on Christmas Day, ⋯ Let's go hiking on Sunday morning. What are you going to do on Christmas eve?

Practice

Grammar Tip

정오, 자정, 밤은 at을 사용하고 월, 연도, 계절과 오선, 오후, 지녁은 in을 사용한다. 또한 특정한 날은 on을 사용한다.

A. 다음 빈칸에 at, in, on 중 알맞은 것을 쓰시오.

1. _____ noon
2. _____ spring
3. _____ April
4. _____ New Year's Day

B. 다음 빈칸에 알맞은 전치사를 〈보기〉에서 골라 쓰시오.

〈보기〉	at	in	on

1. I went skiing _____ December.
2. She goes to bed _____ ten.
3. The leaves turn red _____ fall.
4. Our school starts _____ nine.
5. A man walked on the moon _____ 1969.
6. My mother was very sick _____ that time.
7. We don't go to school _____ Saturdays.
8. I usually drink milk _____ the morning.
9. Can you come to my party _____ May 3rd?

B. turn ~이 되다
moon 달

C. 다음 밑줄 친 부분을 바르게 고치시오.

1. The bookstore closes in Sunday. → _____
2. Harry will arrive here on 4:30. → _____
3. My brother was born at March. → _____
4. Jonathan and Ann married on 2014. → _____
5. Judy's birthday is in June 16th. → _____

C. arrive 도착하다
be born 태어나다
marry 결혼하다

Unit

70 시간의 전치사 2

· 전치사 before, after, for, during은 시간의 전후 관계나 기간을 나타내는 전치사이다.

before	~ 전에	**before** breakfast, **before** 8 o'clock, ⋯ I will come back **before** lunch.
after	~ 후에	**after** dinner, **after** the class, ⋯ He went to the movies **after** dinner.
for	~ 동안(+숫자/구체적인 시간의 길이)	**for** two hours, **for** a week, **for** five years, ⋯ Tina stayed in Paris **for** two weeks.
during	~ 동안(+특정 기간)	**during** summer vacation, **during** this weekend, ⋯ I stayed in Japan **during** summer vacation.

＊ before와 after가 전치사로 쓰일 때는 뒤에 명사가 오고 접속사로 쓰일 때는 절(주어+동사)이 온다.

Practice

A. 다음 밑줄 친 부분을 우리말로 옮기시오.

1. I made a kite <u>for two hours</u>.

2. It rained a lot <u>during the summer camp</u>.

3. She goes to bed <u>before 10:00</u>.

4. What do you do <u>after school</u>?

5. Don't use your cell phone <u>during class</u>.

B. 다음 괄호 안에서 알맞은 것을 고르시오.

1. June comes (before / after) May.

2. Some animals sleep (on / during) the cold winter.

3. James stayed in England (for / during) a month.

4. It is dark (before / after) sunrise.

5. We enjoyed ourselves (for / during) the trip.

C. 다음 우리말과 같도록 빈칸에 알맞은 전치사를 쓰시오.

1. 우리는 그 파티가 끝난 후에 설거지를 했다.
   → We did the dishes _____ the party.

2. 그들은 3시간 동안 자전거를 빌렸다.
   → They rented bikes _____ three hours.

3. 나는 휴일 동안 해변에서 즐거운 시간을 보냈다.
   → I had a good time at the beach _____ holidays.

4. Sophie는 보통 아침 식사 전에 조깅을 한다.
   → Sophie usually jogs _____ breakfast.

Grammar Tip

전치사 for와 during은 '~ 동안'이라는 뜻인데, for 뒤에는 기간을 나타내는 숫자가 오고 during 뒤에는 특정 기간이 온다.

B. sunrise 일출
trip 여행

C. rent 빌리다
holiday 휴일, 휴가

71 장소의 전치사

- 전치사는 장소에 대한 정보를 나타내기도 하는데 at, in, on은 지점이나 장소를 나타낼 때 사용한다.

at	+비교적 좁은 장소, 지점	at the station, at home, at school, … I want to stay at home. She saw Peter at the bus stop.
in	+비교적 넓은 장소	in Seoul, in Korea, in the world, … It snowed heavily in London. My uncle lives in France.
on	~ 위에(표면에 접한 상태)	on the road, on the wall, on the table, … There are pictures on the wall.

*at과 in은 우리말 뜻이 같지만 장소의 크기나 지점에 따라서 구별한다.

 Practice

A. 다음 괄호 안에서 알맞은 것을 고르시오.

1. Japan is (at / in) Asia.
2. There are my photos (on / in) the wall.
3. I want to study Art (at / in) Italy.
4. The actress stayed (at / on) the hotel.

B. 다음 빈칸에 at, in, on 중 알맞은 전치사를 쓰시오.

1. He watched a movie _____ home.
2. There is a mirror _____ the wall.
3. We can see kangaroos _____ Australia.
4. They wait for her _____ the bus stop.
5. I found his key _____ the second floor.
6. Don't make noise _____ the classroom.
7. She and he walk together _____ the road.
8. Henry has many friends _____ the US.

C. 다음 밑줄 친 부분을 바르게 고치시오.

1. Sweden is at Europe. → _____
2. Please write your name at the board. → _____
3. There are many balloons on the sky. → _____
4. I met a strange man in the crosswalk. → _____

Grammar Tip

A. wall 벽
Italy 이탈리아

전치사 at과 in은 뜻은 같지만 좁은 장소는 at을, 넓은 장소는 in을 사용한다. on은 표면에 접한 상태를 나타낸다.

B. mirror 거울
floor 마루, 층
noise 소음, 소란

C. Sweden 스웨덴
crosswalk 횡단보도

Unit

72 위치의 전치사

· 전치사는 사람이나 사물의 위치에 대한 정확한 정보를 나타내기도 한다.

under	~ 아래에	There are children **under** the tree.
over	~ 위에(표면에 접하지 않은 상태)	The plane is flying **over** the building.
in front of	~ 앞에	She stopped **in front of** the store.
behind	~ 뒤에	A dog is sleeping **behind** the sofa.
next to(= by)	~ 옆에	My school is **next to** the bakery.
near	~ 근처에	There is a park **near** my house.
between	~ 사이에	I sat **between** Kate and Andy.
across from	~ 맞은편에	The bank is **across from** the library.

Practice

Grammar Tip

전치사 on은 표면에 접촉하고 있는 상태이고 over는 표면에 접촉하지 않은 상태를 나타낸다.

A. 다음 우리말과 같게 빈칸에 알맞은 전치사를 쓰시오.

1. My bag is _____ the sofa. (그 소파 앞에)

2. The boy was sleeping _____ the tree. (그 나무 아래에)

3. There is a bank _____ the hospital. (그 병원 뒤에)

4. The dog jumped _____ the bench. (그 벤치 너머 위로)

B. 다음 괄호 안에서 알맞은 것을 고르시오.

1. The big ship sailed (over / under) the bridge.

2. Eagles are flying (under / over) that house.

3. Is there a post office (near / between) here?

4. I saw Ryan (across / between) from the bakery.

5. Do you know the girl (under / next) to Tony?

B. sail 항해하다
bridge 다리

C. 다음 우리말과 같도록 빈칸에 알맞은 전치사를 쓰시오.

1. 나는 그 침대 아래에서 나의 양말을 찾았다.
   → I found my socks _____ the bed.

2. 그는 그 서점 맞은편에 서 있다.
   → He is standing _____ the bookstore.

3. 모빌이 그 침대 위에 걸려 있다.
   → A mobile is hanging _____ the bed.

4. 이 근처에 지하철역이 있나요?
   → Is there a subway station _____ here?

C. mobile 모빌(작품), 움직이는 조각
hang 걸다, 걸리다
subway 지하철

Unit 73 방향의 전치사

· 전치사는 사람이나 사물이 움직이고 있는 방향을 나타내기도 한다.

up	~ 위로	She is walking **up** the hill.
down	~ 아래로	The girl came **down** the stairs.
into	~ 안으로	The frog jumped **into** the river.
out of	~ 밖으로	She looks **out of** the window.
from	~로부터	They came **from** Canada.
to	~로	I'm going **to** the library.
for	~을 향하여	We will leave **for** Jeju-do tomorrow.

Practice

Grammar Tip

A. 다음 밑줄 친 부분을 우리말로 옮기시오.

1. The boy climbed up the ladder.

2. A bear went into the forest.

3. The train started for Busan.

4. A gorilla escaped from the zoo.

B. 다음 괄호 안에서 알맞은 것을 고르시오.

1. We went (to / down) the museum yesterday.

2. The tiger came (out of / up) the cave.

3. The train runs south (into / from) Paris.

4. The squirrel went (of / down) the tree.

5. Monkeys move fast (from / for) trees to trees.

C. 다음 우리말과 같도록 괄호 안의 단어들을 바르게 배열하시오.

1. 나무가 땅에 쓰러졌다. (fell, a tree, on, down, the ground)
   → _____

2. 그는 그 바위에서 뛰었다. (from, jumped, the rock, he)
   → _____

3. 토끼가 구멍으로 들어갔다. (a rabbit, a hole, into, went)
   → _____

4. Dan은 산을 올라갔다. (Dan, the mountain, up, climbed)
   → _____

A. ladder 사다리
forest 숲
escape 탈출하다

from *A* to *B*는 'A에서 B까지'라는 뜻으로 출발점과 도착점을 나타내며 출발 시간과 도착 시간을 나타낼 수도 있다.

B. cave 동굴
squirrel 다람쥐

C. ground 땅
rock 바위
hole 구멍

Unit 74 | 그 밖의 전치사

· 전치사를 이용하여 시간, 장소, 위치나 방향 외에도 다양한 정보와 방법을 나타낼 수 있다.

by	~을 타고	I go to school **by** bus.
for	~을 위해	We sang a song **for** her.
with	~와 함께, ~을 가지고	He will go camping **with** his friends. He wrote his name **with** a pencil.
without	~없이	We can't live **without** water.
about	~에 대해	I heard the news **about** the woman.
around	~ 주위에	She planned to travel **around** the world.

Practice

A. 다음 우리말과 같게 빈칸에 알맞은 전치사를 쓰시오.

1. This ring is _____ my friend. (나의 친구를 위한)

2. We went to the museum _____ subway. (지하철로)

3. The earth moves _____ the sun. (태양 주위에)

4. She goes to school _____ Brian. (Brian과 함께)

5. I read the book _____ the insect. (그 곤충에 대해)

B. 다음 괄호 안에서 알맞은 것을 고르시오.

1. I wrote a letter (with / around) a pen.

2. They go to Rome (for / by) airplane.

3. We cannot live (with / without) oxygen.

4. We talked (around / about) robots.

5. John played soccer (with / by) his father.

C. 다음 우리말과 같도록 빈칸에 알맞은 전치사를 쓰시오.

1. Cathy는 그녀의 친구들과 함께 점심을 먹는다.
   → Cathy has lunch _____ her friends.

2. 그의 아빠는 그의 아들을 위해 모형 차를 만든다.
   → His dad makes a model car _____ his son.

3. 학생들은 수채화 물감으로 그림을 그렸다.
   → Students painted _____ watercolors.

4. Ann과 Bill은 호수 주위를 걷고 있다.
   → Ann and Bill are walking _____ the lake.

Grammar Tip

A. insect 곤충

전치사 with는 '~와 함께'라는 뜻과 '~을 가지고'라는 뜻으로 수단과 방법을 나타낼 때도 사용한다.

B. Rome 로마
   oxygen 산소

C. paint 그리다, 칠하다
   watercolor 수채화 물감

A. 다음 빈칸에 알맞은 전치사를 쓰시오.

  1. She lived _____ Korea _____ 2012.

  2. He landed _____ the moon _____ July 16th.

  3. _____ the evening, I met Julia _____ the corner.

B. 다음 밑줄 친 부분을 바르게 고치시오.

  1. Bean was drawing <u>during</u> 40 minutes. → _____

  2. My house is across <u>to</u> the park. → _____

  3. Ann comes <u>for</u> Japan. She is Japanese. → _____

  4. You should brush your teeth <u>after</u> bed. → _____

C. 다음 괄호 안에서 알맞은 것을 골라 빈칸에 쓰시오.

  1. The boat was passing _____ the bridge. (under / over)

  2. He put the bag _____ Tom and Eric. (by / between)

  3. Thursday comes _____ Wednesday. (before / after)

  4. You should not go _____ the fire. (near / about)

D. 다음 우리말과 같도록 괄호 안의 단어를 이용하여 완성하시오.

  1. 나는 월요일부터 금요일까지 수업이 있다. (Monday, Friday)

    → I have classes _____.

  2. 그는 빗속에서 우산 없이 걸어갔다. (walk, umbrella)

    → He _____ in the rain.

  3. 그녀는 이번 주말 동안 여행을 할 것이다. (take a trip)

    → She will _____.

  4. 큰 눈덩이가 그 언덕 아래로 굴러갔다. (roll, hill)

    → A big snowball _____.

E. 다음 빈칸에 공통으로 알맞은 전치사를 쓰시오.

  1. There is an old cabin _____ the river.

    She went to her uncle _____ airplane.

  2. I'll go on a picnic _____ my cousins.

    Cut the cloth _____ these scissors.

1. 다음 빈칸에 공통으로 알맞은 것은?

   · These flowers are _____ Amy.
   · I will leave _____ Japan tomorrow.

   ① with   ② for
   ③ by   ④ to
   ⑤ at

2. 다음 빈칸에 알맞지 <u>않는</u> 것은?

   Harry visited them in _____.

   ① summer   ② 2013
   ③ the morning   ④ April
   ⑤ July 5th

3. 다음 중 밑줄 친 부분이 어법상 옳은 것은?
   ① I feel sleepy <u>at</u> spring.
   ② Joe will come back <u>in</u> Tuesday.
   ③ She drinks tea <u>at</u> the morning.
   ④ They play badminton <u>on</u> school.
   ⑤ I cleaned the room <u>for</u> 30 minutes.

4. 다음 빈칸에 during이 올 수 <u>없는</u> 것은?
   ① She is running _____ an hour.
   ② I felt bored _____ his speech.
   ③ It snowed a lot _____ the night.
   ④ He had a good time _____ the vacation.
   ⑤ I had a cup of coffee _____ the break.

5. 다음 <보기>에서 알맞은 전치사를 골라 빈칸에 쓰시오.

   <보기>   with   without   up   down

   (1) We can't live _____ air.

   (2) She fell _____ and broke her leg.

6. 다음 대화의 빈칸에 들어갈 말이 바르게 짝지어진 것은?

   A: Did you hear _____ Tommy?
   B: No, I didn't. What happened to him?
   A: He had a car accident yesterday. He is _____ the hospital.

   ① about – on   ② with – in
   ③ about – in   ④ around – at
   ⑤ for – at

7. 다음 우리말과 같은 뜻이 되도록 빈칸에 알맞은 말을 쓰시오.

   나는 어제 곤충에 관한 TV 프로그램을 봤다.
   = I watched a TV program _____ insects yesterday.

8. 다음 빈칸에 들어갈 말이 바르게 짝지어진 것은?

   · It's warm _____ spring.
   · I got up _____ 6:30 this morning.

   ① on – at   ② at – in
   ③ in – on   ④ in – at
   ⑤ on – in

[9-10] 다음 빈칸에 들어갈 말이 나머지와 <u>다른</u> 것을 고르시오.

9. ① I saw him _____ the station.
   ② We met her _____ the corner.
   ③ They weren't there _____ that time.
   ④ I don't play the piano _____ night.
   ⑤ It is the longest river _____ the world.

10. ① There is a mirror _____ the wall.
    ② The cat is sleeping _____ the sofa.
    ③ We had a good time _____ the festival.
    ④ They go to church _____ Sundays.
    ⑤ I eat turkey _____ Thanksgiving Day.

11. 다음 중 어법상 <u>어색한</u> 것은?
    ① She walked around the lake.
    ② I have the exam in April 21st.
    ③ He wants to go there without her.
    ④ The dog barks in front of the door.
    ⑤ There are many bees over the flowers.

12. 다음 빈칸에 알맞은 것은?

    His plan is to travel _____ the world someday.

    ① about   ② around
    ③ from   ④ for
    ⑤ with

13. 빈칸에 공통으로 알맞은 전치사를 쓰시오.

    School begins _____ March
    _____ Korea.

[14-15] 다음 중 전치사의 쓰임이 <u>잘못된</u> 것을 고르시오.

14. ① She went into the gallery.
    ② Which is the train for Chicago?
    ③ The ship is sinking out of the river.
    ④ Please wash your hands before meals.
    ⑤ I have something to tell you about Ann.

15. ① I can't live without you.
    ② The boy is hiding behind the door.
    ③ The moon goes to the earth.
    ④ I saw a rainbow over the mountain.
    ⑤ She doesn't know anything about me.

16. 다음 중 어법상 <u>어색한</u> 부분을 찾아 바르게 고치시오.

    He goes to work around bike on sunny days.

    _____ → _____

17. 빈칸에 공통으로 알맞은 것은?

> · I live _____ my cousin.
> · The baby is playing _____ dolls.

① with   ② around
③ on   ④ across
⑤ for

18. 다음 빈칸에 on이 들어갈 수 없는 것은?

① I wear Hanbok _____ Chuseok.
② We moved here _____ August 15th.
③ My sweater is _____ the table.
④ The office is _____ the third floor.
⑤ I usually go skiing _____ winter.

19. 다음 밑줄 친 전치사의 쓰임이 나머지와 <u>다른</u> 것은?

① He went <u>to</u> the park by car.
② A monkey is climbing <u>up</u> the tree.
③ He slept <u>during</u> the flight.
④ I'll leave <u>for</u> Paris next year.
⑤ The boys dived <u>into</u> the water.

20. 다음 대화의 밑줄 친 부분을 바르게 고친 것은?

> A: How often do you exercise?
> B: I go hiking <u>in</u> weekends.

① for   ② to
③ at   ④ on
⑤ by

〈서술형 문제〉

21. 다음 두 문장이 같은 뜻이 되도록 빈칸에 알맞은 말을 쓰시오.

> Jamie sat behind Sally.
> = Sally sat _____ Jamie.

[22-23] 다음 우리말을 참고하여 괄호 안의 단어들을 바르게 배열하시오.

22. Bob은 그 책상 아래에서 그의 열쇠를 찾았다.
(found, the, his, under, key, Bob, desk)
→ _____

23. 6시 전에 극장에서 만나자.
(meet, before, the, let's, at, six, theater)
→ _____

24. 다음 우리말과 같도록 괄호 안의 단어를 이용하여 문장을 완성하시오.

> 개가 그 울타리 위로 뛰어넘었다. (jump, fence)
> → A dog _____.

25. 다음 〈보기〉에서 알맞은 전치사를 골라 대화를 완성하시오.

> 〈보기〉   at   around   up   for

(1) A: What are you doing?
B: I'm planting flowers _____ the wall.
(2) A: When does the bus leave _____ LA?
B: It will leave _____ three.
(3) A: Look at the spider!
B: It is climbing _____ the tree.

149

1. 시간의 전치사

_____	+구체적인 시각, 특정한 시점 (정오, 자정, 밤)	I usually get up _____ seven. Don't stay up late _____ night.
_____	+월, 연도, 계절, 시기 (오전, 오후, 저녁)	He reads the newspaper _____ the morning. The weather is too hot _____ August.
_____	+요일, 날짜, 특정한 날	Let's go hiking _____ Sunday morning. What are you going to do _____ Christmas eve?
_____	~전에	I will come back _____ lunch.
_____	~후에	He went to the movies _____ dinner.
_____	~ 동안(+숫자/구체적인 시간의 길이)	Tina stayed in Paris _____ two weeks.
_____	~ 동안(+특정 기간)	I stayed in Japan _____ summer vacation.

2. 장소의 전치사

_____	+비교적 좁은 장소, 지점	I want to stay _____ home.
_____	+비교적 넓은 장소	It snowed heavily _____ London.
_____	~위에(표면에 접한 상태)	There are pictures _____ thc wall.

3. 위치의 전치사

_____	~ 아래에	There are children _____ the tree.
_____	~ 위에(표면에 접하지 않은 상태)	The plane is flying _____ the building.
_____	~ 앞에	She stopped _____ the store.
_____	~ 뒤에	A dog is sleeping _____ the sofa.
_____	~ 옆에	My school is _____ the bakery.
_____	~ 근처에	There is a park _____ my house.
_____	~ 사이에	I sat _____ Kate and Andy.
_____	~ 맞은편에	The bank is _____ the library.

4. 방향의 전치사

_____	~ 위로	She is walking _____ the hill.
_____	~ 아래로	The girl came _____ the stairs.
_____	~ 안으로	The frog jumped _____ the river.
_____	~ 밖으로	She looks _____ the window.
_____	~로부터	They came _____ Canada.
_____	~로	I'm going _____ the library.
_____	~을 향하여	We will leave _____ Jeju-do tomorrow.

접속사란 무엇인가?

접속사는 단어와 단어, 구와 구, 그리고 절과 절을 연결해 주는
역할을 한다.

Tom is tall **and** strong.

접속사의 종류에는 어떤 것이 있는가?

접속사에는 단어와 단어, 구와 구, 절과 절을 서로 대등하게 연결
해 주는 등위접속사와 주가 되는 문장과 그에 속해 있는 문장을
연결해 주는 종속접속사가 있다.

등위접속사 : and, but, or, so

종속접속사 : when, before, after, that, because, if

Chapter 13. 접속사

75 | and, but

· 접속사 and, but은 서로 대등한 단어와 단어, 구와 구, 그리고 절과 절을 연결하는 역할을 한다.

and	~와, 그리고 : 비슷한 내용을 연결하거나 나열	He has blue eyes **and** brown hair. She watched TV, **and** her sister listened to music. I bought apples, strawberries, **and** bananas.
but	그러나, 하지만 : 서로 반대되는 내용을 연결	He is young **but** very brave. My mother is not a nurse **but** a teacher. It was sunny yesterday, **but** I stayed at home.

＊세 개 이상의 것을 나열할 때는 마지막에 and를 쓴다.

Practice

A. 다음 괄호 안에서 알맞은 것을 고르시오.

1. I ate sandwiches (and / but) salad for lunch.

2. She likes to sing (and / but) dance.

3. Penguins can swim, (and / but) they can't fly.

4. His house is old (and / but) good.

5. Olivia is pretty (and / but) kind.

6. I need some flour (and / but) eggs.

7. Billy had dinner (and / but) he is still hungry.

8. I was born in France (and / but) I am Korean.

B. 다음 두 문장을 and나 but을 이용하여 한 문장으로 쓰시오.

1. It is sunny. It is warm.

→ _____

2. The man is rich. He isn't happy.

→ _____

3. I bought pants. I bought sneakers, too.

→ _____

C. 다음 밑줄 친 부분을 바르게 고치시오.

1. The woman is old <u>and</u> healthy.   → _____

2. She has big eyes <u>but</u> black hair.   → _____

3. Cows <u>but</u> pigs are farm animals.   → _____

4. I met Susan, <u>but</u> we went to see a movie.   → _____

5. It is fine today, <u>and</u> I won't go outside.   → _____

Grammar Tip

A. flour 밀가루
still 여전히

접속사 and와 but으로 연결된 절에서 앞과 반복되는 말은 생략할 수 있다.

B. sneakers 운동화

C. healthy 건강한
farm 농장
fine 좋은, 맑은

Unit 76 or, so

· 접속사 or는 둘 중 하나를 선택하여 말할 때 쓰고, so는 원인에 대한 결과를 나타낼 때 쓴다.

or	~이거나, 또는 : 둘 중에서 선택할 대상을 연결	You can have pizza **or** spaghetti. Which do you like better, coffee **or** tea? Shall we meet at noon **or** at 1 o'clock?
so	그래서, 따라서 : 앞 내용의 결과	I was sleepy, **so** I went to bed early. He was very busy, **so** he couldn't have lunch.

· 'either *A* or *B*'는 'A와 B 둘 중 하나'라는 뜻으로 선택의 의미가 강하다.

Lisa is **either** in New York **or** in London.

Practice

A. 다음 문장의 빈칸에 or 또는 so를 쓰시오.

1. Who is younger, Kate _____ Jane?

2. My sister broke my robot, _____ I was angry.

3. Mr. Johnson will come back Sunday _____ Monday.

4. Which do you want, milk _____ juice?

5. She had a cold, _____ she saw a doctor.

B. 다음 〈보기〉에서 알맞은 것을 골라 그 기호를 쓰시오.

〈보기〉 ⓐ but brave	ⓑ Harry or Bean
ⓒ and hungry	ⓓ so I took off my hat

1. Who is your friend, _____?

2. I was very tired _____.

3. The wind was strong, _____.

4. My brother is short _____.

C. 다음 밑줄 친 부분을 바르게 고치시오.

1. Do you go to school by bike <u>so</u> on foot? → _____

2. I am sick, <u>or</u> I can't go to school. → _____

3. It was dark, <u>or</u> the boy turned on the light. → _____

4. Which do you like better, black <u>and</u> white? → _____

5. I needed vegetables, <u>but</u> I went to the store. → _____

6. Who is your brother, Paul <u>and</u> Samuel? → _____

Grammar Tip

A. cold 감기
   see a doctor 진찰을 받다

접속사 and는 비슷한 내용을, but은 반대되는 내용을 연결한다. or는 선택할 대상을 연결하며 so는 결과를 나타낸다.

B. take off 벗다

C. better 더 좋은
   vegetable 야채

Unit 77 when

- 접속사 when은 '~할 때'라는 뜻의 부사적 의미를 나타내는 절로 문장의 중심이 되는 주절의 내용을 보충한다. 접속사가 이끄는 절을 문장 앞에 쓰면 절 뒤에 콤마(,)를 써 준다.

when	~할 때 : 시간을 나타내는 절(부사절)	Susan was cooking **when** I visited her. = **When** I visited her, Susan was cooking.

- when이 이끄는 절에서는 미래시제를 현재시제가 대신한다.

I will take a trip **when** the vacation starts.
　　주절(미래시제)　　　　　　종속절(현재시제)

 ## Practice

Grammar Tip

A. tired 피곤한
　　ready 준비된

A. 다음 우리말과 같도록 괄호 안의 단어들을 바르게 배열하시오.

1. 가위를 사용할 때 조심해라. (you, scissors, when, use)
   → Please be careful _____.

2. 그녀는 피곤할 때 우유를 마신다. (tired, when, she, feels)
   → She drinks milk _____.

3. 내가 그를 불렀을 때 그는 나를 보았다. (I, him, called, when)
   → He looked at me _____.

4. 나는 소년이었을 때 영어를 배웠다. (a boy, I, was, when)
   → I learned English _____.

5. 그녀가 그를 만났을 때 기뻤다. (when, met, she, him)
   → She was pleased _____.

6. 그는 준비가 됐을 때 외출할 것이다. (is, when, ready, he)
   → He will go out _____.

when이 의문사로 쓰이면 '언제'라는 뜻이고 접속사로 쓰이면 '~할 때'라는 뜻이다. 또한 접속사가 이끄는 절이 문장 앞에 오면 절 뒤에 콤마(,)를 쓴다.

B. 다음 〈보기〉와 같이 두 가지 형태의 문장을 완성하시오.

> 〈보기〉 운전을 할 때는 조심해라. (careful, drive)
> → Be careful when you drive.
> → When you drive, be careful.

1. 그녀는 슬플 때 음악을 듣는다. (listen to, sad)
   → _____
   → _____

2. 내가 어렸을 때 선생님이 되고 싶었다. (young, want)
   → _____
   → _____

78 before, after

· 접속사 before와 after는 시간의 전후 관계를 나타낼 때 사용한다.

before	~하기 전에 : 시간을 나타내는 절(부사절)	Brush your teeth **before** you go to bed. I turned off the light **before** I went out. He did his homework **before** he played soccer.
after	~한 후에 : 시간을 나타내는 절 (부사절)	They took a walk **after** they cleaned the house. He arrived at the station **after** the train left. Let's have dinner **after** we finish the work.

* before와 after는 전치사로 쓰일 수 있는데 전치사 다음에는 명사나 명사구가 온다.

　She goes to bed **before** ten.

Practice

A. 다음 괄호 안에서 알맞은 것을 고르시오.

1. It gets dark (before / after) the sun sets.

2. You can't drive a car (before / after) you're 20.

3. Close the window (before / after) you go out.

4. He washed the dishes (before / after) he had lunch.

5. I bought a hat (before / after) I saved some money.

B. 다음 우리말과 같도록 괄호 안의 단어들을 바르게 배열하시오.

1. 나는 떠나기 전에 그를 보고 싶다. (before, leave, I)
   → I want to see him _____.

2. 나는 식사를 한 후에 양치질을 한다. (I, eat, meals, after)
   → I brush my teeth _____.

3. 그는 외출하기 전에 샤워를 한다. (goes, before, he, out)
   → He takes a shower _____.

C. 다음 두 문장이 같은 뜻이 되도록 빈칸에 알맞은 말을 쓰시오.

1. I watched TV after I did my homework.
   = I did my homework _____.

2. After I had lunch, I took a nap.
   = _____, I had lunch.

3. He ate some cookies before he went to the concert.
   = He went to the concert _____.

4. Wash your face before you go to bed.
   = Go to bed _____.

Grammar Tip

A. save 저축하다

B. meal 식사
　take a shower 샤워하다

before나 after를 이용하여 주절과 종속절의 내용을 바꾸면 같은 뜻이 된다.

C. nap 낮잠
　concert 콘서트

Unit 79 | that

- 접속사 that이 이끄는 절은 명사절로 문장에서 명사 역할(주어, 보어, 목적어)을 한다.

that (명사절)	주어 : ~라는 것은	**That** the man is honest is true. = It is true **that** the man is honest. (가주어 It 사용)
	보어 : ~라는 것(이다)	The problem is **that** he broke his leg.
	목적어 : ~라는 것을	I think (**that**) he is a good man. She hopes (**that**) he will get better soon.

- that절이 목적어로 쓰일 때는 know, think, believe, say, hope 등과 같은 동사의 목적어 역할을 한다. 이때 that은 생략할 수 있다. We believe (that) her dream will come true.

 Practice

A. 다음 중 that이 들어가기에 알맞은 곳을 고르시오.

1. I ① didn't ② know ③ Jamie ④ likes ⑤ David.
2. ① S(s)he ② is ③ a genius ④ is ⑤ a rumor.
3. The reporter ① says ② the weather ③ is ④ cold ⑤.
4. Do ① you ② think ③ the program ④ is ⑤ useful?
5. The good ① news ② is ③ he ④ won ⑤ the game.

B. 다음 두 문장을 접속사 that을 이용하여 한 문장으로 쓰시오.

1. She thinks. He is very smart.
   → _____

2. I know. She is Henry's sister.
   → _____

3. He heard. Linda will leave next Monday.
   → _____

4. We know. He likes Amy very much.
   → _____

C. 다음 괄호 안의 단어들을 바르게 배열하여 문장을 완성하시오.

1. I know _____.
   (my brother, well, cooks, that)

2. She believes _____.
   (her dream, come true, will, that)

3. I think _____.
   (is, the most important, friendship, that)

Grammar Tip

A. genius 천재
   rumor 소문
   useful 유용한

that절은 명사절로 문장에서 명사 역할을 하며 that절 전체가 문장에서 주어, 보어, 목적어 자리에 온다.

B. smart 영리한

C. believe 믿다
   friendship 우정

80 | because, if

· 접속사 because는 '~하기 때문에'라는 뜻의 이유를 나타내는 절을 이끌고 접속사 if는 '만약 ~한다면'의 뜻으로 조건을 나타내는 절을 이끈다.

| because | ~하기 때문에 : 이유를 나타내는 절(부사절) | I was late for school **because** I got up late.
She closed the window **because** it rained.
＊because of+명사(구) → **because** of rain |
| if | 만약 ~한다면 : 조건을 나타내는 절(부사절) | Exercise regularly **if** you want to be healthy.
You can have this hat **if** you like it. |

＊if가 이끄는 절에서는 현재시제가 미래시제를 대신한다. I will stay at home **if** it **rains** tomorrow.

Practice

A. 다음 괄호 안에서 알맞은 것을 고르시오.

1. I was very sad (because / if) Roy left for London.

2. You will get fat (that / if) you eat too much sweets.

3. (Because / If) you feel cold, wear this jacket.

4. Take some rest (that / if) you feel sick.

5. I can't go to the party (because / that) I'm very busy.

6. Raise your hand (if / that) you have any questions.

B. 다음 우리말과 같도록 밑줄 친 부분을 바르게 고치시오.

1. 서두르면 너는 제시간에 거기 도착할 것이다.
   You'll get there in time <u>that</u> you hurry up.　　→ _____

2. 오늘이 일요일이기 때문에 우리는 학교에 가지 않는다.
   We don't go to school <u>if</u> it's Sunday today.　　→ _____

3. 내일 날씨가 좋다면 나는 캠핑을 하러 갈 것이다.
   I will go camping <u>because</u> it's fine tomorrow.　　→ _____

C. 다음 괄호 안의 단어들을 바르게 배열하여 문장을 완성하시오.

1. Please help me _____.
   　　　　　　　　(have, time, if, you)

2. He was angry _____.
   　　　　　　　(because, broken, was, his bike)

3. _____, I'll give it to you.
   　(you, this ball, If, like)

4. The city is popular _____.
   　　　　　　　　(has, it, towers, because, old)

Grammar Tip

A. sweets 단것
raise 올리다, 들다

because와 if는 모두 부사절로 because는 이유를 나타내는 절을 이끌고 if는 조건을 나타내는 절을 이끈다.

C. broken 부서진, 고장난
popular 인기 있는

A. 다음 괄호 안에서 알맞은 것을 고르시오.

1. Thomas has a fever (and / but) a runny nose.
2. He plays the guitar (when / that) he is sad.
3. He is very kind, (because / so) they like him.
4. I believe (that / if) everything will be better.
5. You should wear your helmet (when / after) you ride a bike.

B. 다음 <보기>에서 알맞은 것을 골라 빈칸에 쓰시오.

| <보기> | or | before | if | but |

1. She is either a singer _____ an actress.
2. Think carefully _____ you say something.
3. I knew the answer _____ I didn't tell Judy.
4. Please tell me _____ you need any help.

C. 다음 우리말과 같도록 알맞은 말을 골라 바르게 배열하시오.

1. 난 개를 좋아하지만 고양이는 좋아하지 않는다.
   → I like dogs, _____.
      (cats, I, but, and, like, don't)

2. 나는 그가 Julia의 남동생이라는 것을 몰랐다.
   → I didn't know _____.
      (he, if, that, is, Julia's brother)

3. 우리는 저녁 식사를 마친 후에 후식을 먹었다.
   → We ate dessert _____.
      (we, dinner, before, after, finished)

D. 다음 두 문장을 접속사를 이용하여 한 문장으로 쓰시오.

1. She was very angry. Jim told a lie to her. (because)
   → _____

2. You can lose your weight. You exercise regularly. (if)
   → _____

3. He thinks. The movie is great. (that)
   → _____

4. I worked for sick people. I graduated from school. (after)
   → _____

Grammar Tip

A. fever 열, 고열
   helmet 헬멧

and, but, or, so는 등위접속사로 서로 대등한 것을 연결해 준다. 또한 when, before, after, if 등은 종속접속사로 시간, 조건 등을 나타내며 주절의 문장을 보충 설명한다.

C. dessert 후식, 디저트

D. lie 거짓말
   weight 체중
   graduate 졸업하다

1. 다음 빈칸에 알맞은 것은?

> It was too hot, _____ I turned on the air conditioner.

① and ② but
③ or ④ so
⑤ after

2. 다음 빈칸에 공통으로 알맞은 것은?

> · We will go hiking _____ we have free time tomorrow.
> · Please call me _____ you can't come to the party.

① if ② because
③ that ④ before
⑤ and

3. 다음 밑줄 친 부분을 생략할 수 있는 것은?
① Don't do that.
② I know that old woman.
③ I want to buy that skirt.
④ Oh, that is my puppy.
⑤ I heard that he moved to Rome.

4. 다음 빈칸에 들어갈 말이 바르게 짝지어진 것은?

> · I don't like him _____ he is not honest.
> · Did you know _____ she left for France?

① because – if ② because – that
③ so – that ④ when – before
⑤ and – because

[5-6] 다음 빈칸에 알맞은 말을 〈보기〉에서 골라 쓰시오.

> 〈보기〉 and so if or

5. The food in this restaurant is delicious _____ cheap.

6. Which is better for your lunch, pizza _____ chicken?

7. 다음 밑줄 친 when의 쓰임이 나머지와 다른 것은?
① When I was in Paris, I met Lily.
② Jonathan, when is your birthday?
③ When he feels tired, he drinks milk.
④ He was my best friend when I was young.
⑤ Please lock the door when you go out.

8. 다음 대화의 빈칸에 알맞지 않은 것은?

> A: How about going fishing?
> B: Sorry, I can't. Because _____.

① I feel tired today
② it's really cold outside
③ I have enough time
④ I have many things to do
⑤ I must take care of my brother

9. 다음 빈칸에 알맞지 <u>않은</u> 것은?

> They _____ that their daughter will like the bike.

① hope   ② think
③ believe   ④ know
⑤ talk

10. 다음 두 문장이 같은 뜻이 되도록 할 때 빈칸에 알맞은 것은?

> Tina saved the file before she turned off the computer.
> = Tina turned off the computer _____ she saved the file.

① if   ② when
③ and   ④ after
⑤ because

11. 다음 빈칸에 or이 들어갈 수 <u>없는</u> 것은?
① You can have coffee _____ tea.
② Do you take a bus _____ a taxi?
③ Who is your cousin, Lucy _____ Ann?
④ He is short, _____ he is very brave.
⑤ I'll have a party on Sunday _____ on Monday.

12. 다음 두 문장을 한 문장으로 연결할 때 빈칸에 알맞은 말을 쓰시오.

> I came back home. My father was washing his car.
> → My father was washing his car _____ I came back home.

13. 다음 중 내용상 빈칸에 들어갈 말로 어색한 것은?

> _____ before you go to bed.

① Turn on the TV
② Brush your teeth
③ Clean your room
④ Wash your face
⑤ Put on your pajamas

14. 다음 빈칸에 공통으로 알맞은 접속사를 쓰시오.

> My sister ____ I will make sandwiches for our parents. We need some bread, cheese, eggs, _____ tomatoes.

15. 다음 밑줄 친 ①~⑤ 중 어법상 <u>어색한</u> 것은?

> I ①<u>want</u> ②<u>to call</u> Amy, ③<u>and</u> I don't ④<u>know</u> ⑤<u>her</u> phone number.

16. 다음 밑줄 친 부분의 쓰임이 <u>어색한</u> 것은?
① The man is handsome <u>and</u> unkind.
② I know <u>that</u> the man is a firefighter.
③ Wash your hands <u>after</u> you touch it.
④ He enjoys playing soccer <u>and</u> baseball.
⑤ Knock the door <u>before</u> you enter my room.

17. 다음 빈칸에 들어갈 말이 바르게 짝지어진 것은?

> · She said _____ she was interested in math.
> · I'm getting fat _____ I quit jogging.

① that − so   ② if − after
③ that − after   ④ when − because
⑤ so − before

18. 다음 밑줄 친 부분을 바르게 고치시오.

> Mike and I will go to the amusement park if it will be sunny tomorrow.

→ _____

19. 다음 중 접속사의 쓰임이 어색한 것은?

① My father is thin, but he is strong.
② Be careful when you cross the street.
③ Whose shoes are these, yours or hers?
④ She thinks that the ring is expensive.
⑤ I can't write letters, so I don't have pens.

20. 다음 두 문장이 같은 뜻이 되도록 빈칸에 알맞은 말을 쓰시오.

> It rained heavily, so we couldn't play outside.
> = We couldn't play outside _____ heavy rain.

〈서술형 문제〉

21. 다음 대화에서 어색한 부분을 찾아 바르게 고치시오.

> A: Which country do you want to visit, China or Japan?
> B: I want to visit Japan, so my uncle lives there.

_____ → _____

[22-23] 다음 두 문장이 같도록 빈칸에 알맞은 말을 쓰시오.

22. I opened the window before I cleaned my room.
= I cleaned my room _____.

23. The banks are closed because it's a holiday today.
= It's a holiday, _____.

24. 다음 우리말과 같도록 괄호 안의 단어를 이용하여 문장을 완성하시오.

> 그는 그의 아들이 채소를 더 많이 먹어야 한다고 생각한다. (son, should, more vegetables)
> → He thinks _____.

25. 다음 표를 보고, 날씨에 따른 가족의 토요일 계획을 접속사 if를 써서 완성하시오.

(1) sunny	(2) rainy
go to the beach	watch a movie

(1) We will _____
  this Saturday.
(2) We _____
  this Saturday.

Student Book
Answer Key

Chapter 1. be동사와 인칭대명사

Unit 01. be동사의 의미와 형태
Practice

A. 1. am 2. are 3. He 4. are
B. 1. It's 2. They're 3. I'm 4. She's
C. 1. I am tired today.
  2. They are very long.
  3. He is under the tree.
  4. We are in the park.

Unit 02. be동사의 부정문
Practice

A. 1. I am not a math teacher.
  2. She is not beautiful.
  3. They are not easy problems.
  4. We are not at school.
B. 1. I'm not
  2. They're not[They aren't]
  3. He's not[He isn't]
  4. You're not[You aren't]
C. 1. She is not[She's not/She isn't] in the garden.
  2. It is not[It's not/It isn't] a popular movie.
  3. They are not[They're not/They aren't] very sad.

Unit 03. be동사의 의문문
Practice

A. 1. Is he an actor?
  2. Are you busy today?
  3. Are they in the library?
B. 1. are 2. he isn't 3. Are you 4. it isn't
C. 1. Are the shoes on the table?
  2. Is she a good chef?
  3. Are they baseball players?
  4. Is Mike in the bookstore?

Unit 04. 인칭대명사
Practice

A. 1. You 2. Its 3. him 4. She
B. 1. my 2. her 3. our 4. them
C. 1. ④ 2. ② 3. ③ 4. ④

Unit 05. 소유대명사, 명사의 소유격
Practice

A. 1. yours 2. hers 3. My neighbor's 4. theirs 5. of
  6. Tony's
B. 1. yours 2. Sarah's 3. my, hers 4. Peter's 5. of

Review Test / Unit 01~05

A. 1. are 2. isn't 3. It's
B. 1. They are not[aren't] his grandparents.
  2. Are Tony and Steve late for school?
  3. I'm not a famous cook.
  4. Is he a soccer player?
C. 1. he 2. Tim's 3. they are 4. mine, hers
D. 1. She is not lazy.
  2. Their sons are brave.
  3. She is my art teacher.
  4. The chair is my father's.

Chapter Test / Unit 01~05

1. ④ 2. ② 3. ④ 4. ⑤ 5. ① 6. ① 7. She 8. ④ 9. ⑤
10. ③ 11. ② 12. ③ 13. ③ 14. ③ 15. Hers → Her 16. It
→ Its 17. ③ 18. ③ 19. ② 20. ② 21. My dolls are not
[aren't] in the box. 22. Is he a famous actor? 23. is, Brian,
is 24. is, is, London 25. (1) my, brother (2) His, name
(3) his, favorite, sport (4) He's

1. 주격과 소유격의 관계를 나타내고 있는데, he의 소유격은 his이다.

2. am과 not은 줄여서 쓸 수 없으며 주어 I와 be동사 am을 줄여 I'm
으로 쓴다.

3. be동사는 뒤에 명사가 오면 '~이다'라는 뜻으로 해석하고 전치사구가
오면 '~(에) 있다'라는 뜻으로 해석한다.

4. 주어가 2인칭이거나 3인칭 복수일 경우에는 be동사 are와 함께 쓰며
부정문의 경우에는 are not으로 쓴다. 사물의 경우 단수는 be동사 is를
쓴다.

5. she는 3인칭 단수로 be동사 is를 쓴다.

6. her는 목적격과 소유격의 형태가 같은데, her name에서 her는 소유
격이다.

7. 3인칭 단수명사 a daughter의 경우 여자이고 주격이므로 3인칭 단수
형 she를 쓴다.

8. 복수명사는 대명사의 복수형과 같이 쓰므로 They are my glasses.
가 되어야 한다.

9. 한국 사람인지를 물어보았고 대답에서 중국 사람이라고 했으므로 부정
의 대답을 찾는다.

10. 그것은 Tony의 집이라고 했으므로 부정의 대답을 찾고, 단수는 it으로
쓴다.

11. 긍정의 대답일 때 Yes와 not은 함께 쓰일 수 없다.

12. be동사의 부정문은 be동사 뒤에 not을 쓴다.

13. 단수명사는 be동사 is와 함께 쓰고 각 두 번째 문장의 반대 내용으로
보아 be동사와 부정문으로 쓴다.

14. 명사의 소유격은 명사 뒤에 's를 붙인다. Today's의 경우에는 Today
is를 줄인 형태이다.

15. her는 she의 목적격과 소유격이고 hers는 she의 소유대명사이다. 문
장의 의미상 소유대명사가 아닌 소유격이 와야 한다.

16. '그것의 이름은 ~'이라는 뜻으로 소유격이 와야 한다. it의 소유격은 its이다.

17. like 뒤에는 대명사의 목적격이 와야 한다.

18. '나의 것'이라는 뜻으로 I의 소유대명사 mine을 쓴다.

19. I는 be동사 am을 쓴다.

20. '우리의 것'은 we의 소유대명사 ours를 쓴다.

23. Julie는 13살이고 Brian은 17살이다.

24. Julie는 파리 사람이고 Brian은 런던 사람이다.

25. 해석 : 저를 소개하겠습니다. 나의 이름은 민호입니다. 나는 14살입니다. 나는 한국의 부산 사람입니다. 나는 키가 크지 않지만 내가 가장 좋아하는 운동은 농구입니다. 나는 농구를 잘합니다.

Chapter 2. 일반동사

Unit 06. 일반동사의 의미
Practice

A. 1. × 2. ○ 3. ○ 4. ○ 5. ×

B. 1. fly 2. wash 3. study 4. clean 5. dance

C. 1. play 2. eat 3. live 4. go 5. swim

Unit 07. 일반동사의 3인칭 단수형
Practice

A. 1. swims 2. stays 3. relaxes 4. does 5. sleeps
   6. cries 7. makes 8. has

B. 1. has 2. goes 3. watch 4. need 5. sends

C. 1. fixes 2. drinks 3. sings 4. misses 5. listens

Unit 08. 일반동사의 부정문
Practice

A. 1. doesn't 2. don't 3. don't 4. doesn't 5. wash

B. 1. ② 2. ④ 3. ③

C. 1. Kevin does not[doesn't] ride a bike very well.
   2. You do not[don't] want a new computer.
   3. The coat does not[doesn't] have many pockets.

Unit 09. 일반동사의 의문문
Practice

A. 1. finish 2. know 3. Does

B. 1. Does, does 2. Do, do
   3. Does, doesn't 4. Do, don't

C. 1. Do you buy many flowers?
   2. Does he find a wallet on the street?
   3. Does your sister want a backpack?

Review Test / Unit 06~09

A. 1. have 2. fixes 3. doesn't 4. Does

B. 1. – (c) / 2. – (a) / 3. – (b) / 4. – (d)

C. 1. enjoys 2. sit 3. doesn't, drive 4. Does, like

D. 1. Jack does not[doesn't] sell books at the bookstore.
   2. Does Jack sell books at the bookstore?

Chapter Test / Unit 06~09

1. ③ 2. ② 3. ④ 4. ⑤ 5. ⑤ 6. ① 7. ④ 8. ② 9. ④
10. ③ 11. ③ 12. ① 13. ⑤ 14. sleeps 15. does not
[doesn't] use 16. Does she clean her house every day?
17. ② 18. ② 19. ① 20. ⑤ 21. ② 22. wants, doesn't,
want 23. doesn't, leave, leaves 24. don't like 25. doesn't
like

1. 일반동사를 3인칭 단수형으로 바꿀 때, -o, -s, -x, -ch, -sh로 끝나는 동사는 -es를 붙인다.

2. 주어가 3인칭 단수일 경우 일반동사의 의문문은 Does를 사용해서 만들며 뒤에 일반동사는 동사원형을 쓴다.

3. 일반동사가 3인칭 단수형인 것으로 보아 주어에는 3인칭 단수 주어가 와야 한다.

4. have의 3인칭 단수형은 has를 쓴다.

5. 주어가 3인칭 단수형일 때는 Does를 사용한다.

6. 주어가 Alice이므로 일반동사는 3인칭 단수형을 쓴다.

7. 의문문의 문장 앞에 Does가 있는 것으로 보아 주어에는 3인칭 단수형을 쓴다.

8. 주어가 3인칭 단수형일 때는 have는 has로 쓴다.

9. 주어가 3인칭 단수형인 일반동사의 의문문은 Does를 사용한다.

10. 추운 날씨가 좋다고 답한 문장으로 보아 부정의 대답을 쓴다.

11. 주어가 1, 2인칭과 3인칭 복수인 일반동사의 부정문은 do not[don't]을 사용한다.

12. 주어가 1, 2인칭과 3인칭 복수인 일반동사의 의문문은 Do를 사용하여 나타낸다.

13. 주어가 3인칭 단수인 일반동사의 부정문은 does not[doesn't]을 사용하여 나타낸다.

14. 주어가 My sister로 3인칭 단수이므로 sleeps를 쓴다.

15. 주어가 3인칭 단수이고 부정의 의미가 있으므로 does not[doesn't] use를 쓴다.

16. Does를 써서 의문문으로 바꾼다.

17. 주어가 3인칭 단수일 경우 일반동사 뒤에 -s나 -es를 붙인다.

18. 일반동사의 의문문에서는 주어의 인칭과 수에 상관없이 Do나 Does 뒤에 동사원형을 쓴다.

20. 부정의 대답과 딸이 있다는 문장으로 보아 아들이 있는지 물어본 것을 알 수 있다.

21. 해석 : Alex는 일요일마다 아침에 늦게 일어난다. 그는 아침을 먹지 않는다. 그는 오후에 그의 친구들을 만난다. 그는 저녁에 조깅을 한다.

22. 해석 : Henry는 그의 여동생 생일 선물을 원한다. 그녀는 새 모자를 원한다. 그러나 운동화를 원하지는 않는다.

Grammar Note

1. works, sees, likes, comes, goes, relaxes, passes, washes, teaches, mixes, studies, carries, flies, cries, has

2. don't, don't, doesn't, doesn't

3. Do, don't, Do, don't, Does, 동사원형, Does, play

Chapter 3. 명사와 관사

Unit 10. 명사의 단수와 복수 1(규칙 변화)

Practice

A. 1. cars 2. bottles 3. knives 4. toys 5. pianos
   6. foxes 7. dresses 8. families 9. babies 10. keys

B. 1. potatoes 2. classes 3. shoes 4. flowers

C. 1. babies 2. leaves 3. oranges 4. countries
   5. tomatoes 6. pencils

Unit 11. 명사의 단수와 복수 2(불규칙 변화)

Practice

A. 1. feet 2. Chinese 3. geese 4. women 5. oxen
   6. sheep

B. 1. children 2. deer 3. men 4. teeth 5. Mice

C. 1. snowmen 2. fish 3. Chinese 4. Men 5. teeth

Unit 12. 셀 수 없는 명사

Practice

A. 1. love 2. is 3. rain 4. salt 5. cups

B. 1. pieces of paper 2. glasses of water
   3. bottles of juice 4. cups of green tea

C. 1. Air 2. milk 3. money 4. Korea, Seoul
   5. glasses of juice 6. pieces of cake

Review Test / Unit 10~12

A. 1. teeth 2. men 3. knives 4. pianos 5. benches
   6. watches 7. classes 8. deer 9. cities 10. wolves
   11. ladies 12. Japanese

B. 1. pepper 2. mice 3. shoes 4. Friendship 5. geese

C. 1. sugar 2. paper 3. stories 4. pieces of pizza
   5. scissors

D. ④

Unit 13. 부정관사 a, an

Practice

A. 1. a 2. an 3. an 4. an 5. a

B. 1. × 2. a 3. an 4. a 5. ×

C. 1. an 2. a 3. a

Unit 14. 정관사 the

Practice

A. 1. the 2. a, The 3. the 4. an 5. the

B. 1. The boy 2. The Nile 3. The pen 4. the guitar
   5. The earth

C. 1. the 2. the 3. the

Unit 15. 관사를 쓰지 않는 경우

Practice

A. 1. × 2. × 3. × 4. × 5. ×

B. 1. a 2. × 3. × 4. the 5. ×

C. 1. basketball, school 2. goes, church
   3. eat[have], lunch 4. by, subway

Review Test / Unit 13~15

A. 1. × 2. the 3. an 4. a 5. ×

B. 1. The jacket 2. The computer 3. soccer(the 삭제)
   4. an honest 5. the violin

C. 1. after, school 2. have[eat], dinner 3. in, the, west

D. ③

Chapter Test / Unit 10~15

1. ② 2. ⑤ 3. ④ 4. ⑤ 5. puppies, mice 6. ③ 7. ③
8. ④ 9. ④ 10. the 11. ③ 12. ⑤ 13. (1) cups (2) deer
(3) health 14. ④ 15. a pair of 16. ① 17. ④ 18. ④ 19. ④
20. ⑤ 21. I see four deer in the woods. 22. He eats
two pieces of cake. 23. They are sweet candies. 24. the
(piano 앞) 25. a, a, the, the

1. piano는 -o로 끝나지만 -es가 아닌 -s를 붙인다.

2. leaf의 복수형은 leaves이다.

3. 첫소리가 모음으로 나는 단어는 부정관사 an을 쓴다.

4. two는 복수이므로 뒤에는 명사의 복수형을 쓴다.

5. 〈보기〉는 명사의 단수와 복수를 나타낸 것이다. puppy의 복수형은 y를
i로 바꾸고 -es를 붙이며 mouse의 복수형은 mice이다.

6. 악기 이름 앞에 the를 쓴다.

7. 일주일에 한 번이라고 할 때는 once a week라고 표현하며 여기에서
a는 '~마다'라는 뜻이다.

8. snow는 셀 수 없는 명사로 단수 취급한다.

9. 첫소리가 모음으로 나는 단어는 부정관사 an을 쓴다. 누구나 알고 있는
명백한 것을 가리킬 때는 정관사 the를 쓴다.

10. 앞에 언급한 것을 다시 언급할 때는 정관사 the를 쓰며 자연물도 the
를 쓴다.

11. 교통수단을 나타낼 때는 「by+교통수단」으로 관사를 쓰지 않는다.

13. 물질명사는 복수형으로 나타낼 수 없지만 용기나 단위를 복수로 나타
내어 수량을 표현할 수 있다.

14. 자연 현상이나 자연물은 정관사 the를 쓴다.

15. 항상 짝을 이루는 것은 복수로 나타내며 a pair of socks는 양말 한 켤레이다.

16. 부정관사 a는 하나를 나타내며 뒤에는 단수명사가 온다. 둘 이상은 복수형으로 쓴다.

17. one은 하나를 나타내므로 뒤에는 단수명사를 쓴다.

18. 셀 수 없는 명사는 복수형으로 만들 수 없으며 -o로 끝나는 명사의 복수형은 -es를 붙인다.

19. 앞에 언급한 말이나 방향, 자연 현상은 정관사 the를 쓴다.

21. 부정관사 a를 four로 바꾸면 명사도 복수형으로 바뀐다. deer는 단수형과 복수형이 같다.

23. candy의 복수형은 candies이다.

24. 해석 : 나는 오늘 바쁘다. 나는 2시간 동안 피아노를 연주하고 나의 친구 Jack과 점심을 먹는다. 점심 식사 후에 나는 그와 함께 과학을 공부한다.

25. 해석 : 그는 중학생이다. 그는 교복을 입지만 그 교복을 좋아하지 않는다. 그는 기타를 매우 잘 연주한다.

Chapter 4. 대명사

Unit 16. 지시대명사

Practice

A. 1. This 2. That 3. those 4. These
B. 1. These pants 2. This is 3. boys are 4. Are those
C. 1. This, is 2. Those, are 3. This, is 4. Those, are
   5. That, is

Unit 17. 비인칭 주어 it

Practice

A. 1. 비인칭 주어 2. 비인칭 주어 3. 대명사
   4. 비인칭 주어
B. 1. It 2. It's 3. It, is 4. It's 5. It, is
C. 1. 3월 3일이다. 2. 겨울에는 춥다.
   3. 그것은 나의 지갑이다. 4. 12시다.

Unit 18. 부정대명사 one

Practice

A. 1. It 2. one 3. ones 4. it 5. one
B. 1. one 2. It 3. one's 4. ones
C. 1. one 2. It 3. it 4. ones

Unit 19. another, other

Practice

A. 1. other 2. another, the other 3. another 4. others
B. 1. other 2. another 3. One, others
C. 1. another 2. One, the other 3. One, the others

Unit 20. 재귀대명사

Practice

A. 1. herself 2. themselves 3. himself 4. itself 5. him
   6. himself 7. myself
B. 1. myself 2. herself 3. himself 4. yourself 5. myself
   6. ourselves

Review Test / Unit 16~20

A. 1. This is my math teacher.
   2. Those girls are Ashley's sisters.
   3. Are these your cats?
   4. It is hot in summer.
B. 1. it 2. one 3. it 4. ones 5. it 6. ones
C. 1. it 2. one 3. another 4. others 5. One, other
D. 1. it 2. It 3. towers 4. himself

Chapter Test / Unit 16~20

1. ③ 2. ④ 3. ② 4. That, It 5. ② 6. ① 7. ③ 8. ⑤ 9. ④
10. ③ 11. ⑤ 12. shirt 13. ④ 14. ① 15. This dictionary
16. It is 17. ⑤ 18. ④ 19. ② 20. ③ 21. These
shoes are very comfortable. 22. Those are very tall
buildings. 23. It, is, it, is 24. (1) One is (2) Another is
(3) The other is 25. ⓐ my, myself ⓑ us, ourselves

1. be동사가 are인 경우 지시대명사 복수형을 쓰고 is인 경우 지시대명사 단수형을 쓴다.

2. 날씨, 날짜, 요일, 월, 명암과 거리 등의 주어로 it이 오면 비인칭 주어로 '그것'이라고 해석하지 않는다.

3. 지시대명사 this나 that으로 물어볼 경우에 대답은 it으로 한다. 또한 these나 those로 물어보면 they로 대답한다.

4. 날짜를 말할 때는 비인칭 주어 it을 사용한다.

5. 지시대명사 that으로 물어 보면 it으로 대답한다. 그 물건은 자신의 것이 아닌 Dan의 것이므로 부정의 대답을 한다.

6. 오늘의 날씨를 물어보고 있으므로 날씨를 대답한다.

7. this나 that은 지시대명사나 지시형용사로 쓰이는데 this나 that 뒤에 명사가 오면 그 명사를 수식하는 지시형용사이다.

8. it은 '그것'이라는 대명사인데 날짜, 요일, 날씨, 거리, 명암 등을 나타낼 때는 비인칭 주어로 문장에서 해석하지 않는다.

9. 주어 자신이 즐기는 것이므로 주어 we의 재귀대명사 ourselves를 쓴다.

10. 주어 자신이 스스로 하는 것이므로 주어인 3인칭 단수 남성의 재귀대명사 himself를 쓴다.

11. 앞에 나온 것을 대신해서 대명사로 나타내는데, 복수이면 they를 쓴다. many stories는 복수이고 목적격이 필요하므로 them을 쓴다.

12. 부정대명사 one은 앞에 나온 것을 가리키는 말이다.

13. 앞에 나온 것을 가리킬 때 부정대명사 one, 특정한 것을 가리킬 때 it을 쓴다.

14. '하나는 ~이고 나머지는 ~이다'라고 표현할 때 one ~, the others ~를 쓴다.

15. 지시대명사 문장은 지시형용사 문장으로 바꿀 수 있는데 지시형용사 뒤에 명사를 쓴다.

16. 거리를 나타내는 문장은 비인칭 주어 it을 사용한다.

18. 여러 개 중에서 하나를 제외한 나머지가 복수인 경우 the others를 쓴다.

19. 특정한 것을 가리킬 때 it을 사용한다.

20. '그녀 자신'은 she의 재귀대명사인 herself를 쓴다.

21. '이 신발들은'이라고 할 때는 복수형 지시형용사 these를 쓴다.

22. '저것들은 ~이다'라고 할 때는 복수형 지시대명사를 쓴다.

24. 셋 이상을 나타낼 때는 'one ~, another ~, the other'를 쓴다.

Chapter 5. 동사의 시제
Unit 21. be동사의 과거형
Practice

A. 1. was, was 2. were 3. were 4. were

B. 1. was 2. were 3. was 4. was 5. were

C. 1. He, was 2. We, were 3. They, were 4. was, last

Unit 22. be동사 과거형의 부정문
Practice

A. 1. ② 2. ② 3. ②

B. 1. was not 2. were 3. was 4. were not 5. was

C. 1. Your trip was not[wasn't] exciting.
   2. They were not[weren't] kind to everyone.
   3. I was not[wasn't] interested in sports.
   4. The man was not[wasn't] a great painter.
   5. My brother was not[wasn't] good at history.

Unit 23. be동사 과거형의 의문문
Practice

A. 1. Was he an actor?
   2. Were you sleepy?
   3. Was it good news?

B. 1. Was the water very cold?
   2. Were they thirsty then?
   3. Was he in the bookstore yesterday?
   4. Were you at the party?

C. 1. it wasn't 2. they were 3. they weren't
   4. he wasn't

Unit 24. 일반동사의 과거형 1(규칙 변화)
Practice

A. 1. washed 2. moved 3. fixed 4. visited

5. carried

B. 1. watched 2. played 3. studied 4. lived
   5. stopped

C. 1. worked 2. stayed 3. loved 4. finished
   5. walked

Unit 25. 일반동사의 과거형 2(불규칙 변화)
Practice

A. 1. saw 2. wrote 3. ran 4. cut 5. ate 6. gave
   7. hurt 8. left

B. 1. came 2. began 3. found 4. took 5. did

C. 1. went 2. made 3. got 4. put 5. had 6. read
   7. met 8. bought

Review Test / Unit 21~25

A. 1. were 2. was 3. were 4. was

B. 1. I was not a farmer.
   2. It was not beautiful.
   3. The test was not easy.
   4. They were not dentists.

C. 1. Was he Mr. Smith?
   2. Were they close friends?
   3. Was Kate a good chef?

D. 1. visited 2. went 3. helped 4. met

E. 1. wrote 2. bought 3. learned 4. ate

F. ③

Unit 26. 일반동사 과거형의 부정문
Practice

A. 1. didn't 2. didn't 3. come

B. 1. fix 2. didn't 3. catch 4. didn't 5. meet

C. 1. The train didn't stop at this station.
   2. I didn't go to the amusement park then.
   3. The child didn't make a paper airplane.
   4. He didn't see the movie at the theater.
   5. Lisa didn't help his son with his homework.

Unit 27. 일반동사 과거형의 의문문
Practice

A. 1. have 2. Did 3. like

B. 1. Did 2. they, did 3. she, didn't

C. 1. Did she buy an expensive dress?
   2. Did they do many good things there?
   3. Did Jane read the novel again?
   4. Did my sister play tennis after dinner?

Unit 28. 진행형의 의미와 형태

Practice

A. 1. waiting 2. running 3. sitting 4. buying
   5. carrying 6. driving 7. playing 8. having
   9. cutting 10. tying

B. 1. am going 2. is raining 3. riding 4. lying
   5. is looking

C. 1. making 2. swimming 3. walking
   4. baking 5. watering

Unit 29. 현재진행형과 과거진행형

Practice

A. 1. cooking 2. singing 3. taking

B. 1. am 2. is writing 3. were 4. know 5. was

C. 1. He is taking 2. The boy was playing
   3. They were eating 4. We have

Unit 30. 진행형의 부정문과 의문문

Practice

A. 1. are not 2. weren't 3. Were 4. Is it 5. Was

B. 1. The train was not[wasn't] arriving at that time.
   2. Is he waiting for him at the bookstore?
   3. I'm not doing my homework now.
   4. Was her father finding the treasure map?

C. 1. He was playing soccer.
   2. She is listening to music.

Review Test / Unit 26~30

A. 1. looked → look
   2. told → tell
   3. not took → didn't take
   4. doesn't → didn't
   5. Was → Did

B. 1. The woman didn't put on a hat at that time.
   2. Did she carry the baby in her arm?
   3. You didn't read the comic books last night.

C. 1. It was snowing a lot last night.
   2. My daughter is studying English hard.
   3. I am drinking a glass of milk.
   4. They were living in the apartment.

D. 1. is, talking 2. isn't, riding 3. was, carrying
   4. Are, flying

Chapter Test / Unit 21~30

1. ③ 2. ④ 3. ② 4. ② 5. ⑤ 6. ④ 7. ④ 8. ③ 9. ①
10. ⑤ 11. ④ 12. Was the concert very exciting? 13. ②
14. ④ 15. ② 16. did, not, didn't 17. ② 18. ⑤ 19. ③
20. ⑤ 21. ② 22. ① 23. ③ 24. ① 25. ④ 26. were
27. ② 28. ① 29. ③ 30. ④ 31. ① 32. ③ 33. ② 34. ⑤
35. (1) saw (2) writing (3) hurt 36. (1) Does, wear (2) didn't,
open 37. (1) I caught a cold last week. (2) He had lunch
at noon at that time. 38. She went on a picnic last month.
39. (1) plays, learned, liked (2) goes, was, swam 40. (1) is
playing with his friends (2) is doing his homework (3) is
having dinner (4) is reading books

1. run의 과거형은 ran이다.

2. 일반동사의 과거형은 보통 -(e)d를 붙이지만 catch의 과거형은 caught
이다.

3. eat의 진행형은 eating이다.

4. 단수명사는 be동사 is나 was를 쓴다.

5. 일반동사 과거형의 부정문은 인칭의 수에 상관없이 did+not을 쓴다.

6. 과거를 나타내는 부사(구)가 문장에 있으면 동사는 과거형으로 쓴다. 또
한 now처럼 현재의 사실을 나타낼 때는 현재형으로 쓴다.

7. now는 현재이므로 is reading을 쓴다.

8. clean과 dirty, short와 tall이 서로 반대의 뜻이므로 과거형의 부정문
을 쓴다.

10. be동사 was는 과거의 일을 나타낸다. tomorrow는 '내일'이라는 뜻으
로 미래시제와 함께 쓰인다.

11. 문장에 과거의 부사구인 last가 있으므로 현재형은 쓸 수 없다.

12. be동사의 의문문은 주어와 be동사의 위치를 바꾸고 문장 끝에 물음
표를 붙여서 만든다.

13. at that time은 과거를 나타내는 부사구이다.

14. 일반동사 과거형의 의문문은 인칭과 수에 관계없이 문장 앞에 Did를
쓰고 동사는 동사원형을 쓴다.

15. 그는 바쁘다고 했으므로 didn't를 이용한 부정의 대답을 쓴다.

17. 일반동사 과거형의 의문문에서 일반동사는 동사원형으로 쓴다.

18. 일반동사 read는 현재형과 과거형의 형태가 같은 동사이다.

20. 일반동사 과거형의 부정문에서 didn't 뒤에는 동사의 원형을 쓴다.

22. 주어 she는 과거형 be동사 was와 함께 쓰이며 일반동사는 Did를 이
용하여 만든다. 또한 진행형은 주어에 따라서 알맞은 be동사를 사용하는데,
now가 있는 것으로 보아 현재진행형으로 Are가 들어가야 한다.

23. 주어가 Lucy로 3인칭 단수형인데 과거 부사구인 last가 있으므로
Does가 아닌 Did를 쓴다.

24. have가 소유를 나타내는 경우에는 진행형으로 나타낼 수 없다.

27. 현재진행형 의문문에 대한 대답은 Yes나 No를 이용하여 표현하며 동
사는 be동사를 이용하여 나타낸다.

28. know는 인지, 상태를 나타내는 동사로 진행으로 나타낼 수 없다.

29. 반복적인 일상 생활은 현재형으로 쓰며 과거의 한 시점을 나타낼 때
는 과거형으로 쓴다.

34. tired는 형용사로 문장에 be동사 was가 not 앞에 들어가야 한다. 또
한 진행형 문장은 「be동사+동사-ing형」으로 practicing이 되어야 한다.

39. 해석 : (1) Cindy는 기타를 매우 잘 친다. 그녀는 그것을 2년 전에 그

169

녀의 삼촌에게서 배웠다. 그는 그 당시 유명한 기타리스트를 좋아했다.
(2) Susan은 매주 토요일에 수영장에 간다. 어제는 토요일이었다. 그래서 그녀는 그 수영장에 갔고 2시간 동안 수영을 했다.

Chapter 6. 의문사

Unit 31. who, whose
Practice

A. 1. Who 2. Whose 3. Who 4. Who
B. 1. Whose 2. Who(m) 3. teaches 4. Whose
C. 1. Who is the pretty girl?
2. Who broke the vase?
3. Whose is that car?
4. Who did she meet?
5. Whose dog is this?

Unit 32. what, which
Practice

A. 1. What 2. Which 3. Which
B. 1. What 2. Which 3. What
C. 1. What, subject, does
2. Which, season, do
3. Which, better, or

Unit 33. when, where
Practice

A. 1. When 2. Where 3. When 4. Where
B. 1. Where 2. When 3. When 4. Where
C. 1. What, When 2. When, Where 3. Who, Where
4. Which, When 5. What, Where

Unit 34. why, how
Practice

A. 1. © 2. ⓑ 3. ⓐ 4. ⓓ
B. Why
C. 1. Why, did 2. How, is 3. Why, were
4. How, do, we

Unit 35. how + 형용사/부사
Practice

A. 1. much 2. long 3. often
B. 1. many 2. tall 3. far 4. long
C. 1. How old is your sister?
2. How much is this sweater?
3. How long is that bridge?

Review Test / Unit 31~35

A. 1. Whose 2. How 3. Which 4. When
B. 1. Who, is 2. Why, did 3. Where, did
4. How, old, is
C. 1. Where 2. Who 3. Which[What] 4. Why
D. 1. How often do you clean your room?
2. How tall is she?
3. When do you get up?

Chapter Test / Unit 31~35

1. ⑤ 2. ② 3. ② 4. ④ 5. ④ 6. ④ 7. ① 8. many
9. Who 10. ③ 11. ① 12. ③ 13. ② 14. ② 15. ③
16. ⑤ 17. ⓐ 18. © 19. ⑤ 20. ① 21. When does he
play 22. How many classes do you have 23. How, Why
24. How often, How long 25. How old is Max?

1. 사물이나 물건을 물어볼 때는 의문사 what을 사용한다.
2. 상태나 방법 등을 물어볼 때는 how를 쓴다.
3. 둘 중에서 선택할 때는 '어느, 어느 것'이라는 뜻의 which를 사용한다.
4. whose는 '누구의, 누구의 것'이라는 뜻으로 의문형용사나 의문대명사로 쓰인다.
5. 나이를 물어볼 때는 how old를 이용하여 쓴다.
7. 장소를 물어볼 때는 의문사 where를 사용한다.
8. How many 다음에는 셀 수 있는 명사가 오고 How much 다음에는 셀 수 없는 명사가 온다.
9. 의문사가 주어로 쓰일 수 있는 것은 who와 what인데 주어가 사람이면 who를 쓴다.
10. 방법을 물어볼 때는 how, 기간을 물어볼 때는 how long을 쓴다.
11. 시간을 물어볼 때 의문사 when을 사용한다.
12. 콘서트의 시간이 얼마나 걸리는지 물어보는 것이므로 시간으로 대답한다.
13. 시간이나 기간을 물어볼 때는 how long을 쓴다.
14. 누구의 것인지를 물어보고 있으므로 「소유격+명사」나 소유대명사로 답한다.
15. 고양이의 다리는 4개이고 일주일은 7일이며 우리 손가락은 10개이다.
19. 누구를 좋아하는지 묻는 말에 대한 대답을 해야 한다.
20. 의문사 why로 물어볼 때 because로 대답한다.
23. because로 대답하는 말 앞에 이유를 묻는 의문문을 써야 한다.
24. 빈도를 물어볼 때는 how often을 쓴다.

Chapter 7. 조동사

Unit 36. will, be going to
Practice

A. 1. call 2. be 3. will 4. is
B. 1. She will be here in five minutes.

2. He will learn Chinese this year.

3. Sally is going to buy a bike next week.

4. You are going to the library tomorrow.

C. 1. ⓒ 2. ⓑ 3. ⓐ 4. ⓓ

Unit 37. will의 부정문과 의문문
Practice

A. 1. He is not going to arrive there.

2. Will she join our team this week?

3. Will you open the window?

4. She won't be late for school again.

5. Are they going to go camping this weekend?

B. 1. He is not[isn't] going to see a doctor.

2. Will you visit Janet in hospital?

3. The lady will not[won't] meet the man.

4. Are you going to play soccer after school?

5. Will you play baseball with them tomorrow?

Unit 38. can, be able to
Practice

A. 1. can, ride 2. could, solve 3. can, see
4. could, find

B. 1. He is able to speak Chinese.

2. I am able to run 100 meters in 14 seconds.

3. Judy was able to ski when she was young.

C. 1. 허가 2. 능력 3. 능력

Unit 39. can의 부정문과 의문문
Practice

A. 1. can 2. can't 3. Can

B. 1. Can you 2. Can I 3. Can you

C. 1. She can't understand the book.

2. Can he make spaghetti?

3. Is Mark able to drive a car?

4. We weren't able to count to ten.

Unit 40. may
Practice

A. 1. 허락 2. 추측 3. 허락

B. 1. You may catch a cold.

2. She may sing the song on the stage.

3. They may not believe your story.

C. 1. It may be cold outside.

2. He may not come to the meeting.

3. You may use my dictionary.

4. May I borrow your umbrella?

Unit 41. must, have to, should
Practice

A. 1. has, to 2. have, to

B. 1. must 2. should, help 3. have, to
4. must/should, put

C. 1. She should save her money.

2. You had to go home yesterday.

3. They should be quiet in the gallery.

4. Tom has to wear his school uniform.

Unit 42. must, have to, should의 부정문과 의문문
Practice

A. 1. should/must, not 2. Do, have, to
3. must/should, not

B. 1. don't have 2. should 3. doesn't have

C. 1. 우리는 늦으면 안 된다.

2. 너는 그 박물관에서 뛰어서는 안 된다.

3. 그녀는 콜라를 너무 많이 마셔서는 안 된다.

4. 너는 점심을 가져올 필요가 없다.

Review Test / Unit 36~42

A. 1. have to/should 2. Is he able to 3. has to
4. are going to

B. 1. will, be 2. must, be 3. should/must
4. doesn't, have, to 5. can't/shouldn't

C. 1. can't 2. want 3. had 4. may not

D. 1. I won't be there tomorrow.

2. You must not talk to strangers.

3. Is she going to change her mind?

4. He was able to speak Korean.

Chapter Test / Unit 36~42

1. ② 2. ③ 3. ③ 4. ⑤ 5. will 6. ④ 7. ① 8. ② 9. ⑤
10. ④ 11. No, you don't have to. 12. ③ 13. ① 14. ⑤
15. ③ 16. ⑤ 17. ② 18. ① 19. ② 20. ④ 21. Can[Will]
you pass me the butter? 22. It will be a nice day tomorrow.
23. she can't come to my birthday party 24. You don't
have to get up early tomorrow. 25. should, should not

1. 춥다는 것을 추측하고 있으므로 조동사 must를 쓴다.

2. 훌륭한 피아니스트라고 했으므로 가능의 조동사 can을 쓴다.

3. 핸드폰이 가방에 있을 것이라고 추측하고 있으므로 추측을 나타내는 조동사를 쓴다. be going to는 미래를 나타내는 말이다.

4. 조동사 뒤에는 동사원형을 쓰고 조동사의 부정은 조동사 뒤에 not을 붙인다.

5. 앞으로 일어날 일을 나타낼 때 미래의 조동사 will을 쓴다.

6. 미래의 will은 be going to로, 가능의 can은 be able to로, 부탁의 can은 will로 바꿔 쓸 수 있다. 또한 의무는 should나 have to로 나타낼 수 있다.

7. 조동사 may는 허가와 추측으로 쓰이는데, 허가를 부탁할 때는 May I ~?로 물어본다.

8. 조동사 must는 의무나 강한 추측으로 사용되는데, ②는 강한 추측으로 쓰였다.

9. 사람들에게 친절해야 한다는 의무의 must를 써야 한다.

10. 대답에 is가 있는 것으로 보아 질문은 be동사 의문문으로 해야 한다.

11. have to 의문문의 대답은 Yes나 No로 하며 긍정은 have to, 부정은 don't have to로 답한다.

12. 조동사의 의문문은 조동사를 문장 앞에 쓰고 「주어+동사원형」의 형태로 쓴다.

13. 허가의 may는 can으로 바꿔 쓸 수 있다.

14. 의무의 must는 have to로 바꿔 쓸 수 있는데 주어가 3인칭 단수형이므로 has to로 쓴다.

15. 〈보기〉의 조동사 must는 의무와 추측 중 추측을 나타낸다.

16. 주어가 3인칭 단수형이므로 doesn't have to를 쓴다.

18. 춥다고 했으므로 그것에 대한 대답으로 창문을 닫는 것이 맞다.

19. 부탁을 할 때는 can이나 may를 쓰며 다시 전화하겠다는 말은 미래를 나타내는 will이 와야 한다.

20. be going to는 미래를 나타내는 문장으로 미래를 나타내는 부사(구)와 함께 쓰인다. last는 과거를 나타내는 말이다.

21. 상대방에게 부탁할 때는 조동사 can이나 will을 쓴다.

22. tomorrow는 미래를 나타내는 부사로 조동사 will과 같이 쓴다.

25. *A*: Eric, 너 오늘 농구를 하면 안 된다.
    B: 엄마, 하지만 이번 주말에 시합이 있어요. 나는 연습을 해야 돼요.
    A: 너는 열이 있어. 감기에 걸릴까봐 걱정이 돼. 너는 집에 있으면서 쉬어야 해.

Chapter 8. 형용사와 부사

Unit 43. 형용사의 역할
Practice

A. 1. red 2. tired, hungry 3. delicious 4. new
   5. healthy 6. brown 7. two, cute

B. 1. old 2. easy 3. Japanese 4. different 5. wonderful

C. 1. smart 2. beautiful 3. empty 4. wide 5. scary

Unit 44. some, any
Practice

A. 1. some 2. some 3. any 4. some 5. any

B. 1. some, presents 2. any, birds 3. any, famous

C. 1. We don't need any help.
   2. Did he catch any fish?
   3. Robert has some pets.

4. I didn't make any mistakes on the exam.

Unit 45. many, much, a lot of
Practice

A. 1. many 2. many 3. much 4. much 5. many
   6. many 7. much 8. many

B. 1. any 2. some 3. many 4. many 5. juice

C. 1. lots, of 2. a, lot, of 3. much 4. much 5. many

Unit 46. (a) few, (a) little
Practice

A. 1. a little 2. A few 3. little 4. few

B. 1. water 2. cars 3. eggs 4. cheese

C. 1. a little 2. little 3. a few 4. Few

Review Test / Unit 43~46

A. 1. a beautiful dress 2. a big city
   3. a blue bicycle 4. fresh vegetables

B. 1. the new library 2. a very kind person
   3. the wrong answer 4. an interesting history

C. 1. many 2. a lot of 3. much 4. a little

D. 1. little 2. a few 3. lots of 4. any 5. Few

Unit 47. 부사의 역할과 형태
Practice

A. 1. really 2. easily 3. slowly 4. too, carefully
   5. quite, well

B. 1. 형 2. 형 3. 부 4. 부 5. 부

C. 1. late 2. strongly 3. clearly 4. happily

Unit 48. 빈도부사
Practice

A. 1. always 2. often 3. sometimes 4. never

B. 1. ① 2. ① 3. ② 4. ②

C. 1. I will never forget his smile.
   2. We often go shopping on Saturday.
   3. He sometimes walks his dog in the evening.
   4. What does he usually do in the evening?

Unit 49. 비교급, 최상급
Practice

A. 1. shorter, shortest 2. wider, widest
   3. smaller, smallest 4. more difficult, most difficult
   5. busier, busiest 6. thinner, thinnest
   7. cuter, cutest 8. younger, youngest

B. 1. taller 2. bigger 3. longest 4. hottest 5. colder

Unit 50. 비교 구문
Practice
A. 1. older 2. heaviest 3. popular 4. smarter 5. in

B. 1. strong 2. faster 3. happiest 4. sweet

C. 1. as, crowded, as 2. as[so], difficult, as
   3. the, biggest 4. more, expensive, than

Review Test / Unit 47~50
A. 1. lately, late 2. easy, easily 3. slow, slowly
   4. heavy, heavily

B. 1. well 2. hard 3. loud 4. fast

C. 1. He often goes to the movies.
   2. She could never find her ring.
   3. I usually have toast for breakfast.
   4. We will always remember that day.

D. 1. bigger, than 2. better, than 3. the, coldest
   4. as[so], exciting

Chapter Test / Unit 43~50
1. ③ 2. ③ 3. ② 4. ③ 5. It is really cold today. 6. ②
7. ② 8. ③ 9. ④ 10. ⑤ 11. ② 12. ⑤ 13. more expensive
14. taller, tall 15. ① 16. ③ 17. ⑤ 18. ④ 19. ③ 20. ④
21. ③ 22. (1) older than (2) as, as (3) the heaviest 23. an
exciting movie 24. baseball well 25. What do you usually
do on Sundays?

1. be동사 뒤에는 형용사나 명사가 온다.

2. some과 any는 '약간의, 몇몇의'의 뜻으로 같지만 some은 긍정문에 사용하고 부정문과 의문문에는 any를 사용한다.

3. hard는 형용사와 부사의 형태가 같은 단어로 형용사는 '어려운, 딱딱한'이라는 뜻이고 부사는 '열심히'라는 뜻이다.

4. 다른 단어들은 형용사와 부사의 관계인데 much와 more는 형용사와 비교급의 관계이다.

5. 부사는 보통 일반동사 앞에, be동사 뒤에 위치한다.

6. 동사를 수식할 때는 형용사가 아닌 부사를 사용한다.

7. '많은'이라는 뜻으로 셀 수 있는 명사 앞에는 many나 a lot of, lots of를 사용한다.

8. Jason은 David보다 키가 크다.

9. 비교급은 '~보다'라는 뜻의 than을 사용하여 나타낸다. best는 최상급으로 범위를 나타내는 전치사 in이 들어간다.

10. 부탁이나 권유를 나타낼 때는 의문문이라도 some을 사용할 수 있다.

12. 빈도부사는 일반동사 앞에, 조동사나 be동사 뒤에 위치한다.

13. expensive의 비교급은 앞에 more를 쓴다.

14. 「as+원급+as」 문장으로 taller는 비교급이므로 원급이 와야 한다.

16. 빈도 순서를 적은 것부터 나타내면 never > sometimes > often > usually > always이다.

17. 동사나 부사 뒤에 쓰인 fast는 모두 부사이고 명사 앞에 쓰인 fast는 형용사이다.

18. 셀 수 있는 명사는 many와 셀 수 없는 명사는 much와 함께 쓴다.

19. snow는 셀 수 없는 명사로 much와 함께 쓴다.

20. important의 비교급과 최상급은 more important, most important 이다.

21. old의 반대 의미를 가지는 형용사를 사용하고 비교 대상을 서로 바꾸면 된다.

25. 빈도부사 usually는 일반동사 앞에 위치하는데, 이 문장에서 일반동사는 두 번째 do이다.

Chapter 9. 문장의 종류
Unit 51. 명령문
Practice
A. 1. Wash 2. Don't be 3. Don't 4. Turn

B. 1. Be quiet in the library. 2. Don't tell a lie.
   3. Don't be noisy. 4. Pass me the salt.

C. 1. be, a 2. Don't, waste 3. Don't, be 4. Sit, down

Unit 52. 청유문
Practice
A. 1. go 2. Let's not 3. Let's 4. Let's not 5. not throw

B. 1. Let's 2. Let's 3. Let's 4. Let's not 5. Let's
   6. Let's not

C. 1. Yes, let's. / Sure. / Why not? / That's a good idea.
   2. No, let's not. / I'm afraid I can't.

Unit 53. 명령문+and/or
Practice
A. 1. Turn, and 2. Hurry, or 3. Open, and 4. Be, or

B. 1. and 2. or 3. or 4. and 5. or

C. 1. Push, and 2. Start, or 3. Stop, or 4. Come, and

Unit 54. 감탄문
Practice
A. 1. What 2. people 3. How 4. the animals are

B. 1. How 2. What 3. How 4. What 5. What

C. 1. How long the bridge is!
   2. What a lovely dress it is!
   3. How easy the problems are!
   4. What amazing stories they are!

Unit 55. 부가의문문
Practice
A. 1. aren't you 2. won't they 3. can she 4. doesn't he

5. didn't you   6. isn't he   7. will they

B. 1. wasn't, it   2. doesn't, she   3. were, they
   4. didn't he   5. do, they   6. aren't, they   7. did, you

C. does, he, he, does

Unit 56. 선택의문문
Practice
A. 1. or   2. Which, or   3. Who, or   4. or   5. or

B. 1. I go to school by bus.
   2. I ordered sandwiches.
   3. That one is mine.
   4. I want yogurt.
   5. My sister sings better.

Unit 57. 부정의문문
Practice
A. 1. Didn't you see a ghost yesterday?
   2. Isn't she a great musician?
   3. Wasn't the soccer player famous?
   4. Won't they wait for her at the bus stop?
   5. Can't Sally arrive here soon?

B. 1. Didn't, No   2. Yes, he did.   3. Yes, it is.
   4. No, he doesn't.   5. Can't, Yes

Review Test / Unit 51~57
A. 1. Opens → Open   2. Let's not → Let's   3. Not → Don't
   4. or → and

B. 1. do you?   2. did he?   3. won't they?   4. isn't it?

C. 1. What, an, exciting   2. How, beautifully
   3. Drink, and   4. Invite, or

D. 1. she doesn't   2. he will   3. I want
   4. I take a shower

Chapter Test / Unit 51~57
1. ③   2. ⑤   3. ③   4. ③   5. ②   6. ①   7. ⑤   8. ①   9. ②
10. ③   11. ②   12. ①   13. ④   14. ③   15. ④   16. What, a, big,
How, big   17. Don't   18. ③, ④   19. ④   20. ⑤   21. didn't
Mike → didn't he, he does → he did   22. Let's open the
window.   23. Let's not go to the movies.   24. Yes, he does.
25. He teaches math.

1. 느낌표가 있는 것으로 보아 감탄문인 것을 알 수 있고 명사가 있기 때문에 what이 와야 한다.
2. house와 apartment 중에 선택하고 있으므로 or를 쓴다.
3. 둘 중에서 어느 것을 필요로 하는지 물었으므로 선택한 하나를 답하면 된다.

4. 부가의문문으로 be동사 were가 있으므로 be동사의 부가의문문을 만들면 된다. 명사는 대명사로 써 주고 긍정문이면 부가의문문은 부정형으로, 부정문이면 긍정형으로 쓴다.
5. What 감탄문은 명사를 강조할 때 사용하고 How 감탄문은 형용사를 강조할 때 사용한다.
6. 명령문은 동사원형으로 문장을 시작하며 부정명령문은 「Don't+동사원형」으로 시작한다.
8. 감탄문으로 영리한 강아지를 강조하고 있으므로 What을 이용하여 감탄문을 만들면 된다.
9. swimmers가 복수명사이므로 What fast swimmers they are!가 되어야 한다.
10. 선택의문문의 대답은 둘 중에서 선택한 하나를 답하면 된다.
11. 명령문은 동사원형으로 문장을 시작하며 부정명령문은 Don't를 이용한다.
12. 게으른 남자를 강조한 감탄문으로 What을 이용하여 만들어야 한다.
13. 청유문의 부정은 Let's 다음에 not을 넣어서 만든다.
14. 조동사 will이 있는 문장의 부가의문문은 조동사를 이용하여 만든다.
15. 감탄문은 what이나 how를 이용하여 만들며 동사원형으로 시작하는 문장은 명령문이다.
17. 부정명령문은 일반동사나 be동사가 있는 문장에 모두 Don't를 앞에 붙여서 만든다.
19. 부가의문문을 만들 때 긍정문이면 부가의문문은 부정형으로 쓴다.
20. 「명령문, and」는 '~해라, 그러면 ~할 것이다'라는 뜻이고 「명령문, or」는 '~해라, 그렇지 않으면 ~할 것이다'라는 뜻이다.
21. 부가의문문에서 앞에 나온 명사 주어는 대명사로 바꿔 써야 하며 과거로 물어본 경우에는 과거로 답해야 한다.

Chapter 10. to부정사와 동명사
Unit 58. to부정사의 명사적 용법
Practice
A. 1. to visit   2. to collect   3. To play   4. to see

B. 1. 보어   2. 목적어   3. 주어   4. 목적어   5. 주어

C. 1. to teach   2. to play   3. To swim   4. to be
   5. to buy

Unit 59. to부정사의 형용사적 용법
Practice
A. 1. something   2. a dress   3. palaces

B. 1. to, read   2. to, drink   3. to, go   4. to, open
   5. to, help

C. 1. with   2. with   3. on   4. with   5. about

Unit 60. to부정사의 부사적 용법
Practice
A. 1. 나의 목걸이를 찾아서

2. 자라서 요리사가 되었다

3. 그들을 만나기 위해서

4. 에너지를 절약하기 위해서

B. 1. ⓑ 2. ⓐ 3. ⓒ

C. 1. to play with his friends

2. to become a famous model

3. to lose their dog

4. practice the piano to be a pianist

Review Test / Unit 58~60

A. 1. 형용사 2. 부사 3. 명사 4. 부사

B. 1. It, to, visit 2. happy, to, pass

C. 1. to be 2. to have 3. to live in

D. 1. to lose her wallet

2. to say goodbye

3. to stay here

4. to read magazines

E. 1. ③ 2. ①

Unit 61. 동명사의 용법

Practice

A. 1. taking 2. Getting up 3. swimming 4. helping

B. 1. 보어 2. 주어 3. 목적어 4. 목적어 5. 주어

C. 1. playing 2. writing 3. watching 4. telling

5. baking

Unit 62. 동명사와 to부정사

Practice

A. 1. watching 2. answering 3. to read 4. to have

B. 1. to work 2. having 3. cleaning

C. 1. riding a horse 2. eating carrots 3. to lose weight

4. washing the dishes

Unit 63. 동명사와 현재분사

Practice

A. 1. getting 2. singing[to sing] 3. calling

4. Talking[To talk] 5. driving 6. laughing 7. making

8. drawing[to draw]

B. 1. crying 2. sitting 3. are playing 4. climbing

5. is wearing

Review Test / Unit 61~63

A. 1. going 2. cooking 3. to meet 4. to buy

5. collecting[to collect]

B. 1. to hear the news

2. breaking your window

---

3. to become a great artist

4. telling the truth

C. 1. meet → to meet

2. got → get

3. changing → to change

4. to lend → lending

5. taking → to take

D. 1. 동명사 2. 현재분사 3. 동명사 4. 현재분사 5. 현재분사

6. 동명사 7. 동명사 8. 현재분사

Chapter Test / Unit 58~63

1. ④ 2. ③ 3. ⑤ 4. ③ 5. ① 6. ② 7. ④ 8. ② 9. ②

10. (1) 목적어 (2) 주어 (3) 보어 11. ④ 12. ① 13. ③ 14. to

15. ⑤ 16. ② 17. ②, ③ 18. to buy 19. ① 20. ① 21. to

open, opening 22. hope to be a famous singer 23. to read

[reading] books, to clean[cleaning] her room 24. to visit

the museum, to play[playing] soccer 25. (1) to buy (2) to

give (3) to choose

1. decide, want, plan, hope는 목적어로 to부정사를 쓰는 동사이다.

2. enjoy는 목적어로 동명사를 쓰는 동사로 riding이 와야 한다.

3. to부정사의 부사적 용법(목적)으로 쓰였으므로 to buy가 되어야 한다.

4. 전치사의 목적어로는 명사, 대명사가 오며 동사가 올 경우에는 동명사
가 와야 한다.

5. like는 to부정사와 동명사를 모두 목적어로 쓸 수 있는 동사이며 give
up 뒤에는 동명사가 온다.

6. '마실 무언가를'이라는 뜻으로 앞에 있는 명사를 수식하고 있으므로 형
용사적 용법으로 쓰였다.

7. love, start, like, begin은 to부정사와 동명사를 모두 목적어로 쓸 수
있는 동사이다.

8. to부정사가 주어, 보어, 목적어의 자리에 오는 경우는 명사적 용법이고
to부정사가 앞에 있는 명사를 수식하는 경우는 형용사적 용법이다.

9. finish는 목적어로 동명사를 쓰는 동사로 cleaning이 되어야 한다.

11. to부정사는 '~해서 ~하다'라는 뜻의 부사적 용법으로 결과를 나타내기
도 한다.

12. to부정사의 명사적 용법과 동명사는 공통으로 명사의 역할을 하며 주
어, 보어, 목적어 자리에 올 수 있다. enjoy 뒤에는 동명사만 올 수 있다.

13. 전치사의 목적어로는 동명사만 올 수 있다.

15. be동사 뒤에 동명사가 오면 보어의 역할이 된다.

16. begin 뒤에는 to부정사나 동명사가 오고 plan은 to부정사가 온다.

17. love는 목적어로 to부정사와 동명사 모두 올 수 있으므로 riding과 to
ride가 된다.

20. 주어를 to부정사로 표현하면 To speak English ~.가 되고 동명사
로 표현하면 Speaking English ~.가 된다.

21. mind는 목적어로 동명사를 쓰는 동사이다.

25. 해석 : 나는 나의 여동생을 위한 선물을 사기 위해 백화점에 가고 있

175

어. 나는 그녀에게 옷을 주기를 원하지만 무엇도 고를 수가 없어. 나는 좋은 것을 고르기 위해 너의 도움이 필요해. 나에게 좀 와줘.

Chapter 11. 문장의 형식

Unit 64. 1형식 문장과 There is/are

Practice

A. 1. Tigers, run 2. We, go 3. She, sings
   4. The sun, sets

B. 1. are 2. aren't 3. milk 4. is 5. are

C. 1. There are a lot of dolls on the sofa.
   2. There are not[aren't] many caps on the shelf.
   3. Is there a blue house on the hill?

Unit 65. 2형식 문장과 감각동사

Practice

A. 1. soft 2. angry 3. sweet 4. well 5. great 6. sad
   7. delicious 8. like

B. 1. The clothes feel smooth.
   2. The girls look beautiful.
   3. This lemon tastes sour and sweet.

C. ⑤

Unit 66. 3형식 문장과 4형식 문장

Practice

A. 1. to sing 2. me 3. cookies

B. 1. 3 2. 4 3. 3

C. 1. He teaches us science.
   2. She made me spaghetti.
   3. I passed him a ball.
   4. She can give them good advice.
   5. They will send you a gift.

Unit 67. 4형식 문장의 3형식 전환

Practice

A. 1. to 2. for 3. of 4. to

B. 1. ② 2. ① 3. ②

C. 1. My uncle showed a camera to me.
   2. She bought a new bike for her daughter.
   3. They told interesting stories to him.
   4. Can you bring some juice to me?

Unit 68. 5형식 문장

Practice

A. 1. me 2. found 3. to win 4. call 5. to read

B. 1. clean 2. to brush 3. sad 4. to play

C. 1. him, Jack 2. to, drink 3. the, exam, easy
   4. her, to, come

Review Test / Unit 64~68

A. 1. 간접목적어 2. 주격보어 3. 직접목적어 4. 목적격보어

B. 1. to go 2. for 3. good 4. Is

C. 1. bitter and sweet
   2. There are many stars
   3. made a pie for me

D. 1. to help 2. to clean 3. to come

E. 1. study → to study 2. are → is 3. tiredly → tired
   4. for → to

Chapter Test / Unit 64~68

1. ② 2. ③ 3. ① 4. ⑤ 5. ② 6. ⑤ 7. ② 8. good, bad
9. ② 10. ④ 11. to the students 12. There is 13. ⑤
14. ① 15. ① 16. ②, ⑤ 17. to 18. ① 19. ① 20. ④
21. sounds strange 22. take pictures, to take pictures
23. (1) to be (2) dangerous 24. Is there my watch on the table? 25. They want me to read many books.

1. 감각동사 뒤에 오는 보어는 부사처럼 해석하지만 형용사가 와야 한다.
2. 「주어+동사+목적어+목적격보어」로 이루어진 5형식 문장으로 ask, tell, want, expect는 to부정사를 목적격보어로 쓴다.
3. show는 수여동사로 간접목적어와 직접목적어의 순서로 오며 간접목적어를 뒤로 이동할 경우에는 전치사 to를 간접목적어 앞에 쓴다.
4. There is 뒤에는 단수명사나 셀 수 없는 명사가 온다.
5. 4형식 문장은 「주어+동사+간접목적어+직접목적어」로 이루어져 있으며 간접목적어를 뒤로 이동하여 전치사(to, for, of)와 함께 써서 3형식 문장으로 바꿀 수 있다.
6. 주격보어는 주어의 성질이나 상태를 나타내고 목적격보어는 목적어의 성질이나 상태를 나타낸다.
7. 셀 수 없는 명사는 단수 취급하며 단수동사와 함께 쓴다.
9. buy, make, cook, find는 4형식 문장을 3형식 문장으로 전환할 때 간접목적어 앞에 전치사 for를 쓴다.
10. send, show, tell, give, write, teach 등의 동사는 4형식 문장을 3형식 문장으로 전환할 때 간접목적어 앞에 전치사 to를 쓴다.
12. There is/are 문장으로 가지고 있는 것을 표현할 수 있다.
13. allow는 목적격보어로 to부정사를 쓰므로 to watch가 되어야 한다.
16. 4형식 문장은 3형식 문장으로 전환할 수 있으며 give는 3형식 문장으로 전환할 때 간접목적어 앞에 전치사 to를 쓴다.
18. 4형식 문장을 3형식 문장으로 전환할 때 ask는 간접목적어 앞에 전치사 of를 쓴다.
19. find를 이용하여 5형식 문장으로 나타낼 수 있다.
20. 〈보기〉는 목적격보어로 목적어의 상태를 나타내고 있다.

Chapter 12. 전치사

Unit 69. 시간의 전치사 1

Practice

A. 1. at 2. in 3. in 4. on
B. 1. in 2. at 3. in 4. at 5. in 6. at 7. on 8. in
   9. on
C. 1. on 2. at 3. in 4. in 5. on

Unit 70. 시간의 전치사 2

Practice

A. 1. 2시간 동안 2. 여름 캠프 동안 3. 10시 전에 4. 방과 후에
   5. 수업 동안
B. 1. after 2. during 3. for 4. before 5. during
C. 1. after 2. for 3. during 4. before

Unit 71. 장소의 전치사

Practice

A. 1. in 2. on 3. in 4. at
B. 1. at 2. on 3. in 4. at 5. on 6. in 7. on 8. in
C. 1. in 2. on 3. in 4. at

Unit 72. 위치의 전치사

Practice

A. 1. in front of 2. under 3. behind 4. over
B. 1. under 2. over 3. near 4. across 5. next
C. 1. under 2. across from 3. over 4. near

Unit 73. 방향의 전치사

Practice

A. 1. 그 사다리 위로 2. 그 숲 안으로 3. 부산을 향해
   4. 그 동물원으로부터
B. 1. to 2. out of 3. from 4. down 5. from
C. 1. A tree fell down on the ground.
   2. He jumped from the rock.
   3. A rabbit went into a hole.
   4. Dan climbed up the mountain.

Unit 74. 그 밖의 전치사

Practice

A. 1. for 2. by 3. around 4. with 5. about
B. 1. with 2. by 3. without 4. about 5. with
C. 1. with 2. for 3. with 4. around

Review Test / Unit 69~74

A. 1. in, in 2. on, on 3. In, at
B. 1. for 2. from 3. from 4. before

C. 1. under 2. between 3. after 4. near
D. 1. from Monday to Friday
   2. walked without an umbrella
   3. take a trip during this weekend
   4. rolled down the hill
E. 1. by 2. with

Chapter Test / Unit 69~74

1. ② 2. ⑤ 3. ⑤ 4. ① 5. (1) without (2) down 6. ③
7. about 8. ④ 9. ⑤ 10. ③ 11. ② 12. ② 13. in 14. ③
15. ③ 16. around, by 17. ① 18. ⑤ 19. ③ 20. ④ 21. in
front of 22. Bob found his key under the desk. 23. Let's
meet at the theater before six. 24. jumped over the fence
25. (1) around (2) for, at (3) up

1. for는 '~을 위해'라는 뜻과 '~을 향해'라는 뜻이 있다.
2. 시간을 나타내는 전치사 in 뒤에는 연도나 계절, 월, 하루의 시기 등을
나타내며 날짜를 나타낼 때는 on을 사용한다.
3. 요일 앞에는 전치사 on을 쓰며 장소는 at을 사용한다. 시간을 나타내는
for 뒤에는 숫자가 나온다.
4. during과 for는 '~ 동안'이라는 뜻인데 during 뒤에는 특정 기간이 오
며 for 뒤에는 주로 숫자가 온다.
7. '~에 대하여'라는 뜻의 전치사는 about이다.
8. 계절 앞에는 전치사 in을 쓰고 시간 앞에는 전치사 at을 쓴다.
9. 작은 공간이나 기점을 나타낼 때는 at을 쓰고 넓은 공간이나 지역을 나
타낼 때는 in을 쓴다.
10. 요일이나 특정한 날은 전치사 on을 쓰며 표면과 맞닿아 있는 상태에
서 위에 있는 경우에도 on을 쓴다.
11. 시험을 보는 특정한 날을 나타내고 있으므로 전치사 on을 쓴다.
12. '세계 여행을 하다'라고 할 때는 around를 사용하여 travel around
the world라고 한다.
13. 월을 나타내는 시간의 전치사와 넓은 지역을 나타내는 장소의 전치사
가 들어가야 한다.
14. 배가 침몰하고 있으므로 out of가 아닌 into를 써야 한다.
15. 달은 지구 주위를 돌고 있으므로 around를 써야 한다.
16. 교통수단을 나타낼 때는 전치사 「by+교통수단」으로 쓴다.
17. with는 '~와 함께'라는 뜻과 '~을 가지고'라는 뜻이 있다.
19. during은 특정 시간을 나타내고 나머지 전치사들은 방향을 나타낸다.
21. Jamie가 Sally 뒤에 앉은 것은 Sally가 Jamie 앞에 앉은 것이다.

Grammar Note

1. at, at, at, in, in, in, on, on, on, before, before, after, after,
   for, for, during, during
2. at, at, in, in, on, on
3. under, under, over, over, in front of, in front of, behind,
   behind, next to/by, next to/by, near, near, between,

between, across from, across from
4. up, up, down, down, into, into, out of, out of, from, from, to, to, for, for

Chapter 13. 접속사

Unit 75. and, but
Practice
A. 1. and 2. and 3. but 4. but 5. and 6. and 7. but
   8. but
B. 1. It is sunny and (it is) warm.
   2. The man is rich but he isn't happy.
   3. I bought pants and (I bought) sneakers.
C. 1. but 2. and 3. and 4. and 5. but

Unit 76. or, so
Practice
A. 1. or 2. so 3. or 4. or 5. so
B. 1. ⓑ 2. ⓒ 3. ⓓ 4. ⓐ
C. 1. or 2. so 3. so 4. or 5. so 6. or

Unit 77. when
Practice
A. 1. when you use scissors
   2. when she feels tired
   3. when I called him
   4. when I was a boy
   5. when she met him
   6. when he is ready
B. 1. She listens to music when she is sad. /
      When she is sad, she listens to music.
   2. I wanted to be a teacher when I was young. /
      When I was young, I wanted to be a teacher.

Unit 78. before, after
Practice
A. 1. after 2. before 3. before 4. after 5. after
B. 1. before I leave
   2. after I eat meals
   3. before he goes out
C. 1. before I watched TV
   2. Before I took a nap
   3. after he ate some cookies
   4. after you wash your face

Unit 79. that
Practice
A. 1. ③ 2. ① 3. ② 4. ③ 5. ③
B. 1. She thinks that he is very smart.
   2. I know that she is Henry's sister.
   3. He heard that Linda will leave next Monday.
   4. We know that he likes Amy very much.
C. 1. that my brother cooks well
   2. that her dream will come true
   3. that friendship is the most important

Unit 80. because, if
Practice
A. 1. because 2. if 3. If 4. if 5. because 6. if
B. 1. if 2. because 3. if
C. 1. if you have time
   2. because his bike was broken
   3. If you like this ball
   4. because it has old towers

Review Test / Unit 75~80
A. 1. and 2. when 3. so 4. that 5. when
B. 1. or 2. before 3. but 4. if
C. 1. but I don't like cats
   2. that he is Julia's brother
   3. after we finished dinner
D. 1. She was very angry because Jim told a lie to her.
   2. You can lose your weight if you exercise regularly.
   3. He thinks that the movie is great.
   4. I worked for sick people after I graduated from school.

Chapter Test / Unit 75~80
1. ④ 2. ① 3. ⑤ 4. ② 5. and 6. or 7. ② 8. ③ 9. ⑤
10. ④ 11. ④ 12. when 13. ① 14. and 15. ③ 16. ①
17. ③ 18. is 19. ⑤ 20. because of 21. so, because
22. after I opened the window 23. so the banks are closed
24. (that) his son should eat more vegetables 25. (1) go to the beach if it is sunny (2) will watch a movie if it is rainy

1. 매우 더워서 에어컨을 틀었다고 했으므로 원인과 결과를 나타내는 접속사 so를 쓴다.
2. '~하다면'이라는 뜻의 조건을 나타내고 있으므로 조건의 접속사 if를 쓴다.
3. 접속사 that이 있는 문장이 목적어 역할을 하는 경우에 that은 생략할 수 있다.
4. 첫 번째 문장은 결과와 원인을 나타내기 때문에 원인을 이끄는 접속사

because가 필요하다.

5. 두 단어가 동급으로 연결되어 있으므로 '~와, 그리고'의 뜻을 가진 접속사가 와야 한다.

6. 둘 중에서 하나를 선택하는 경우에는 접속사 or를 사용한다.

7. when은 의문사로 쓰이면 '언제'라는 뜻으로 의문문을 이끌고 접속사로 쓰이면 '~할 때'라는 뜻으로 시간을 나타내는 접속사 문장을 이끈다.

8. 낚시를 가자고 했는데 거절하는 뜻으로 because 뒤에 못 가는 이유를 말하면 된다.

9. hope, think, believe, know 동사들은 목적어로 that절이 올 수 있다.

11. 키가 작지만 용감하다고 했으므로 반대의 의미를 가지는 접속사 but을 쓴다.

12. '~할 때'라는 뜻의 접속사 when이 와야 한다.

15. 전화를 하고 싶지만 전화번호를 모른다고 했으므로 and가 아닌 but이 와야 한다.

18. 조건의 부사절에서는 현재시제가 미래시제를 나타낸다.

19. 결과와 원인으로 이루어진 문장이므로 so 대신 because가 와야 한다. 원인과 결과로 이루어진 문장은 so를 사용한다.

20. because 뒤에는 절이 오고 because of 다음에는 단어나 어구가 온다.